GOA AND THE REVOLT OF 1787

XCHR STUDIES SERIES

No. 1. João de Barros : Portuguese Humanist and Historian of Asia – *C.R. Boxer*

No. 2. Coastal Western India : Studies from the Portuguese Records – *M.N. Pearson*

No. 3. The Black Legend of Portuguese India : Diogo Couto, His Contribution to the study of Political Corruption in the Empires of Early Modern Europe – *George Davison Winius*

No. 4. Health and Hygiene in Colonial Goa (1510-1961) – *Fatima da Silva Gracias*

No. 5. Trade and Finance in Portuguese India : A Study of the Portuguese Country–Trade, 1770-1840 – *Celsa Pinto*

No. 6. Goa and the Revolt of 1787 – *J.H. da Cunha Rivara,* Editor: *Charles, J. Borges*

About the Editor and the Author

Fr. Charles J. Borges has been with the Xavier Centre of Historical Research (Goa) since 1981 and is presently its Director. He holds a doctorate in history from the University of Bombay. He has written *The Economics of the Goa Jesuits 1542-1759* (New Delhi: Concept) and is co-editor of *Jesuits in India: In Historical Perspective* (Macau, 1992) and *Proceedings of the Seventh International Seminar on Indo-Portuguese History* (Lisbon: *Mare Liberum,* no. 9, July 1995). He contributes regularly to national and international journals and seminars.

Joaquim Heliodoro da Cunha Rivara, author of *A Conjuração de 1787 em Goa e varias cousas desse tempo* was born at Arraiolos (Portugal) on 23 June 1809. He studied Latin, Greek, English, French and German as a youth, took a degree in medicine at Coimbra and in 1836 was at Evora to practise. But the following year he entered the administrative service of the district and was appointed chief secretary. A year later he was appointed librarian at the Public Library at Evora and soon came to be known for his remarkable familiarity with documents and for his efficiency. His interest in journalism led him in 1841 to collaborate with the *Revista Universal.*

In 1855 he was sent to the overseas province of Goa and on 1 November of that year appointed chief secretary of the State. His wide interests led him to write much in defence of the Portuguese Padroado, and to publish among other things *Boletim do Governo, O Oriente Portugues, Ensaio Historico da Lingua Concani,* and *Dicionario Portugues Concani.* As travel writer himself, he translated the work of *François Pyrard de Laval,* and edited *Cronista de Tissuari.* He remained in Goa till 1877 to write a history of India and returned to Portugal where he passed away on 20 February 1879.

XCHR Studies Series No. 6

GOA AND THE REVOLT OF 1787

by

Joaquim Heliodoró da Cunha Rivara

Editor

Charles J. Borges

Director, Xavier Centre of Historical Research, Goa

Translator

Renato da Cunha Soares

Introduction by

Teotonio R. de Souza

Member, Portuguese Academy of History, Lisbon

CONCEPT PUBLISHING COMPANY, NEW DELHI-110059

ISBN 81-7022-646-5

First Published 1996

Published and Printed by
Ashok Kumar Mittal
Concept Publishing Company
A/15-16, Commercial Block, Mohan Garden
NEW DELHI-110059
Phones: 5554042. 5504042

PREFACE

The Xavier Centre of Historical Research is pleased to bring to a wider readership the work of J.H. da Cunha Rivara *A Conjuraçã de 1787 em Goa e varias cousas desse tempo: Memoria Historica* first published at the Imprensa Nacional, Panjim, in 1875. It has been translated from the original in Portuguese into English by Mr. Renato da Cunha Soares at the request of the late Capt. E.L. Pinto (IN), and has been edited by me for publication. I am grateful to Dr. Teotonio R. de Souza who has written an introduction situating the importance of the book in Goan history, to Lt-Col. António Pinto (Retd) who was instrumental in getting financial support for the present publication from the extended Pinto families listed in the family chart mentioned in this book and for updating the Pinto family chart itself, to Mrs. Lalita Victor for making available the computer texts, to Fr. Caetano da Cruz Fernandes who translated some of the passages from the Latin, and to Ms. Ernesta Bhobe for all her able computer assistance. I am also grateful to Concept Publishing Company, New Delhi, for undertaking this its sixteenth publication of the XCHR since 1979.

Fr. Charles J. Borges, S.J.
Director, XCHR

1 September 1996

CONTENTS

INTRODUCTION

When the so-called "Conspiracy" of Pintos completed two centuries I was still in Goa, and my contribution to the celebration of the second centenary of this event was intendedly a muted one. As an eminent Indo-Portuguese historian Prof. S. Subrahmanyam put it explicitly in his recent and much acclaimed book, I too had no intention of fighting the colonial wars all over again. I only edited and published (and with an unavoidable delay of two years) a collection of essays presented by Goan researchers at the Indian History Congress (Goa University, November 1987). But to these was added one more on my initiative, and that was related to the "Conspiracy" of Pintos by Mariano Dias. It was meant to complete and balance another thought-provoking paper already forming part of the collection and dealing with the "protesting priests of Goa". The book appeared as *Essays in Goan History* (1989). The centenary passed pretty unnoticed, though some stray write-ups did not fail to appear both in Goa and in Portugal. In Goa Dr. Carmo Azevedo celebrated the bi-centenary by starting his article in the Goan daily *Herald* (Panjim, Aug. 10, 1987, p. 2) in a nationalist tone: "It is a matter of legitimate pride for Goans that they organised the second anti-colonial revolt in modern history. (...) It took place only fourteen years after the Boston Tea Party (1773) which led to the generalized revolt among the American colonies and their War of Independence (1775-83) and two years before the Minas Gerais Conspiracy (1789) which likewise, eventually led to the independence of Brazil (1822)". The author further suggested that relevant documentation in Goa and Portugal was kept under wraps lest the unpalatable truths should come to light. Much of the information that is available to us has come through the book that is now being introduced in its first English translation. However, in 1985 a Portuguese researcher found in the Municipal Archives of Porto a very important document relating to the "Conspiracy" and entitled *Copia da Sentença de Conspiração e alta traição contra o Estado*. Based on it he wrote "Há dois seculos: Revolta frustrada para a independência de Goa" *(História,* no. 75, pp. 32-46). My attention was drawn to it by my old professor and friend, Leopoldo da Rocha, author of the classic work on the *Confrarias de Goa* (Lisbon, 1973). He arranged to send me a photocopy of the document traced by Ivo Carneiro de Sousa in Porto. It is very likely that this document reached Porto with the personal belongings of the Judge José da Rocha Dantas e Mendonça (former judge of the High Court at Porto) who came to Goa as judge of the High Court and conducted the inquiry and gave the sentence in the case of the "Conspiracy". He died in Goa in August 1792.

We believe that this English version of J. H. da Cunha Rivara's *A Conjuração de 1787 em Goa* will make this event better known to a wider readership and to researchers worldwide. Fresh interest and re-evaluation of the event can thus be expected, and with new linkages and evidence that may be available or found by researchers on the period and related subjects elsewhere. Mr. Dias in his above-mentioned chapter in the *Essays in Goan History,* refers to Cunha Rivara's research efforts as *disinformation.* He sees Rivara, who was Chief Secretary of the Goa government from 1855 to 1877, as disturbed by the events in the neighbouring British India where the colonial rule was severely shaken by the so-called "Sepoy Mutiny" of 1857, and by various rebellions of Sawant Desais and Ranes from Kolhapur and Sawantwadi on Goa border in the previous decades. The fears of the much weaker Portuguese administration in Goa should not be ignored in such a situation. There is much evidence of this in the official correspondence in Goa Archives *(Monções* 232 & 233B, *Estrangeiros,* and *Confidenciais).* The Portuguese feared that these Maratha insurgencies would spill into Goa, and his fears were not unfounded. The Portuguese had allowed telegraph linkage between Bombay and Surat crossing Daman. The British troops were also allowed passage through Goa for undertaking some operations to check the rebels. Some rebels from Sawantwadi had sought refuge in Goa. The Portuguese had accepted their request for asylum, but proposed to take them to Africa, which they flatly refused on grounds of pollution. The British tried to have them extradited, but the Portuguese administration tried its best to honour its pledge of refuge and to take the rebel Desais of Sawantwadi to Timor as a compromise solution. The British reluctantly yielded and offered a steam vessel "Prince Arthur" to ensure that they were transported to the agreed destination. Incidentally and strangely, no one seems to remember today this rebellious component of Timor population when so much is been said and written in Portugal about the Timorese identity and their will to fight for their autonomy against Indonesia ("L.F. Thomaz, *De Ceuta a Timor*, Lisboa, 1994. This collection of essays includes one on Goa and four on Timor. *Cf.* Review in *Indica* (Bombay, Sept. 1995). The author provides no answer to our question on Timor. While providing a good picture of social relations in Goa of the time of *Conjuração* and citing Rivara's contribution to historiography, he has nothing to say about his political predilections and involvement, which is essential for a critical assessment of his overall performance and contribution as historian). Where did the rebel Desais disappear? Goa Government, and Rivara as its representative, collaborated fully with the British administration and its representatives Lords Canning and Elphinstone in quelling the revolt or mutiny, as the British chose to call it. Rivara had therefore reasons to be suspicious of anything that smacked of nationalist pride in Goans. His research on *Conjuração* has to be seen in the background and not necessarily aimed at minimising the revolutionary nature of the plot as was done by the British historiography with reference to the Mutiny of 1857. However, the claim for meticulous research and free from all bias (*limpa da macula da paixão*) needs to be more critically checked. Rivara was certainly aware of the efforts of *Ultramar* and *Illustração Goana* to rehabilitate the Goans who had fought the Portuguese colonial pretensions and suffered for it, like Bernardo Peres da Silva or Mariano José Conceição da Rocha. The Portuguese liberalism gave the Goan intelligentsia an opportunity to attempt this, and Rivara's *historical research* may be seen as a counter-exercise. Barreto Miranda's description of the *Sentença de Conspiração e Alta Traição* as a judicial murder of the martyrs of Bardez is seen by Mr. Dias as the red rag that provoked Rivara's research on *Conjuração*, specially in the sensitive context of comments on the elections in Nagoa (Bardez) in 1861, as it is plain from p. 115 of the original Portuguese text of the book. Rivara was personally and emotionally involved in these elections on behalf of white interests and had referred in the *Boletim do Governo* to the mean and duplicitous character of the Goan natives. For him (as to many Europeans and Americans even today) the innate Indian subtlety was always an expression of meanness and machiavellism. Hence, this book is not just a contribution to the history of Goan nationalism, but also to the history of the colonial mentality of the author and of the time when he wrote it.

There is much evidence of emotionalism in Rivara's published reactions (called *reflexões*) on the issue of Portuguese crown patronage (*Padroado*) that was being cut to size by the Propaganda Fide in the changed political-military scenario in the East, where the British had taken over as the dominant colonial power. Some of these *reflexões* of Rivara appeared without appending his name to them, and simply as authored by a Portuguese. But that does not fail to reveal how emotional and hysterical the man could become over the issues that touched his patriotic feelings, while the issue of "conspiracy" being used for electoral purposes by the natives of Bardez is condemned by Rivara as fanning "pseudo-patriotism of crude mob". His impressive and voluminous *Archivo Portugues-Oriental* and his interest in Konkani writings have left many a Goan historian and nationalist obliged to his historical contribution. A more critical assessment needs to be undertaken of Rivara as documentalist and historian of Portuguese India.

One could draw here a parallel to the Conspiracy of Goa with a similar development in the Philippines under the Spanish rule (one can find more parallels in the colonial histories of Goa and the Philippines but with chronological delays in the Philippines). There too the anti-colonial feelings manifested themselves in the narrow struggle of the Filipino clergy for justice. Its most noted spokesman was Fr. Jose Burgos. He and some other priests lost their lives in their campaign for the "filipinization of the parishes". Jose Rizal's *El Filibusterismo* and *Noli Me Tangere* have recorded the representative value of this struggle in the wider anti-colonial resistance. The colonial discrimination seen as colour discrimination was not exclusively a Portuguese fault, neither was it entirely absent despite greater degree of integration achieved by the Portuguese in the colonial societies, chiefly due to their interest in religious activities. It was not greatly different with the Spanish situation, but these had to deal with less developed native populations than did the Portuguese in the East, except in the Philippines where the Hindu and Muslim influences were already sufficiently marked. It was the educated clergy among the natives who experienced the discrimination first, and when the white colonialists had no other superiority to display, they usually fell back on the colour superiority. Racism has always been the last desperate resort of the dominant groups to assert their right for domination. If Rivara believes that this was not true in the context of the Conspiracy of Goa in 1787 he was not reading all the facts for reasons best known to him and also to us. Prof. Boxer has already drawn the parallel between the Conspiracy in Goa and *Inconfidencia* of 1787 in Minas Gerais. He points to the difference in the treatment meted out to those found guilty. In Brazil only one of the eleven condemned to death was executed, but in India the repression was more savage, and fifteen Goans were executed with great barbarity. He concludes: "It is difficult to believe that this different treatment was due to anything else but colour prejudice, since those reprieved in the *Inconfidencia Mineira* were all white and the Goan victims were all coloured" (*The Portuguese Seaborne Empire*, London: Hutchinson & Co., 1969, pp. 199-200).

The conspiracy, wrongly linked by tradition almost exclusively with Pintos (a psychiatrist-friend of mine with whom I discussed this matter some years ago, jokingly asked me if it was really a *conspiração* or a *constipação* of Pintos. He seems to have made a point: the native colonial society represented by the Pintos seems to be felt left in the coid), had three priests leading it, and one of them from Pinto family, namely Fr. Caetano Victorino de Faria, Fr. José António Gonçalves and Fr. Francisco Couto, who had felt their talents and self-dignity hurt by the dominant Portuguese colonial interests of the time and as represented by the metropolitan whites and by the Goa-based *mestiços* or *descendentes*. But when these Goan priests were bypassed in favour of the South Indian St. Thomas clerics for the appointment to the vacant sees of Cranganore and Mylapore, they did not seem to realise that they were contradicting themselves by their colonial and discriminating attitude towards the local candidates of South India. The Malabar clergy certainly had greater right to rule over their churches than Goa-born clerics. Rivara gloats on this point to ridicule the ambitions of the Goan priests. However, a more recent piece of evidence in the form of the published diary of Bishop Cariattil and written by the priest who accompanied him (*Varthamanapusthakkam*, trans. & edit. by Placid J. Podipara, Rome, 1971) discloses the large game-plan of Fr. Caetano Victorino de Faria, the real mastermind of the plot to displace the Portuguese and to take over the control of responsible posts in Goa. He was not opposed to Cariattil's appointment to the Cranganore See, but he would do it after taking over the metropolitan See of Goa. He had even shown special interest in ordering from Milan specially cut Malayalam letter-types which were better than those of the Propaganda. It appears from the new evidence that the departure of the priests Francisco Couto and José António Gonçalves to Rome for further studies was not their own move as presumed by Rivara, but on instructions of Fr. Caetano Victorino de Faria. It was only when Cariattil was appointed and his own claims were ignored that Fr. Caetano Victorino de Faria seems to have decided on the revolt. And was the death of Bishop Cariattil in Goa and before reaching his See natural, or part of the conspiracy? It remains unclear.

One could usefully consult the documents appended to the *Refutação Analytica* published by a Goan in Bombay, and of which Rivara served himself to draw the information on the inquiry. He could not find any original, but only the doc. 24 of *Refutação Analytica*, which copied the original from the Archives of the High Court in 1835 and had found it already in a bad condition. Curiously, the orthography of this document does not tally fully with the document found in Porto District Archives. What is also curious is the arrangement chosen by Rivara to present the details of the inquiry and punishments meted out to the condemned. By grouping them under similar penalties, Rivara found a way of avoiding the unpalatable expressions in the original of the inquiry text which refers to tortures administered to extort confessions. Rivara has no use for these details, but seeks rather to distract the reader by referring to the Frenchman serving as Sergeant Major of Cavalry in Bardez and was very kind in the way he effected the arrest of two Pintos in Saligao. Incidentally, a study of local rebellions in the bordering region under British rule in 1844 by Dr. P. P. Shirodkar (*Purabhilekha-Puratatva*, III, no. 2, 1985) reveals direct link of some Pintos of Candolim with the rebels. It is only on the basis of these continued links of Candolim Pintos with the rebel elements during the time of Rivara that perhaps justify his appending a genealogical tree of the family to his book. The native discontent in Goa sensed by Rivara was not of his imagining, but despite his long title of the book suggesting a wider scope than just the event of 1787, he failed to go beyond the condemnation of the Conspiracy to the study of the roots of the problem and its many manifestations. The whole issue is still awaiting a well-documented research on the Goan native society in the 18th century and later. We can look forward to the posthumous publication of Mira Mascarenhas in the *History of Christianity in India* (edited by the Church History Association of India). A doctoral dissertation on late 18th century Goa has recently been published by M. J. M. Lopes. Unfortunately it limits its scope to quantifying and presenting graphically the results of the Pastoral Visitations to which I had drawn public attention twelve years earlier, and does not bring any substantially new interpretation into the debate.

The Viceroy of Goa in 1760 (not too far before the "Conspiracy" date) had studied the reluctance of Goan natives to participate in the Portuguese military service and wars of the New Conquests, and he decided among other things to issue an ordinance banning under heavy penalties the use of the expression *negro* (black) or *cachorro* (dog) to refer to the Goan natives. His ban was aimed at the Portuguese, including expressly the *mestiços* (*porque nestes ainda mais que nos mesmos Europeos reina aquelle luciferino vicio*). He was referring to the vice of pride (*soberba*) or what we may describe as the "white superiority", smacking of racism, which he considered greatly responsible for the native difference towards the Portuguese colonial interests. The growing white superiority of the *luso-descendentes* needs to be understood as a reaction to their losses in Daman and Bassein where they owned large estates and which had been overrun by the Marathas in 1739. It was a bitter experience for the *mestiços* to swallow. A growing pressure of Goan natives to deprive them also of their monopoly over the local army made them more insecure and hostile. The Viceroy deserves credit for the boldness of his assessment, which was not a virtue of many of his countrymen then or later. The official cultural openness was also an expression of short-lived Pombaline reforms. To be fair to Portugal, its policy during the colonial times (at least in Goa) and even in the post-colonial period has not denied its citizenship to its former colonial subjects. In practice, the integration of the colonial subjects into the metropolitan society may not have been always free from certain prejudices based partly on conscious discrimination, or more often on problems of cultural adaptation.

Just a few years before the year of publication of *Conjuração*, the Goan natives had succeeded in obtaining the abolition of the local army, heightening thereby the insecurity of the *descendentes* and also the patriotic fears of Rivara. Various revolts of the Ranes should not be considered seriously as any freedom struggles of Goans. Their revolts were largely in defence of feudal rights that were being challenged by the Portuguese administration and by new plantation interests that had come into Satari in the wake of demand for teak for the construction of the new railway line. Satari forests were the real target, when plantation concessions were being sought by some foreign companies ostensibly for coffee and cotton cultivation. Lands were also being usurped by a State sponsored *sociedade patriotica de baldios* as a hopeful project of reducing pressure on cultivable land in the Old Conquests of Goa, and thereby hoping to stem the tide of emigration. All this came after the time of Rivara, but his great interest in the preservation of the Goa village communities was also a covert expression of preserving an institution which was by its very nature caste-oligarchical and opposed to any structural change in the property relations as demanded by needs of modernisation and as analysed by Francisco Luis Gomes in his *A Liberdade da Terra e a Economia Rural India Portugueza* (1862). Was Cunha Rivara trying to ignore the non-Brahminical sage from Salcete? He sought to pamper the traditionally entrenched rural interests, predominently of the Brahmin caste and keeping them thereby satisfied with their inherited pride, rather than meddling into the general public issues. He seems to have had little influence on the Bardez and Tiswadi

Brahmins who led the Conspiracy of 1787. His defence of the Goan village communities should not be interpreted as an exercise of political altruism. We must, therefore, note that he belonged to the historical trend of his contemporary Alexandre Herculano in Portugal, as a champion of middle class gentry and its municipal and corporate institutions. His publications and those sponsored by him through Felippe Nery Xavier or Miguel Vicente Abreu reveal this preference. His historical intervention was therefore not devoid of political orientation, just as in the case of Herculano in Portugal. Despite their great stress on archival documents, they saw in history a guide for the political needs of their present. Rivara's *Archivo Portugues-Oriental* was an extension of *Portugaliae Monumenta Historica* to the colonial history in the East. His patriotic defence of Padroado rights also reflects Herculano's special concern. Rivara did honour the Portuguese colonial administration as a worthy parallel to his contemporary and able administrator-historians of British India, such as Elphinstone, Duff, Maine, etc. Rivara was convinced that history was an essential tool for a successful colonial administration.

Some other considerations before we conclude: Whether there were links of the Goan conspirators with Tipu Sultan or not, we have had more research recently coming out from Ernestina Carreira on the basis of the contemporary French documentation. The Mhamai link of this period of Goa's history and their greater involvement in Malabar trade at this juncture needs perhaps to be better explored to obtain more clues to the conspiracy episode and events of the time. There are also some other lines of analysis that have not been pursued: What was the British reaction to the episode? Did they take notice of it at all? Had the conspiracy succeeded, what would be its fate under the growing British hegemony, let alone the interests of the French or of the neighbouring native chieftains, including the Marathas and Tipu Sultan? There is another curious side-issue of the conspiracy to which very recently a Goan writer, Carmo de Noronha, had made a reference. He refers to one of the consequences of the brutal suppression of the conspiracy on the psyche of the Goans from Bardez, unlike those of Salcete who were not involved in the conspiracy (with one single exception?) and consequently did not have to face the repressive measures. These responded enthusiastically to State sponsored programmes and subsidies for Goans wishing to proceed to Portugal for higher studies. Hardly anyone from Bardez opted for it for a very long time. It appears to be a reasonable historical explanation for the preference shown by Bardez people to emigrate to non-Portuguese territories instead.

To conclude, I wish to touch on another characteristic Goan trait (perhaps reinforced by Portuguese heritage of *má lingua*) in the attitude of two outstanding Goan disciples of Rivara, namely, Felippe Nery Xavier and Miguel Vicente Abreu. Both made notable contribution to Goan historiography under the direction and patronage of Rivara. While Abreu was an employee of the Government Printing Press, Xavier was a first grade official in the Department of Finance. They did not seem to be above petty academic rivalry, and Abreu felt victimised by the other, when he saw his pay cut to half of what was approved in the State budget. I am not sure what was the final outcome, but he pleaded with Rivara, the then Chief Secretary of the government, to protect his interests. The text is thought-provoking in the context of the history of mentalities: "If Your Excellency feels that I have the law on my side, please do not leave it to the interpretation of Mr. Felippe Nery, because this country chief (I am sorry to say so) does not seem to be inclined to help his own subject as you Portuguese officials do, whenever you have an opportunity to help. It is for this reason that God has been kind to place you over us. May the Lord keep your Excellency, my chief and protector, for many years." (translated from the correspondence of Rivara at Evora Public Library). Abreu seems to reflect what is contained in an old Konkani proverb of Goa: *Firgyanchea payam mel'lem borem, punn Kan'dyachea sangata jiel'lem nhoi*, meaning it is better to die at the feet of a Portuguese man, than to live in the company of a Goan Christian (*Canarim, kan'dy*). But João de Barros tells us that a Portuguese does not suffer as much by being forgotten as with the praise of another! (*Decada I: da Asia*). We need a more human portrait of Joaquim Heliodoro de Cunha Rivara and a clearer picture of his involvement and response in the Goan cultural and political ambience. Such an attempt is bound to reveal that "historical objectivity" is only a qualified human achievement. Perhaps this publication of Rivara's work in English translation may motivate wider interest in this man who is barely known in his own country.

Dr. Teotonio R. de Souza,
Lisbon

---

*Dr. de Souza was formerly director of the Xavier Centre of Historical Research, Goa (1979-1994) and is a member of the Portuguese Academy of History. He is author of *Medieval Goa* (1979), and *Goa to Me* (1994) and has edited a number of books including *Indo-Portuguese History: Old Issues, New Questions* (1985), *Goa through the Ages: An Economic History* (1990), and *Discoveries, Missionary Expansion and Asian Cultures* (1994).

PROLOGUE

The confused legends about the conspiracy, commonly known as *The Revolt of Pintos*, which are current in the country, have impelled us to find, through documents which are authentic, the exact details of how these events took place. While presenting the results of our investigations, we place, with historical exactness, the significance of these documents, now compiled for the first time.

Together with the incidents of the conspiracy and the people involved in it, there are other contemporary incidents not yet made public, which one would like to know more about and which would, at this stage, serve to give a better understanding of that time.

We trust the reader will find this report devoid of any bias which unfortunately despite the lapse of a century still percolates everytime it is discussed or written about. This may probably be due to the fact that little or incorrect information about these events is available.

Everyone desires that historical events should be reported truthfully and therefore each of us should endeavour to contribute his mite to see that truth continues to prevail in history where it is not less important than in the course of our normal lives.

J.H. da Cunha Rivara

1 September 1875 Nova Goa,

SECTION I

1

DISCOVERY OF THE CONSPIRACY AND ARRESTS OF THE ACCUSED

The Governor and Captain-General of the State of India, Francisco da Cunha e Menezes was in 1787 burdened with many grave problems. On the one hand, though the war declared against the Bhosales had a temporary lull due to suspension of hostilities, the army was kept in readiness to block their advance and to defeat that bad neighbour and perpetual enemy. On the other hand, the fear of invasion by Tipu Sultan was ever present as he was increasing, day by day, both in power and haughtiness after the annexure of the territories of Kanara and Sunda upto the fortress of Piro, bordering the frontiers of our State and he was threatening to extend his conquests to further annex some or all the territories belonging to us.

Furthermore, on the other hand, the King of Sunda, deprived of his territories and sheltering under the hospitality of the Portuguese, was scheming, both at the court of Pune and with other rulers to recover his kingdom which comprised the provinces which he had handed over to the Marathas and from whom we had, later, won. He should have, therefore, been the last person to be a hindrance to us against the evil designs of Tipu Sultan.

In addition to this, which, in itself was sufficient to keep the Governor in a state of constant anxiety and worry, the following event took place. On 5 August of 1787, early in the morning, António Eugenio Toscano, a clerk in the communidade of Aldona, a village in the province of Bardez, came to report to the Governor that some priests were plotting to subvert the natives with the objective of expelling the whites from here. The Governor did not attach much importance to this report as he thought it preposterous and a matter to be laughed at and probably the effect of some personal grudge. However, that night, Manoel Godinho de Mira, Colonel Governor of Alorna and Commander of the Legion of Bardez, came, together with Nicolau Luiz da Costa, Lieutenant of the same Legion, who had earlier reported the matter to him, to confirm the first report. Accordingly a detailed report was submitted the next morning before Mr. Justice and Secretary of State. On the same day, Archbishop D. Fr. Manoel de Santa Catharina sent a summary of the depositions made before him on 31 July 1787, by Fr. Pedro Caetano José Lobo, Vicar of Tivim and subsequently by two more priests who, questioned by the Vicar-General on 3 August, gave a more detailed statement on the case.

From the first information reports it became evident that the conspiracy was far advanced and that the appointed day to give effect to the plot was 10 August. There was, therefore, little time to lose and so, on the same day, secret orders were issued by the Governor of the State to arrest, that very night, all the persons indicated as leaders and also their accomplices.

Naval Captain, Xavier de Mendonça was instructed that immediately on receipt of the order, with the help of personnel with him, he should proceed to arrest Fr. José António Gonçalves or José Felippe Gonçalves, residing at Piedade, for having committed an act of high treason and for being the mastermind of an attempted uprising against the State. He was to be taken, with due respect and proper security, to Reis Magos fort, where necessary orders would be sent to detain him. A thorough search was to be made of all his papers which were to be confiscated and personally handed over to the Governor. He was to see if the priest had any large sum of money with him and, if so, it was to be kept under the Captain's custody or of any other person of his confidence, until a final report was made.

Colonel Manoel Godinho de Mira was ordered to detain Fr. José Vaz of Anjuna and Fr. António Felippe Vaz, Vicar of Moira. The Governor instructed him to delegate this task only to European officers of his Legion and to those of his confidence. They were to take the detainees with decorum and proper security to Reis Magos fort. The officers who carried out this task were also to effect a search of all the detainees' papers which were to be sent duly bound, packed and sealed to the Governor. They were to see if the priests had any large sum of money in their houses and, if so, to call the constable and the clerk of the village, or in their absence, the money was to be counted in the presence of witnesses and handed over after recording the details thereof, to any local person who resided in the same house or to be kept in his custody and to make a final report of the case. However, if any of the detainees resided with a relative or friend, the amount found was to be handed to such person, but if he was alone, the house was to be locked and the constable of the village was to maintain a guard on the house, the keys being kept in the custody of the Colonel. If any of the priests was not arrested either because he was not at home or not found elsewhere, then a search was to be conducted with utmost urgency and his residence subjected to the same search as mentioned above. As the Governor was fully aware that the Colonel had already detained the Lieutenant of his Legion, Ignacio Toscano, he was asked to send the Lieutenant with proper security to Reis Magos fort.

Orders were also issued to Brigadier António de Assa Castelbranco, Commander of the Legion of Ponda province, to arrest the Dessai, Narba Naik, resident of that province, Manoel Caetano Pinto of Candolim and Pedro de Souza of Pilerne, Lt. and 2nd Lt. respectively, and that the three should be arrested simultaneously, so that any of them, learning of the arrest of the other, might not make bold his escape. The Dessai, Narba Naik, was to be sent, with decorum and proper security to Aguada fort and the Lieutenants to Reis Magos fort.

The Governor further instructed the said Brigadier that under the present circumstances, as there might be a few people of doubtful loyalty who might plot to throw us out, greater vigilance was to be exercised over the province under his command and he was to, minutely, observe what exactly went on, especially with regard to the King of Sunda, against whom the most caution was required as it was not desirable, at present, to make any open move or one that might alarm him.

The officers who were to effect the arrest of Sardessai, Narba Naik, were to be instructed to make a search of all the papers they could find, and the Brigadier was to bind, seal and submit them to the Governor. He should also try to find out if any other officers of the Legion were, in any way, sympathetic with the sedition movement of those arrested.

Mr. Justice António Rebello do Amaral was assigned the duty of going, at 5 a.m. the following day, 7 August, to the convent of the priests of the Congregation of the Miraculous Cross. After ordering the Fr. Superior to confine Frs. Sebastião Baptista and Pedro Delgado in separate cells, in his presence, (and for whom the prelate would be responsible) and after duly locking the cells and keeping the keys with him, he was to proceed to seize all papers in that cell, on completion of which, he had to repeat the similar performance with the other cell, submitting, thereafter, the seized papers to the Governor, who ends his order with the following warning: "Though I do not expect that there will be any resistance on the part of the prelate, I have, however, sent fifteen men and one officer whom you will find near the pillory of the city, with instructions to extend to you any military help that you may need."

The pillory of the city still exists together with its walls and is not far from the convent, and the church, though desecrated and without adornments, is intact (1875).

These were the actions taken on the first day, which were successful, barring the arrest of Fr. José António Gonçalves considered as the main architect and leader of the conspiracy, who was not found at home at 11 on the night between the 6th and 7th, when the officers knocked at his door, though it was well-known that he had had his dinner on the 6th at the house of Fr. Vicente Alvares, brother of the Vicar of Pilerne, who lived within the limits of the same village.

The Governor ordered Colonel Manoel Godinho de Mira, on the 7th to dispatch his subordinates whom he deemed competent, with minimum delay, to search and arrest the said priest wherever he might be found within the province of Bardez, authorising the Colonel to deploy some soldiers with these officers and to issue necessary instructions in the villages that they be given all help. The Governor also issued orders, on the 7th, to the commanders of the river passes of St. Lourenço and St. Tiago to be on maximum alert and to foil any attempt of the priest to escape.

The Sergeant-Major Commander of Canacona, Fernando Caetano de Souza Pereira, was issued written orders to arrest the said priest should he reach that province and to bring him, posthaste, personally, with decorum and proper security to the secretariat of the State. Since it was possible that the priest might go about in disguise, without his habit, he was informed that the priest was cock-eyed, and if he was in doubt he was to detain any suspicious person, but, in such case he was not to leave the province but the detainee was to be sent through a person of his confidence. Further, if it so happened that the said priest had already passed through the province before receipt of these orders, he should immediately send his subordinates to follow and detain the priest.

In the order issued to Colonel Manoel Godinho de Mira, he was entrusted the task of arresting Fr. José Manoel Ribeiro and one Gerardo Ferreira who had also dined, on the 6th, with Fr. Vicente Alvares, mentioned earlier, and also to arrest one Italian who lived with the Vicar of Pilerne and who had not been found there. The Canacona authorities were also alerted to arrest the said Italian. The Italian was José Luiz Guineti of Milan, who had come as a servant of the Archbishop of Cannanore, D. José Cariattil.

On the same day, orders were also issued to Field Marshal Francisco

António da Veiga Cabral, Commander of the Salcete province, to expeditiously arrest Sebastião de Noronha, married, residing at Nagoa of Salcete province, one of the conspirators who had gone that day or earlier to that place, and to detain him at the Rachol fortress with maximum security, in solitary confinement and to search and confiscate all papers found in his possession or at his residence. He was arrested and sent to the Reis Magos fort.

As the Governor was aware that the conspirators in Salcete province had among them a large number of priests as well as laity; that people of Cuncolim were ready in thousands to be of service; that they were provided with false seals which could be easily mistaken as those of the Governor and thereby cause confusion in the regiment under the command of the Field Marshal, the latter was ordered to arrest any suspicious looking person trying to commit any offence and to inform the Governor if there were sufficient number of persons at Cuncolim who could confirm the above news. With regard to the false seals, the Field Marshal was informed that it would be easy to distinguish them from the real ones in his possession.

All officers in the villages were ordered to render any assistance asked for by the persons assigned to these tasks. The Commanders of prisons of Aguada and Reis Magos were instructed to disburse to the prisoners the necessary supplies, which were being sent for this purpose.

On completion of these initial steps, the Governor committed the case, as was his duty, to the Tribunal, ordering, on 9 August, the Chief Justice of the State, José Joaquim de Sequeira Magalhães e Lançôes, to begin the proceedings in the case, with Mr. Justice José Ferreira Barroco as secretary, for which purpose relevant papers and documents from which proof could be adduced to ensure that the accused of such an abominable crime might be given a proper and just punishment, were duly forwarded.

The Governor also wanted them to ascertain if there was any involvement of any enemy nation or of any person holding high position in the State that could be fomenting this uprising.

Together with the letter to the Chancellor, the Governor also enclosed a list of persons whose arrests he had ordered, the list which is on record. But as various other documents also record who were actually arrested or who were arrested later through warrants from the court and who evaded arrest, we give below as exhaustive a list as could be ascertained from details available.

Arrested

1. Pedro Luiz Gonzaga of Nerul, Lt. of Ponda Legion.
2. Manoel Caetano Pinto of Candolim, Lt. of the same Legion.
3. Ignacio Caetano Toscano of Aldona, Lt. of Bardez Legion.
4. Nicolau Luiz da Costa, Lt. of the same Legion.
5. David Francisco Viegas, chief surgeon of Ponda Legion.
6. Caetano Xavier da Costa, Corporal of the same Legion.
7. Ignacio Caetano Lopes of Mandur, Captain of Auxiliaries.
8. Salvador Alvares da Costa.
9. Balthazar Caeiro, Sergeant of the Legion of Ponda.
10. Manoel Ferrão, Corporal in same Legion.
11. António Fernandes, Corporal in the same Legion.
12. João Vaz, soldier of the same Legion.
13. José Monteiro.
14. Miguel António da Costa, brother of Caetano Xavier da Costa.
15. Bernardo Mesquita.
16. José Luiz Guineti of Milan, former servant to the Archbishop of Cannanore.
17. Sebastião de Noronha of Nagoa, Corporal off-the-shore of Salcete.
18. Manoel Luiz, brother-in-law of Fr. Caetano Francisco do Couto.
19. Vicente de Abreu, fisherman of Chorao.
20. Francisco Pereira, helper of the surgeon.
21. Felippe Fernandes, farmer of Chorao.
22. Victorino Vaz, farmer of Chorao.
23. Vicente Gomes, farmer of Chorao.
24. Manoel Silvestre, student.
25. João de Souza, of Honavar.
26. Sebastião Paulo de Noronha.
27. Fr. António Felippe Vaz, Vicar of Moira.
28. António Dias of Saligão.
29. Manoel Pinto of Saligao, cousin and brother-in-law of Manoel Caetano Pinto of Candolim.
30. Narba Naik, Dessai of Ponda.
31. Manoel Francisco Gonçalves, physician, of Piedade, brother of fugitive Fr. José António Gonçalves.
32. Fr. Sebastião Baptista, of the Congregation of Oratory.
33. Fr. Pedro Delgado of the same Congregation.
34. Fr. Caetano Francisco da Silva, Vicar of St. Lourenço of Linhares.
35. Fr. Manoel Expectação, Vicar of Ponda.

36. Fr. João Alvares de Souza, Vicar of Pomburpa.
37. Fr. Miguel Alvares de Souza, Vicar of Pilerne.
38. Fr. Vicente Alvares.

(The last three are brothers)

39. Fr. Caetano Francisco do Couto of Panjim.
40. Fr. Mathias Bernardo da Fonseca of Chorao.
41. Luis Antonio Gonçalves, seminary student of Piedade, brother of fugitive Fr. José António Gonçalves.
42. Luis Caetano de Souza of Moira.
43. Fr. José Manoel de Menezes, Vicar of Guirim.
44. Fr. José António Vaz of Anjuna.
45. Fr. João Baptista Pinto of Candolim.
46. Fr. Diego Benedicto Lobo of Serula.
47. Fr. Jorge Dias of Candolim.

Absent

1. Fr. Diogo Caetano do Couto, perhaps the brother of Fr. Caetano Francisco do Couto.
2. Fr. Pedro Fernandes of Assagao.
3. Fr. José António Gonçalves of Piedade.
4. Fr. Ignacio de Noronha.
5. Xavier dos Remedios Noronha.

(the last two are brothers who escaped to Bombay)

6. Josefa de Noronha.

Persons whose names do not figure in the warrants of arrest and of whom there is no information

1. Fr. José Manoel Ribeiro.
2. Gerardo Ferreira.

(both included in the order issued to Col. Manoel Godinho de Mira).

3. Pedro de Souza of Pilerne, 2nd Lt. in the Legion of Ponda under the command of Brig. António Assa de Castelbranco.

Immediately thereafter the Governor sent the report, on the 9th to the royal court, via Bombay, together with his letter addressed to the Secretary of State, Martinho de Mello e Castro, in which, after describing the case in detail, he added: "I hasten to inform Your Excellency, not because the case deserves it, but merely to save the embarrassment that it could cause in the Court if such news were reported by less trustworthy or ill-advised persons, and I solicit Your Excellency to keep me advised of any orders from H. Majesty, with utmost urgency possible so that I may be able to know what action I should take against the accused priests".

The move for the arrest of the accused and the return of Fr. José António Gonçalves, as well as the charge-sheets were carried out by the Governor and the authorities in Goa with utmost secrecy so that no more than what was inevitable would leak outside the State and so that the neighbours would attach little or no importance to it. Otherwise, being enemies and some of them powerful, one could expect any hostile movement from any of them, particularly from Nawab Tipu Sultan who, being always in readiness, could easily avail of this opportunity of domestic unrest to attack us.

2

BEGINNING AND PROGRESS OF THE CONSPIRACY

From 1780 to 1785 many people born in Portuguese India had migrated to Lisbon, among whom the oldest resident in that capital was Fr. Caetano Victorino de Faria who managed to win acceptance among the nobility and also in the Palace and therefore was considered the patriarch and protector of the Indian community.

A short mention of those resident in Lisbon whose names are known to us is appropriate at this stage and a more detailed one of some others will be made later.

Fr. Caetano Francisco do Couto had been Governor of the bishopric of Cochin and after being divested of that post by the Bishop D. Fr. Manoel de Santa Catharina, went to Lisbon, as is believed, in 1781 with complaints against the Bishop and demanding his dues.

Fr. José Francisco Gonçalves, ex-parish priest, professor of philosophy at the Seminary of Chorao, appointed by the said Bishop of Cochin who was also the Governor of the archbishopric of Goa, also proceeded to Portugal in 1781 after tendering his resignation or being allowed to leave, being unhappy with the bishop and aspiring to a higher position. He obtained a doctorate in Rome in 1782.

Fr. Custodio de Santa Maria, an Augustinian, who pretended to get revelations, shepherded a flock of sanctimonious ladies in Lisbon in the church of Sacrament.

Joaquim António Vicente, a naval rating, Narciso Vicente, who appears to be the latter's brother, José António Pinto of Candolim, a student, Fr. José Custodia de Faria, son of Fr. Caetano Victorino de Faria. There were, probably, many others of whom we have no knowledge.

Since they lived together, it was but natural that they should discuss matters concerning their motherland, and in their conversations and debates, it appears, the first signs of a secret plot to expel the Portuguese from the State of India and to transfer power to the natives, preferably to the Brahmins to which caste they belonged, took root.

It seems that Fr. Caetano Francisco do Couto and Fr. José António Gonçalves aspired to the vacant bishoprics in India which, then, existed at Cannanore, Mylapore and Malacca. Fr. Custodio de Santa Maria considered more versatile in his Order was also trying for a bishopric.

It so happened that at about the same time two Catanar priests of the Syro-Chaldean rite from Malabar were also in Lisbon who, we understand, went to that court and to Rome with the intentions of finding means to calm down the Christians of their rite who were always fighting among themselves and more so because of the seeds of antagonism that a Nestorian archbishop was sowing, thus driving them towards schism and heresy.

These two Syro-Chaldean priests received the protection of the Queen D. Maria I and also the benevolence of Pope Pius VI, and in common accord one of them, Fr. José Cariattil was elected and confirmed as Archbishop of Cannanore.

Such a promotion, the first of its kind, must have deeply hurt the feelings of the two Goan priests who, belonging to the Latin church and being more erudite, considered themselves more deserving to occupy the See of Cannanore than the Malabar Syrians. Therefore, because their ambitions were not fulfilled and more so because a Catanar was preferred over them, the moment the first signs of sedition were known, it was immediately attributed to them. As soon as this news was conveyed to the Secretary of State, Martinho de Mello e Castro, he wrote to the Governor in his letter of 21 July 1788, "regarding the first item, that of sedition, we have a fair knowledge of those who are known as the masterminds; they are two priests who came to this kingdom with pretensions to be employed in India, one of them very garrulous, and I have no doubts that they had hoped to get a bishopric like the one conferred on the Archbishop of Cannanore; they spoke to me, many times, of things in India trying to impress me that they were very capable, but I listened to them with the indifference that their discourses deserved; finally I told them to return to Goa with the certainty that their Archbishop and Prelate would employ them according to their merits. It is also true that while they made friendship with their compatriots, sons of India, one called José António Pinto, another Joaquim António Vicente, and yet another Narciso Vicente (the second of these young men studied in the navy) and what you refer to in your letter happened with me.[1] I have but a faint recollection as the information that I have of his ability and capability is almost negligible. I understand, however, that presently both he and the two priests who are in jail here, José António Gonçalves and Caetano Francisco do Couto[2] and some Indians who might have assisted them were bitterly complaining of the contempt with which the Portuguese treated them in that State. If instead of the Portuguese that this kingdom was sending to India the government and general administration were handed to the locals, giving them ecclesiastical, military and civil positions, Portugal would derive greater benefits from that State and only then would that country be rich and prosperous. However, little notice was taken here about such absurdities, both because of their nature and the inconsequence of the authors, and it seems quite natural that after their return to Goa they continued with the same or different brain-washing. That is, probably, where the warnings and complaints that you received against them had their origin".

"If it is true that there are men who foment and propagate ideas so pernicious as noted above, when they take place in Portugal, they merit the indifference and contempt with which they were treated here, but it cannot be likewise in the State of India where they may have very unpleasant consequences if due caution is not taken before it grows. In this context, it was very prudent on your part to have ordered the arrests of the said priests and their accomplices and begin inquiries into the case under reference and likewise it was very correct to have carried out searches of the arrested persons to find out if there were any links with neighbouring rulers of those States, particularly with Tipu Sultan. This is the most important aspect towards which utmost care and attention should be devoted."

It is obvious, therefore, that the Secretary of State had no doubts that the two clerics toyed with the idea of getting bishoprics though they never made any specific mention of it but always pretended to be capable men, revealing, indirectly, their intentions of being employed in India.

Having, however, occupied in India positions of certain importance and being doubtlessly well-educated, it is all too evident that they were also aspiring for positions not inferior to bishops, especially so, after the precedent of the bishopric of Cannanore being conferred on a Syro-Chaldean.

There is nothing singular in a priest, and a learned one at that and with experience, aspiring to become a bishop nor can one condemn such an ambition for that high position. What is condemnable in them is their attempt at inciting an uprising in their homeland to hand it over to some barbarian ruler in vindication of ambitions not satisfied by the ministry in Lisbon. The reasons why their requests were turned down are recorded in the very letter of the Secretary of State mentioned earlier. The minister disliked their loquacity, their exaggerated show of being very capable men, their nonsensical plan for the betterment of India, their importunate pleadings before the minister to be employed, though not daring to openly solicit a bishopric.

There is nothing extraordinary in the pretensions of the two clerics to episcopal positions. In 1772, Fr. Caetano Victorino de Faria, then a recent arrival in Lisbon, recounting his first activities in that court, recorded in his letters, to which we shall revert, the favourable acceptance he had, through the good offices of Prof. Fr. João Baptista de S. Caètano and on the part of the Archbishop Nuncio of Tyro, a Benedictine, who was said to be a lover of Goans and who after learning from Fr. Caetano about the ecclesiastical and secular state of affairs in India, went so far as to indicate to him that, just like St. Paul and other apostles, he would not rest until he had bestowed the mitre and the staff on the said natives. Fr. Caetano avers that the Nuncio was quite capable of doing this as he had the ears of the ministry, was listened to in the Board of Censors, of which he was a representative, was a person who could not be influenced and was a good and religious man and of nobility.

Fr. Caetano Victorino was accepted not only at the house of the Nuncio but also of Cardinal da Cunha and of many other noblemen and even in the royal palace, as is mentioned in detail elsewhere. By order of H. Majesty he was consulted in matters regarding India, especially ecclesiastical ones.

In the notes he made, on royal instruction, by way of comment about the ecclesiastical state of affairs in India, on the reports sent by the Bishop of Cochin, Governor of the archbishopric of Goa in 1781 (documents to which we shall revert later) and which were evidently compiled with the help of Fr. Caetano Francisco do Couto, who had recently arrived in Lisbon, the idea of nominating natives for bishoprics in India is well set.

The Bishop of Cochin stated at paragraph no. 10 of his Report or information that he would have liked as Archbishop of Cannanore any person from Portugal who would be inclined to live amidst the rudest and crudest people of Asia, to which Fr. Caetano Victorino, obviously with full concurrence of Fr. Caetano Francisco, replies: "With regard, however, to that of Cannanore, the learned Bishop has erred in stating that a metropolitan archbishop be sent because those people were the rudest of Asia. In fact, a stranger who does not know and cannot acclimatize to the customs of such people would never be able to deal with rude and crude people. On the contrary, one from their midst who, getting educated in Europe, acquiring those customs, being civilised and learned, would more easily and effectively be able to tame such people, educate them and bring them to greater perfection".

This "one from the same Asians who has been educated in Europe" clearly points to himself, Fr. Caetano Victorino, to Fr. Caetano Francisco, to Fr. José António Gonçalves, (both of whom were, at that time trying to obtain a doctorate in Rome) or to some other Goan. But little did the priest or priests who commented on the information of the Bishop of Cochin realise that H. Majesty and the Pope would take their comment to the letter and choose as Archbishop of Cannanore not a Latin Goan but a Malabar Syrian who rigorously met the requirements demanded by them.

The Bishop of Cochin continued at paragraph no. 11 of his Report, stating that he saw nothing in secular priests which could be of any use (for governors of bishoprics, superiors of missions) nor were the natives of India accepted in those regions even as missionaries. An exaggeration, perhaps, but pardonable because of those initial problems which the Bishop found himself in and to which Fr. Caetano or the two Caetanos replied in this manner, "We should not have replied to this paragraph because it bares the passionate blindness with which you speak because, no one but one who is out of his mind, will believe or make himself believe that if out of 3,000 clerics, it is not the tenth or the hundredth, it would, at least, be the thousandth. Therefore one could expect to find at least three, while you found none?"

"This indicates that you are ill-advised because while you were able to appoint Fr. Joaquim Furtado of Salcete and Fr. José Felippe[3] of Divar as professors of philosophy at the college of Chorao, if you wanted priests not only as professors and bishops but also to teach others how to become bishops, you would have found here more than a hundred, at least."

Such being the stand taken by the Goan priests residing in Lisbon, one can now understand better how great would have been their resentment on seeing themselves farther away from the mitre which they coveted so much. The resentment was further aggravated, as we have mentioned, with the nomination and confirmation of one Syrian Catanar whom they could not have but considered far inferior to themselves intellectually, morally, politically and in erudition.

The two priests, José António Gonçalves and Caetano Francisco do Couto, left Lisbon bound for India in April 1785, on board the *Senhor Jesus Resuscitado, Santa Zeferina* and *Princeza do Brazil* which reached

Goa on 1 May 1786. Some documents mention that the priests arrived in 1785, but this should be taken as their departure from Lisbon. The ships called at the port of Galle in Ceylon, where Fr. José António disembarked, reaching Goa, we are not exactly sure, either by the end of 1786 or beginning of 1787.

As the conspiracy was discovered in August 1787 much before the arrival of the ship which made the voyage that year, the Governor had the good sense of ordering the confiscation, on arrival of the ships, of any letters addressed to any of the suspects in Europe. They found among others the following: one from a boy called José António Pinto, belonging to the Pinto family of Candolim, of which family the Governor, while reporting to the Secretary of State, says (in his letter of 9 October 1787), they are known here as the haughtiest natives and most opposed to everything known as whites. That letter was addressed to one of his brothers, Fr. João Baptista Pinto, who at the time the Governor wrote, was already under arrest for being the brain behind the conspiracy, according to ample and undeniable evidence available against him. In that letter the boy, José António Pinto showered praises on Fr. José António Gonçalves, with arrogance made references about Fr. Custodio, an Augustinian, also of Goa, and stated that he had considered deeply in his mind and conversed with serious-minded people on the ways for the future prosperity of his homeland. From the enquiries made with some post office employees, suspicions in this case that the said José António Pinto and Fr. Custodio were both involved in the conspiracy were found well-founded.

The other letter was addressed to the said Fr. José António Gonçalves by another boy with whom he seemed to be very intimate, Joaquim António Vicente, a Goan too and one who had shared quarters with Eloy José Correa Peixoto. In this letter, besides other news, the writer shows his repugnance to speak to the Secretary of State, Martinho de Mello e Castro, fearing that he might be pressed into some service of H. Majesty that might embarrass him later on his return to India in the monsoon of 1787, and he indicates his intentions of getting in the service of Tipu, admitting having made known his intentions to someone called Calama or Jalama Brandão and Manoel Rodrigues, friends of the same Fr. José António, and ends his letter with protestations in these words, "I am a man of one word and deed and, therefore, I place myself entirely at your disposal. You may take it or consider it as done what has to be done there. I think I have made myself very clear." Mysterious words and indicative of some secret understanding between the two! The remaining portions of the letter were protestations of great friendship between him, José António Pinto, the author of the first letter, and the said Fr. Custodio.

Who Calama or Jalama Brandão and Manoel Rodrigues, referred to in the previous letter, were, is not known to us till this day; but we have more details than the Governor seemed to have about Eloy José Correa Peixoto with whom Joaquim António Vicente shared quarters in Lisbon. Speaking about the said Eloy José, at that time, in his letter of 16 January 1788 to the Secretary, the Governor only says that he was given to understand that he (Eloy) had served in this State, but seems to ignore what the Governor D. José Pedro da Camara had written to the same Secretary of State in his letter dated 29 December 1787, describing him as an adventurer, irrepressible, dissolute and whose inconsistency made him lose interesting fortunes that he had acquired and that he served for many years under the Nawab Hyder Ali and under the King of Tanjore. "I believe (added D. José Pedro da Camara) that he is going to rest in his house at Azeitão after all the trouble he faced through his long and continuous pilgrimages in Asia. It is possible that he may not be able to adjust himself to the lifestyle of his homeland which he will find very different from the one he was accustomed to (a very licentious one) and knowing him I am certain it will not be long before he returns in search of that life again. I am given to understand that he goes with the intentions of proposing to Your Excellency big projects, apparently very advantageous to the establishments and dominions of H. Majesty, and I am certain that he will embellish them with exaggerated offers but without solid foundations, which you will perceive soon." (Doc. no. 2)

The events around this man would have been important for new investigations in Lisbon regarding the plans of the conspiracy but forgotten as they were in Goa and to a greater extent in Portugal, no further action was taken.

Finally, other letters confirmed what the first two had stated corroborating the suspicions which surfaced from them. Also from judicial inquiries there were various indications that Fr. Caetano Victorino de Faria, who for many years was in Lisbon and was the protector of all Goans, as mentioned earlier, was an accomplice and had prior knowledge of the conspiracy.

With all this information the Governor decided to write to his counterpart in Mozambique to arrest José António Pinto, Joaquim António Vicente, Fr. Custodio and Fr. Caetano Victorino de Faria, should they happen to transit through that port in any boat originating from the kingdom during the monsoon of 1788 and which was very probable according to what was written in one of the above mentioned letters. The captain of the ships *Nossa Senhora da Arrabida and Santo António de Lisboa* which were now proceeding to the kingdom in 1788, was ordered to avoid any communication with any other ship which might reach Lisbon ealier than his, and, if he happened to call at any of the ports in the Azores, to show the order to the Governor or the respective commander so that he, on H. Majesty's service, should not let any other vessel which might carry letters or news to Lisbon depart before his ship. On reaching Lisbon he should not permit entry of any person on the ship, not even the normal courtesy visits, but should, instead, find immediate means of delivering to the Secretary of State the documents he carried and to await positive orders from the Secretary of State so that H. Majesty could make known his royal pleasure before divulging the details of the conspiracy to that court and letting the above mentioned suspects get the news or letters.

The Secretary of State, Martinho de Mello e Castro, in his letter of 21 July 1788 adds that no sooner was the missive of the Governor delivered to him, then he ordered the arrest of the Indians, authors of the letters that were seized here, copies of which were sent to Lisbon. Some of the Indians were, however, not found in that court. It transpired that José António Pinto, Joaquim António Vicente, Narciso Vicente and with them a priest called José, son of the famous Fr. Caetano Victorino de Faria, had left Lisbon with the assistance of the same Fr. Caetano, for France from where they would proceed to India. Joaquim António confided in some of his friends, before leaving Lisbon, that in France he would meet the ambassadors that Tipu Sultan, periodically, sent to Versailles and would discuss with them some business deals. This tallied with what Joaquim António had written to Fr. José António Gonçalves in the letter that was confiscated, in which he cautioned the greatest care so that he may succeed in being taken into service of Tipu.

The Secretary of State further informed the Governor that these facts and the journey of the four Indians via France to their homeland, renouncing the better comforts available on Portuguese vessels which made regular sailings to that State, and the very opportune time when the journey was undertaken to coincide with the arrival in France of the three ambassadors sent to that court by Tipu Sultan with whom, confides one of the Indians, he had matters of business to discuss, are details that deserve closer scrutiny vis-a-vis the results of the investigations ordered. He cautions him to keep in mind the need to keep a careful watch on the steps of these three Indians immediately on their arrival in that State.

where they had not yet reached, so that they might not be forewarned of the disclosures of the conspiracy.

The Secretary of State, finally, reports that by virtue of the contents of the letter that was intercepted he had ordered the arrest, from the convent of the Paulists in Lisbon, where he resided, of Fr. Caetano Victorino de Faria, the only person in Lisbon who could be suspected of being involved in the conspiracy, as is evident from the contents of the letters sent from India. A search of all his papers was carried out but nothing incriminating and that could throw some light on the case, was found. However from the findings of the inquiry, from the contents of a letter written from Lisbon by António José Castrioto and from the depositions of witnesses who were interrogated in this regard, it could be amply proved that he had prior knowledge of the attempted uprising and was propagating the results of the conspiracy which, he thought, had already percolated here.

The son of this priest, born out of legal marriage, and who also became a priest, called José Custodio de Faria, became world famous later, in France, as L'Abbe Faria. We shall revert to him and his father later.

As stated earlier, after the departure of Frs. Gonçalves and Couto in 1785, it transpired that during the voyage they discussed ways and means they could avail of to carry out their nefarious plans. On arrival in Goa, these were carried out in accordance with their deliberations, details of which are recorded in the proceedings of the case, in the confessions of the accused, in the depositions of the witnesses of the inquiries and other legal proceedings abridged in the sentence delivered on 9 December 1788. Here it is recorded that the conspirators had intended to free the entire State from the subjection, obedience and government of H. Majesty, the Most Faithful, to bringing down this government and implant a new republic where the natives would govern themselves under a system of parliamentary assembly and be a sovereign nation in this part of the empire. With this objective in view, they had, first, instilled a sense of rebellion in the minds of their colleagues in the ecclesiastical profession and influenced them and the vicars that, as parish priests, they could mix with religion the seeds of dissatisfaction and sedition.

For this purpose, meetings of the leaders were arranged at the house of Fr. Couto and of others and they also managed to attract into their party many native military officers so that with their help they could bring into their fold the troops of the State. To persuade people, they had recourse to horrible lies and coersion, assuring them, very confidently, that this rebellion was not a sin but the will of God and that it had the blessings of the High Pontiff himself.

The sentence records that they had boasted of the assistance of foreign powers, of having thousands of arms and unlimited funds, while, in fact, they had nothing. This was a mere disinformation spread by the two priests and their accomplices to attract, by deceit, their victims to their side.

Regarding assistance of foreign powers allow us to make a point or a reservation that it should not be, totally, taken to be a part of disinformation. We shall leave detailed consideration of this to a more appropriate occasion. Continuing with the perusal of the sentence, we find that the rebellion did not stop at vague and verbose speeches and idealistic slogans but it was found that the masterminds, with the assistance of their accomplices and sympathisers, had worked out minute details of the ways of operation, deploying the corps of rebels who would attack squares, market places, guards and more important houses, assigning those who would surprise persons in high positions and authority, agreeing on signals to be used to herald the so-called freedom simultaneously in various places, threatening to kill anyone who opposed the rebellion and finally fixing the date for the execution of the revolt for the 10 of August 1787. Unfortunately, their plans were foiled because of the information received the preceding days.

FOOTNOTES

1. **Intercepted in Goa after the discovery of the conspiracy.**
2. **The Secretary of State wrongly thought that Fr. José António Gonçalves was in prison.**
3. **The same Fr. José António Gonçalves.**

3

TRIAL AND SENTENCE

It has already been stated that on 9 August, immediately after the first investigations, which followed the receipt of complaints, were completed, the Governor committed the case to the Chief Justice of the State, José Joaquim de Sequeira Magalhães e Lanções, for trial on the attempted revolt, at which trial Mr. Justice Sebastião José Ferreira Barroco would serve as secretary. The Chief Justice had barely begun the trial, when during the same monsoon of 1787, his successor José da Rocha Dantas e Mendonça arrived. This minister was a judge of the High Court of Oporto and, by royal order of 17 February 1787, he was rewarded by H. Majesty with the position of Chief Justice of the High Court of Goa for a period of six years, or more or until orders to the contrary. Furthermore, considering his erudition, merits and services and confident that he would perform his duties to the satisfaction of H. Majesty, in any assignment given, H. Majesty did, likewise, grace him with a position of Counsellor of the Overseas Council, a charge he was to take and hold only after serving as Chief Justice satisfactorily, as was expected of him.

Justices Manoel Vicente Teixeira de Carvalho and José Caetano Pacheco Tavares also came during the same monsoon. Consequently, during the monsoon of 1788, Chief Justice José Joaquim de Sequeira Magalhães e Lanções, who had been promoted to the Supreme Court, and Justice Joaquim José Mendes da Cunha, returned to the kingdom. The High Court, thus, had the full complement of judges when the successors arrived.

In the same monsoon of 1788, the Governor sent to the court at Lisbon whatever details of the investigations were, then, available. The new Chief Justice, José da Rocha Dantas e Mendonça, continued with the case from 14 January 1788, but could not complete it in time to forward it to the court at Lisbon during the same monsoon, because there were still some examination of witnesses to be conducted and because he had fallen ill soon after his arrival.

In his letter to the Governor written on 21 July 1788, the Secretary of State, Martinho de Mello e Castro, acknowledged receipt of the investigations sent by the vessels *Nossa Senhora da Arrabida* and *Santo António de Lisboa,* and on behalf of H. Majesty, ordered that the people, who were found implicated in this revolt, be duly tried and sentenced after complying with all the legal formalities and undergoing all processes of law. This was, presently, being done.

The accused that were in jail were being guarded by European troops as it was neither safe nor convenient to use any other, and this during a time of war was of considerable loss to the Exchequer.

In October 1788, there was a change of jail for some of the accused, probably due to the information that kept coming from the investigation. Fr. Luis António Gonçalves, cleric *in minoribus,* was shifted from the gunpowder room to Reis Magos fort and Sebastião Paulo de Noronha from Reis Magos to the gunpowder room in the same cell where Luis António was incarcerated. Similarly, Thomas António Dias was shifted from the gunpowder room to Reis Magos fort and Luis Gonzaga, Lieutenant of the Legion of Ponda, from Reis Magos fort to the gunpowder room and prison of Thomas António.[1] Manoel Luis and Lt. Ignacio Toscano exchanged cells from Reis Magos fort to the gunpowder room, respectively. Fr. Jorge Dias of Candolim was shifted from the gunpowder room to the fort of Reis Magos.

On 14 October, an order was issued to the Captain of the gunpowder room to allow José Pedro de Araujo, defence lawyer of the accused, to meet and talk to them so that the accused could instruct their lawyer regarding their defence. He was also asked to allow the solicitor of the Casa de Misericordia (House of Mercy) to talk to the accused and also to hand over to the solicitor some letters or papers from the defence advocate, leaving it to the solicitor or any of the accused to make whatever notes they deemed necessary and to relay their instructions.

On the same day the Governor ordered Field Marshal Francisco António da Veiga Cabral, Commander of the troops, to discharge Lieutenants of the 2nd Legion, Ignacio Caetano Toscano and Nicolau Luis da Costa, accused of the attempted revolt against the State. He was also asked to issue a certificate stating that the undermentioned had taken the oath of allegiance: Manoel Caetano Pinto and Pedro Luis Gonzaga, both Lieutenants, Balthazar Caeiro, Sergeant, Manoel Ferrão, António Fernandes and Caetano Xavier da Costa, all Corporals, João Vaz, Orderly, David Francisco Viegas, Chief Surgeon, and Francisco Pereira, assistant to the surgeon. All the above were from the Legion of Ponda.

Nicolau Luis da Costa and Ignacio Caetano Toscano, Lts. of Bardez Legion.

At the end of the trial, the final sentence was passed on 9 December 1788, which was certified by the Governor in his capacity as magistrate of all courts. The Chief Justice Rocha (José da Rocha Dantas e Mendonça), Justices Amaral (António Rebello do Amaral), Tavares (José Caetano Pacheco Tavares) and Teixeira (Manoel Vicente Teixeira de Carvalho) were present, also the Procurator of the Crown, Justice and Secretary of State, Barroco (Sebastião José Ferreira Barroco).

A transcript of the proceedings and of the sentence was sent to Lisbon, the remaining portions being sent now, under cover of a letter from the Governor, dated 18 March 1789 and addressed to the Secretary of State. No copy was kept in the secretariat of the government of the State of India and the original was filed in the archives of the High Court and, presumably believed lost today as even in 1835, when the Governor of the State ordered a copy of the trial and sentence to be taken, the file was found full of omissions and printed in the second condition in the Manifesto do Governo Provisional and in the *Refutação Analytica* of the same *Manifesto* (Doc. no. 3). It is quite probable that the copy sent to Portugal has been preserved in good condition, but as it was not available to us, we were compelled to avail of the printed copies. Despite their omissions (some of these we were able to fill with details from other documents) they still throw sufficient light, to enable one to follow the deduction of proof and learn the decisions of the court regarding each civilian accused. The priests, who were indicted, were not tried here but were sent to Lisbon, in accordance with the orders from the court, as we shall see later.

After duly considering the evidence on record, judgement was delivered on 9 December 1788. It was established that the masterminds behind the conspiracy were Frs. José António Gonçalves and Francisco Caetano do Couto. Sentences to various terms of punishment were awarded as follows:

Death Sentence

1-2. Pedro Luis Gonzaga and Manoel Caetano Pinto, Lts. of the Ponda Legion, accomplices and agent provocateurs. From the depositions of various co-accused and the confessions of the very persons who endeavoured to subvert the Legion which, they claimed, was totally suborned, it was found that Pedro Luis Gonzaga had gone to Mandur. He had gone with the main purpose of discussing with Ignacio Caetano Lopes, also a member of the rebellion, the confinement of Sebastião Dias, Corporal in his company, as he was opposed to the revolt and to elicit from the same Ignacio the extent of the assistance of his Company of Auxiliaries, of which he was the captain, with whose help and that of other members of the Legion, they expected to attack some forts. Ignacio Caetano Lopes confessed this to be true.

The said Lts. Pedro Luis Gonzaga and Manoel Caetano Pinto, were condemned to be bound with ropes and to the accompaniment of the town crier, were to be dragged by the horses' tails through the streets of the city to the gallows, which were to be erected, and there, let to die a natural death. While still alive, their hands were to be chopped and after their death their heads severed and staked on poles and their bodies quartered and displayed on high poles in public places of the island of Goa, provinces of Salcete and Bardez and especially in the villages of Candolim and Nerul, where they resided, and also in the villages of Pilerne, Piedade, Mandur and Nagoa, till they decayed with time.

3. David Francisco Viegas, chief surgeon of the Ponda Legion. He incited other accused of the same Legion to revolt. His useless and persistent denials were negatived by proofs surfaced from confessions of the accused António Fernandes, Corporal in the same Legion, and were sustained in the examination of Pedro Luis Gonzaga, corroborated by the pointed references he made to two conversations that he had had with the accused.

The accused was condemned to be taken to the gallows bound with ropes and to the accompaniment of the town crier and there let to die a natural death. While still alive, his hands were to be amputated and after death his head severed and both staked on high poles raised in the place of his residence, till they decayed with time.

4. Caetano Xavier da Costa, Corporal in the same Legion, was condemned to the same punishment as the previous accused, David Francisco Viegas.

5-6. Nicolau Luis da Costa and Ignacio Caetano Toscano, Lts. in the Bardez Legion. Having joined the rebellion they promised their best efforts in recruiting friends and acquaintances to the revolt. There were reasons to believe that they had committed themselves to suborn the Legion of Bardez, where they were officers. This Legion as well as that of Ponda consisted of native soldiers and Costa and Toscano were Lieutenants in that Legion. During the trial no evidence was adduced that any other person or officer was entrusted with a similar mission of suborning the troops. It is, therefore, safe to conclude that the accused had undertaken this task of subverting the Legion and drawing it into the fold of the rebels, in the same way as they did to that of Ponda. They confessed that they were being asked by other accomplices what people they had recruited for the cause. This is fully established from the confessions of the accused and corroborated by other witnesses and Fr. Couto who made a mention of an extraordinary and cruel way that the accused had proposed to use, namely, to poison the bread supplied to the troops.[2] The belated report made by Nicolau Luiz da Costa, personally, and by Ignacio Caetano Toscano, through his brother António Eugenio, could not be considered as a mitigating circumstance, because both of them were well aware of the conspiracy, its circumstances and the stage it had reached much before they made the report on 5 and 6 August, a time when the revolt had already been discovered. This was proved by a number of witnesses questioned on 3 August by the Vicar General of the archbishopric, who enjoyed the position of a Archbishop Primate. Fr. Pedro Caetano José Lobo, then Vicar of Tivim. who refused to be influenced by Fr. Couto and had tried to dissuade other rebels from this treacherous act, reported on 31 July the details of the rebellion to the Archbishop who, convinced about the reality of the revolt, submitted to the Governor a summary of the details he had obtained[3].

They were condemned to be bound with ropes and accompanied by the town crier to be taken to the gallows and, there, let to die a natural death and after their deaths their heads to be severed and staked on high poles erected in places of their residence till they decayed with time.

7. Miguel António da Costa, brother of Corporal Caetano Xavier da Costa. It was established, not only from his confession but also from those of the leader Fr. Couto and Sebastião Paulo de Noronha and Lt. Gonzaga, that he was fully aware of the conspiracy and had joined the rebels with great enthusiasm, recruiting new members, agreeing to detain the Field Marshal, promising to do everything possible and carrying messages from Lt. Gonzaga to other leaders. He was condemned to the gallows and his head was to be severed after his death and staked on a high pole erected at his place of residence.

8. Ignacio Caetano Lopes, Captain of Auxiliaries from Mandur having been asked by the leader Fr. Couto and by his other brother to join the rebel group, agreed and promised to give the help of his company of Auxiliaries to attack the forts and to confine, in his house, the Corporal of his company, Sebastião Dias, whom Lt. Gonzaga was afraid of, as he was hostile to the conspiracy. This is established from the confessions

of the accused and co-accused Gonzaga and Fr. Couto. He was condemned to the same punishment as the previous one.

9. Salvador Alvares da Costa was invited by the leaders to join the group and after associating with them, he revealed the number of Portuguese soldiers in the first Regiment, where he was a soldier, and the state of fortifications in the fortress of Rachol. He was so imbued with the spirit of rebellion that, when he was arrested, he stated before the Lt. and the soldier who was handcuffing him, that he was doing what he had to do and repeated this a second time. This is recorded in his confessions and tallies with the confessions of the leader Fr. Couto. He was awarded the same punishment as the previous one.

10. Balthazar Caeiro, Sergeant of the Ponda Legion.
11. Manuel Ferrão, Corporal of the same Legion.
12. António Fernandes, Corporal of the same Legion.
13. João Vaz, soldier.
14. José Monteiro.
15. Bernardo de Misquita. He confessed that he was called by Sebastião Paulo de Noronha and that he had had dealings with the leader Fr. Couto.

All of them were sentenced to the same punishment as that of Salvador Costa. In addition, all their assets were confiscated and their memories, their children and grandchildren were branded infamous forever.

Deportation

1. José Luiz Guineti of Milan, servant of Archbishop of Cannanore, D. José Cariattil. The mastermind, Fr. Couto, confessed that this accused knew of the conspiracy because, during the voyage they had undertaken together from Lisbon to India, the conspiracy was discussed by all of them. Besides, on the death of his master, the Archbishop, which occured briefly after his reaching Goa, the accused had associated with the leaders and especially Fr. José António Gonçalves whom he would always accompany and follow in all his trips, meetings and functions. Though the accused denied, even under torture, full knowledge of the conspiracy, it is hard to believe that he was ignorant of it, when the leaders themselves were relying on him to make use of his expertise in agriculture, manufacture of glass and paper after winning the so-called freedom and independence. The accused deposed that the others would curse the Portuguese, in his presence, and show their resentment to have to live under their subjection

and obedience in this State and avers that from that attitude he understood that the leaders were attempting something and had some secret plans, though he was never sure if it was to request assistance from some ruler to start an uprising or to secede to him. However, from his confession the only conclusion that could be drawn was that he had full knowledge of the enmity, ill will and perverse intentions that other accused had against the State. From other declarations and depositions it was evident that this accused was one of the conspirators and the very fact that he remained a fugitive as soon as the other accused were arrested contributed to give more weight to this conclusion.

He was condemned to be bound with ropes and to the accompaniment of the town crier, to be flogged in public roads of the city and to be deported for life to serve in the galleys of Angola.

2. Sebastião de Noronha, Corporal at the shore of Salcete. It is established from his confession and those of Lt. Toscano and borne out from the examination of witnesses that everything tallies with the declarations made by Lt. Nicolau Luiz da Costa, that this accused was aware of the conspiracy before 26 July and refrained from reporting it to the proper authorities, though he now pretends to defend himself with the excuse that he did not understand the implications of the conspiracy nor had sufficient details to make a report, so much so that Lt. Toscano had promised that he would explain it to him again, and in detail at some other opportune occasion. Yet from his confession it is obvious that he had sufficient knowledge to understand that this was a revolt against the State and this simple information and circumstance should have made him duty bound to report the matter to the authorities.

He was condemned to be bound with ropes and accompanied by the town crier, to be flogged on the streets of the city and deported for life to Bengal.

3. Manoel Luis, though it is not proved that he was aware of the conspiracy except from the confessions of the leader Fr. Couto, which, being the only evidence on record, does not constitute full proof, still from other circumstances underlying the depositions of the leader Fr. Couto and considering that the accused was his brother-in-law between whom there was no known discord, there are sufficient reasons, in an offence of this nature, to condemn the accused, despite the fact that he maintained in his denials during his examination.

He was condemned to be deported. From the omissions in the copies of the sentence one cannot ascertain to which country he was deported but one can safely conclude that it must have been some place in East Africa. He was also flogged.

4. Vicente de Abreu was a farmer. At the request of Fr. Mathias Bernardo da Fonseca, he sheltered and hid in his house Fr. José António Gonçalves, according to his own confessions. It is improbable, therefore, that he did not know the reasons why the priest became a fugitive soon after the arrests of various accused and also of his own brother. Furthermore he was aware of the road blocks placed on the way to the frontier. It was he who engaged the three labourers to accompany and guide Fr. Gonçalves to the limits of the frontier as confirmed by the said three labourers.

He was condemned to be flogged through the streets of the city, bound with ropes and accompanied by the town crier, and to be deported for 10 years to Senna.

5. Francisco Pereira, helper to the surgeon. He was awarded the same punishment and 10 years deportation to Mozambique.

All the deportees were sentenced to confiscation of their assets to the Exchequer and Royal Council and threatened with death should they ever return and be seen in any fort, island, province or place of this State or captaincy general of Goa.

Galleys

1. Lourenço Fernandes, farmer, servant of Fr. Mathias Bernardo da Fonseca. It is established from his confessions and from those of others that, at the request of the said priest, he went and called the accused, Vicente de Abreu to an empty house next to his, where, earlier on the night of the 7th, the fugitive Fr. Gonçalves, whom he brought to the said house, had slept and where, he knew, the priest had stayed upto the 11th, when he ran away crossing the frontier. He was fully aware of the reasons why the priest had run away and also that he was the mastermind of the revolt which, by then, was common knowledge.

He was sentenced to flogging after being bound with ropes and accompanied by the town crier. He was deported to the galleys of Goa.

2-4. Felippe Fernandes, Victorino Vaz and Vicente Gomes. It has been proved that they guided the leader, Fr. Gonçalves, who leaving the island of Chorao, at the dead of night, went to Mahem, thereafter across the borders, through a circuitous route, to Azarem, dominion of the Court of Pune. This secretive, devious and surreptitious way of the priest was sufficient to raise one's suspicion that the priest was one of the conspirators who was attempting a revolt against the State and that many other suspects had been arrested which was already known to the public on the 11th. Furthermore they were aware that they were doing something that was illegal and forbidden and could not have ignored that helping a fugitive from justice, besides being prohibited, was a criminal act.

They were condemned to be bound with ropes and accompanied by the town crier, to be flogged in the streets and deported to the galleys of Goa.

5. Manoel Silvestre was a student. The charges against him were that he accompanied the mastermind Fr. Gonçalves from Guirim to Chorao, on 7 August, through unused paths when the priest was trying to evade arrest. He confessed that he learnt that the priest was to be arrested, from the priest himself and from what he had seen and heard at Pilerne. He cannot now excuse himself that he thought that the arrest was ordered by the Prelate. Neither can the candid answers which he gave to all the questions during his interrogation be taken as mitigating circumstances because he is endowed with sufficient intelligence to understand the import and gravity of that action. He was deported to the galleys.

All the above accused were also sentenced to pay the costs. It was also ordered that those not sentenced to death were to be taken to the gallows to witness the entire execution.

The executions took place on 13 December 1788, in the Mandovi maidan, near the Customs House, where the gallows were erected. The Mandovi maidan was situated, as its name indicates, adjacent to the Customs House with the river Mandovi to the north, the public road from the city to Santa Luzia to the east and the Convent of St. Dominic on the other side of the road. To the west were various government offices, among which were the Civil Supplies godowns and, today, they face the actual limits of the Convent of St. Cajetan. The place was the most populated of the city where everybody collected. Today, the Mandovi maidan has been turned into a walled palm grove and belongs to some Hindu gentleman. There, amidst the palm grove, one can see the old gallows, made of two stone pillars with a wooden beam across the top portion and a noose in the middle. Now there remain only loose stones of the old pillars.

The sentence of 9 December states that the accused should be taken to the gallows which will be erected. In fact, for the occasion, two more, made of wood, were erected at the side of the old one.

There are no records about who were the priests who accompanied the sentenced men to the place of their hanging nor of any other incident that took place in that gloomy place deserving special mention.

There are, however, two official reports on record, regarding the conspiracy and the execution, from the Senates of the Municipalities of Goa and Bardez, in the beginning of 1789, mentioning the event as noteworthy, copies of which were sent to Lisbon (Doc. no. 4).

It is worth, at this stage, comparing the above two reports, one made by noblemen of Goa, Europeans and descendents of Europeans, and the other by the native councillors of the Bardez municipality. Those from noblemen, Europeans and descendents of Europeans who naturally were happy with the punishment meted out to the rebels, reported the events without emotion, while those from Bardez, shocked with the execution of their compatriots, friends and relatives, after referring broadly to the event, commented, saying: "The people, the nobility and the members of the Senate of this Council of Bardez applaud, with great satisfaction, the punishment imposed on the rebels. On the appointed day, we all gathered, together with officers, the nobility and the troops of the province, which stood in formation before the gallows, and witnessed the execution".

One can notice, from this, the precautions the government took on such a solemn occasion. The name of de Tonnelet, as a member of the Senate of Bardez Municipality, is noteworthy. He was a Sergeant-Major of the Cavalry of the Legion of that province and his full name was Henrique Claudio Desanges de Tonnelet, a French officer serving in our army. According to the existing law, at that time, military officers had to form part of the Senate of the municipalities, and in the list of members of the Senate of Bardez for that year 1789, was Lt. Col. José Lobato Gameiro de Faria, who had, just then, been transferred to the government of Anjediva. On the government being advised by the Senate of this transfer, by a notification of 5 January 1789, he appointed S. M. de Tonnelet as member, because it was mandatory that among the members of the Senate there should be a person endowed with zeal, intelligence and be capable of managing the factories at Mapusa, put up by the municipality, and reduce the losses they had been suffering since their inception and manage them, profitably, with judicious and zealous economy. There was, at that time, a craze for opening cloth mills in the country, at the cost of the government and municipalities. These never produced anything nor could they compensate for the huge losses that they suffered right from their inception.

Another noteworthy coincidence was that of de Tonnelet and Felippe Nery Pinto, relative of some of the rebels, being members of the Senate. It is a legend with the house of the Pintos of Saligao, as confirmed by

Mr. Luis Xavier Correa da Graça, who married a lady from that family, that S. M. de Tonnelet was given the charge of arresting Manoel Pinto, one of the wealthy landlords and heir to the estate. For this purpose the S. M. had his house and that of his relative and neighbour, Felippe Nery Pinto, Captain of Auxiliaries (this is how it was recorded in the Senate) surrounded and after arresting Manoel Pinto, he treated him and the families of both the houses kindly and with deference.

De Tonnelet, eventually rose to the rank of Colonel Commandant of the Corps of Sepoys at Bicholim and died on 30 September 1821. But coming back to the sentence, it makes mention of:

João de Souza of Honavar, who was absolved of all charges and set free on 16 December.

Regarding the accused Sebastião Paulo de Noronha, who died in prison, his defence lawyer was given the opportunity to plead on points of facts and law on behalf of his client. He was found guilty of high treason and sentenced that his memory, his children and his grandchildren be branded as infamous and their assets confiscated in favour of the Exchequer and Royal Council.

These were the accused who figured in the sentencing of 9 December 1788. There were, however, others whom the sentence does not mention and who, by order of the High Court dated 15 December, (Doc. no. 5) were acquitted. Among these, set free on 17 December, the birthday of the Queen, were: Fr. António Felippe Vaz, former Vicar of Moira, António Dias and Manoel Pinto of Saligao who were imprisoned in the fort of Reis Magos; the Dessai of Ponda, Narba Naik, who, it appears, was in the fort of Alorna because the order of acquittal was sent to Col. Manoel Godinho de Mira, although when he was first arrested, he was taken to Fort Aguada; the physician Manoel António Gonçalves, brother of Fr. José António Gonçalves, whose place of incarceration was unknown to us, as the order was addressed to Captain of Grenadiers, João António de Moraes Sarmento, without any details; the priests of the Congregation, Sebastião Baptista and Pedro Delgado who were imprisoned in their convent cells and the order of their acquittal was sent to the Prefect of the Congregation, Fr. Sebastião Mascarenhas.

FOOTNOTES

1. Regarding Thomaz António Dias we have not found any other record besides this, order. Is he being mistaken for António Dias of Saligao who was set free at the end of the trial?

2. From the plans of action suggested by these accused, which are not known to have been accepted by the rest of the accomplices, a false legend was created and is still current among the classes hostile to Brahmins. It seems that the conspirators decided to poison the bread supplied to the troops and because of this, it is said, the Brahmins were prohibited from baking bread in Goa, as they were doing before, and this trade is now being carried by the Kshatriyas. There is no evidence that before the discovery of the revolt, Brahmins were bakers in Goa, nor do we find the least trace in this alleged prohibition. Besides, there was no reason for it, and there is nothing to prove that such a despicable plan formed part of the revolt or that bakers had concurred with this plan.

   From the tenacity, however, with which certain classes defend the veracity of such a legend, we give an example.

   Long ago, while a criminal trial was in progress in a court, in which various Brahmins were accused of having murdered a military officer, descendant of an European, we received through a native, an anonymous and libelous note against the Brahmins, wherein, among other wrong doings attributed to them, was this alleged plan of poisoning of the bread of the troops, as a strategy to be employed for the success of the attempted revolt. The signatories demanded the issuance of an order prohibiting them from exercising their trade of bakers. They also demanded immediate publication of this order in the government *Gazette* and since the trial was nearing its end, it was not difficult to discern that the objective was to prejudice the minds of the public and influence the judges against the accused. We, summarily, rejected this claim and it was not without a touch of surprise that we found, later, that the claim was being patronized by the highest persons, who indicated their desire of publication, despite our insistent refusal. Eventually, it never came into print.

3. The priest who made the complaint was considered a traitor among the families that suffered because of him and, perhaps, they still look down on him.

4

PRIESTS IMPLICATED IN THE REVOLT AND SENT TO LISBON

The Governor knew how embarrassing the trial of the priests implicated in the revolt would be. Therefore, in the first letter he addressed to the Court in Lisbon via Bombay on 9 August 1787, informing them of the discovery of the revolt and the arrest of many priests, he wrote to the Secretary of State, Martinho de Mello e Castro: "And I request you to let me know, with the least possible delay, the orders of H. Majesty so that I may know how to proceed with the priests."

In his letter of 17 January 1788, he repeated: "As the majority of the accused in this premeditated revolt against the State are the priests, I find myself in the horns of a dilemma, not knowing how to proceed in this respect; if I should send them to Portugal or if I should hold them here till H. Majesty takes a final decision. This I have already requested for in my earlier letter."

The reply came immediately through the next sailing. In his letter of 21 July 1788, the Secretary of State replied: "If the two priests who are imprisoned[1] are found during the investigations to be involved in the revolt and their residences dangerous (against which you must take necessary precautions) they should be sent under proper security, to this kingdom together with the charge-sheets."

In another letter of the same date, after informing him that H. Majesty had ordered that the accused found implicated in the conspiracy should be duly put on trial and proceeded with in accordance with the provisions of law and other legal formalities, he adds: "Regarding the priests, they should be arrested and sent to this kingdom with their respective charge-sheets, to be tried here in accordance with the orders of H. Majesty."

While this was being written in Lisbon, doubts were being raised in Goa regarding the trial of the priests. The statutes in Book 2, ch. 1 dealt with cases where clerics and religious persons had to appear before secular courts. One was not sure if these statutes were comprehensive enough to cover all or any of the offences committed by ecclesiastical persons. This issue was referred to the High Court for its opinion and in its order of 20 July 1788, it opined that the arrested persons, being priests, but charged with offences of sedition and high treason and considering that they had masterminded the revolt, they should not be tried by ecclesiastical courts, as crimes of that nature were outside the jurisdiction of such courts. The present case came under the provisions of the law dated 24 October 1764 (no. 4), incorporated in the said statutes. In conformity with the existing law and practice followed here as well as in all Catholic kingdoms, ecclesiastics charged with similar offences had to be detained in H. Majesty's prisons, in which they were presently held until specific orders from H. Majesty who had already been informed about the case. Furthermore, the trial against the civilians had to proceed without further delay. (Doc. no. 6).

In compliance with the orders of H. Majesty issued during the monsoon of 1788, the Governor ordered that the 14 priests be sent on board *St. Luis* and *Santa Maria Magdalena* and handed over to the authorities in Lisbon. The captain of the vessels, Lt. Cmdr. António Joaquim dos Reis Portugal, took charge of the prisoners on 29 March 1789 and the Governor ordered the receiver of the court to return to the priests all the clothes seized from them and as it was found that some had none and others very little, he ordered that they be issued whatever clothes they might need from the Royal magazine stores, in addition to what they had and what their relatives had contributed.

The priests who embarked here were:

1. Caetano Francisco da Silva, Vicar of St. Lourenço de Linhares.
2. Manoel da Expectação, Vicar of Ponda.
3. João Alvares de Souza, Vicar of Pomburpa.
4. Miguel Alvares de Souza, Vicar of Pilerne.
5. Vicente Alvares.
6. Caetano Francisco do Couto of Panjim.
7. Mathias Bernardo da Fonseca of Chorao.
8. Luis António Gonçalves, seminary student of Pilerne.
9. Luis Caetano de Souza of Moira.
10. José Manoel de Mendes of Piedade, Vicar of Guirim.
11. José António Vaz of Anjuna.
12. João Baptista Pinto of Candolim.
13. Diogo Benedicto Lobo of Serula.

14. Jorge Dias of Candolim.

Of these, thirteen reached Lisbon, one expired on the way and his name was not recorded. They were immediately taken to the tower of St. Julião de Barra, where they were lodged at the expense of H. Majesty.

After a few days, Fr. Caetano Francisco do Couto was sent to the convent of St. Francis of the city to be examined if he was mentally sound, because while all the others behaved normally and with decorum, he was just the opposite, to the extent that he could not be controlled as he, sometimes, refused to eat and at other times broke the crockery. This is stated by the Secretary of State in his letter to the Governor written on 9 May 1790.

We do not know how long Fr. Couto was kept at St. Francis, or if he was hospitalised and later brought back to the Tower, or if he was shifted to another prison, or if he was eventually cured or not of his malady.

The priests remained in their cells, without being produced before any magistrate or Court, and, as in India there was no news from them, the Governor Francisco da Cunha e Menezes, was compelled to write to the court on 8 March 1793, informing that the Chief Justice Sebastião José Ferreira Barroco, who was acting as Chief Justice on the demise of José da Rocha Dantas e Mendonça on 29 August 1792, had advised that the properties confiscated from the priests accused of the uprising against the State in 1787 were, noticeably deteriorating in the hands of the receivers of the court and, as they had not been sentenced no action could be taken here in this regard. It was, therefore, imperative that H. Majesty take a decision before the properties were totally ruined. He attached a list of the income derived from the said properties which was not, however, copied.

The Governor thought that the case merited a decision from the royal court. Those at the court thought otherwise, and no reply was forthcoming. The same old custom!

The priests remained in the jail without trial or legal processes.

All had almost forgotten them when, in the monsoon of 1802, it became known that, at least one of them was alive. It so happened that the vessel making the voyage that year, brought two official notes or dispatches from the Secretary of State, Viscount of Amadia, to the Governor, Francisco António da Veiga Cabral, one of which dated 12 March, stated that in pursuance of the information received from the Archbishop of Goa to the effect that the priest Fr. Manoel da Expectação, who had been arrested with others, was innocent, the Prince Regent was pleased to set him free and permit him to return to his homeland aboard the same vessel with orders that he should be reinstated in the same position he held prior to his imprisonment or be employed in the service of the church, in accordance with his merits (Doc. no. 7).

By another dispatch of 30 March, H. Highness ordered that he be paid from the royal coffers, a life pension of 400 *reis* per day, a privilege he was already enjoying from that court by virtue of an act of kindness on the part of H. Highness (Doc. no. 8).

We do not know what action the Archbishop took regarding the priest, but we are sure that he must have employed him, not only to comply with the royal orders but also because he himself was instrumental, with his information, in obtaining his freedom. On his side, the Governor by his ordinance of 16 November 1802, sanctioned a pension account to be opened in the Accountant-General's office, on behalf of the priest, to be effective from the date of the order of the Secretary of State (Doc. no. 9).

The priests were forgotten again, until 18 years after they had departed from Goa, during which time, many fruitless attempts were made to obtain their freedom and pardon, the prayers of those who were still alive were, eventually, heard and in the monsoon of 1807 the following were sent back to Goa: Jorge Dias, Caetano Francisco da Silva, Miguel Alvares, Vicente Alvares, Mathias Bernardo da Fonseca, Diogo Benedicto Lobo, João Baptista Pinto, and Luis António Gonçalves, seminary student.

All of them were pardoned by H. Highness of any charge that might have been levelled against them and he ordered that their confiscated properties be duly returned to them so that they could administer them as their own, with the exclusion of whatever income from the said properties had already been collected by the revenue office, prior to this order (Doc. nos. 10-11).

Similarly, H. Highness, in the same monsoon, after duly considering the representations made by the heirs or constituted attorneys of the priests João Alvares de Sousa, José António Vaz, Luis Caetano de Souza and José Manoel de Menezes, who died on the way to the kingdom, ordered the return of all assets and properties belonging to the said deceased priests, as it was done in the case of others (Doc. no. 12).

It is strange that while the official note from the Secretary of State dated 9 May 1790 states that only one priest had expired during the voyage, the one dated 23 May 1807 should mention that four had expired while being taken as prisoners to the kingdom. This contradiction may, perhaps, be explained by the fact that after a lapse of so long a time, one could not exactly remember when the other three had died, whether during the voyage or while in prison. We feel that the first information is correct and it seems that one died during the voyage and the other three in prison. After the return of Fr. Manoel da Expectação in 1802, there remained only Fr. Caetano Francisco do Couto, to whom we shall revert in a special chapter.

At the same time that pardons were being granted, one more was received on behalf Fr. Ignacio de Noronha and his brothers Xavier dos Remedios de Noronha and Josepha de Noronha who had run away to Bombay. H. Highness pardoned them also of the crime they were accused of enabling them to return to Goa. He also ordered the release of their confiscated properties (Doc. no. 13). There is no mention of these Noronhas in the sentence and other documents pertaining to the conspiracy. Perhaps they belonged to the family of Sebastião Paulo de Noronha, who died in prison before the sentence was delivered and against whom very serious charges had been levelled. However, we found mention of other fugitive priests whose properties were also confiscated and, besides Fr. José António Gonçalves are Frs. Diogo Caetano do Couto and Pedro Fernandes, the latter from Assagao and the former, we do not know from where, probably from Panjim, and brother of Fr. Caetano Francisco do Couto, none of whom was pardoned nor their properties released.

All the above referred orders were carried out by the Viceroy, Count of Sarzedas, as he confirms to the Court, in his official note of 25 February 1808 (Doc. no. 14). And thus came to an end the tragic history of the conspiracy of 1787, which became commonly known as the revolt of the Pintos, though it cannot be said to have been a revolt in the strict sense of the word nor that it was planned and executed by Pintos, though some of them were active members and participants in its execution.

It is pertinent to ask the reasons why the priests were not put on trial in Portugal, notwithstanding the fact that the case with full proof of guilt was conveyed to the court. The existing documents in India do not explain the mystery. One may well presume that the clergy having regained in the reign of D. Maria I part of the power and perquisites they had lost in the previous reign, the government finding very clear proof of guilt in the suit, at least against some of the accused, did not dare accept the opinion of the High Court of Goa that the case was within the competence of civilian courts, fearing protests from the courts and clergy. Neither did they wish to refer the case to the ecclesiastical court, lest carried away by solidarity of the class, they either absolve them all or fail to do proper justice. So it took recourse to what seemed most conducive to avoid change or conflicts among the power of the State and kept the priests in prison until they either died or the time came when they could, without great noise or notice say that they had atoned for their guilt, and that age and aches had drained from the survivors the desire to scheme new plots.

FOOTNOTE

1. Mr. Martinho de Mello believed there were only two priests who had been arrested: namely Fr. José António Gonçalves and Fr. Francisco Caetano do Couto.

5

FR. CAETANO FRANCISCO DO COUTO

According to the personal biodata he gave to Fr. Caetano Victorino de Faria, which the latter recorded in his notes for the information of the Bishop of Cochin, Governor of the archbishopric of Goa in 1781, Fr. Caetano Francisco do Couto was born in Panjim to Pascoal do Couto and Pascoela Pereira. He did his minor and major studies upto theology in the college of Chorao, where there were, according to Fr. Faria, more than 500 students. He appeared for the public examination under the guidance of Archbishop D. António Taveira de Neiva Brum and of the secular court, arguing with masters of religion, one of whom, according to Fr. Faria, happened to be in Lisbon at the time when he wrote this.

He distinguished himself so much in his studies that, on completion, the Archbishop took him as his personal assistant and secretary of Inspections, from which he graduated to Vicar Forane of Honavar in the kingdom of Kanara. He served there so satisfactorily that the next Archbishop D. Francisco de Assumpção e Brito promoted him to Governor of the bishopric of Cochin, a position which he held for three years, with great zeal and spiritual gains, and according to Fr. Faria, who adds that it was a notable feat, at Vencort, where he brought 5,000 souls, who were later baptised, to the fold of the Catholic Church, besides the countless apostates who rejoined the church.

After the expulsion of the Jesuits, Franciscans whose behaviour was abhorent to the precepts of the Gospel, were as missionaries to Malabar. The Archbishop D. Francisco de Assumpção e Brito, in accordance with the instructions he brought from the Court, sent some Goan priests to the bishopric of Cochin to fill the vacancies created by the Franciscans, appointing Fr. Couto, Governor of that bishopric. This gave rise to the formation of two rival camps; one of the friars and the other of the priests. There followed a fierce fight among themselves.

The Christians who preferred the priests, petitioned their king to expel the friars, disclosing all the scandals committed by them and offering a good sum of money for their expulsion.

This was confirmed to Fr. Faria by two Malabar priests who happened to be in Lisbon two years earlier, namely Fr. José Cariattil, later Archbishop of Cannanore and Fr. Thomas Pariemakel, who was the Governor of the same archbishopric in the See which fell vacant due to the demise of its Archbishop. The King rejecting with contempt the offer of money, yielded more to persuasion and merits of the Governor of the bishopric, Fr. Couto, and bestowed on him powers to expel those missionaries from the kingdom. However, Fr. Couto decided to proceed in accordance with the instructions given by his Archbishop which were more conciliatory. Fr. Caetano Victorino de Faria further states that the Malabar Christians seeing the gentle ways, good behaviour and continuous sermons of the new missionary priests, realised how horrible were the ways of the friars and therefore, produced before the King the wives and children of the deceitful missionaries, because they knew that the Governor could not expel the missionaries as they lived under the protection of the pagan king.

What Fr. Caetano Victorino de Faria wrote in his notes, apparently dictated by Fr. Couto, had already been written to the Archbishop of Goa, in Tamil on a palm leaf in 1777 on behalf of the same Christians. Among other things, they complained that the Franciscans used to forcibly take Malabar women and girls as their concubines, forcing the Christians afterwards to bring up and maintain their children.

If we compare the contents of the palm leaf (Doc. no. 15) with those of the notes (Doc. no. 35, 1) one will easily discern that they are the handiwork of the same author. The writings in the palm leaf carry no date; but Fr. Couto was in Cochin with other priests in 1777, and that document (the palm leaf) was received in Portugal in the monsoon of 1779. It is, therefore, obvious that the contents of the palm leaf were written in 1777, in time to catch the mail to Portugal in the monsoon of 1778.

It is hard to believe that the Malabar Christians could suddenly become so enamoured of the improved behaviour and purity of faith that they should take within a span of a few months, so hostile an attitude towards the Franciscans who were supposed to be under the protection of the king's ministers, that they dared complain, of their own accord against the Franciscans, as stated in the palm notes of this book.

It is very clear from a mere reading that the Governor Fr. Couto and his clerics were instrumental in provoking and formenting this revolt among the people.

This fight was in its apogee when the Bishop of Cochin, Fr. Manoel de Santa Catharina, Governor of the bishopric of Goa, arrived and being fully conversant with the role that Fr. Couto had played in the Malabar disturbances, he removed Fr. Couto from the governorship of the bishopric replacing him with Fr. José da Soledade, a Discalced Carmelite who had accompanied the bishop from the kingdom. Fr. Caetano Victorino, in his drive to criticize every action of the prelate, accuses him of having sent Fr. José da Soledade to Cochin to take charge of the governorship of that bishopric, on his behalf, before he, the bishop of Cochin, could take charge as Governor of the bishopric of Goa; a criticism which reveals little knowledge of canonical law on the part of Fr. Caetano Victorino. The Bishop of Cochin had sufficient authority delegated to him not only to take charge of his bishopric, by proxy, but to appoint a governor because he had been entrusted with the twin charge as bishop and governor of the archbishopric of Goa. For this purpose he was using his episcopal jurisdiction and did not require the one conferred on him by the archbishopric of Goa, which he would need only in connection with other suffragan dioceses, as for instance, if he was acting as a Metropolitan.

Fr. José da Soledade left for Cochin in November 1779, but it is believed, that he did not go beyond Calicut (Doc. nos. 16-21). If Fr. Caetano Francisco do Couto promptly handed over charge of the governorship of the diocese to the new governor and returned to Goa, he did no more than his duty as he had done earlier when he obeyed the orders of his Metropolitan than that of the pagan king.

There are different reports of the first actions taken by Fr. José da Soledade. According to Bishop Fr. Manoel de Santa Catharina in no. 2 of his information (if the records left by Fr. Caetano Victorino are to be believed), Fr. José da Soledade settled the differences in the bishopric of Cannanore, returned to Goa to report on his mission and went back to govern the bishopric of Cochin. In his notes, the reference that Fr. Caetano Victorino makes to that paragraph is that the assignment that Fr. José da Soledade carried out there was to hand over the governorship of that archbishopric to the Jesuit Excerpentel, author of Propaganda and friendly with the Franciscans. Fr. Caetano Victorino further adds in his notes at no. 1 that Fr. José da Soledade, joining forces with the Franciscans, disturbed the peace and tranquility of the bishopric of Cochin, that he was arrested and that after four months in prison he ran away coming to Goa and that it was doubtful if he would ever return to Cochin for fear of reprisals from the Catholics. What, however, surfaces from the documents (nos. 22-25) is that Fr. José da Soledade did neither settle the disturbances of the two bishoprics nor was he in prison and ran away to Goa. Taking residence in Calicut he was safe from any violence, protected as he was, in the farm, by the Portuguese flag, and his protracted stay there should be attributed more to his desire to put things in order in the archbishopric of Cannanore than to difficulties in getting into the bishopric of Cochin. Had he been in prison for four months it is inconceivable that no such reference is made in any document, when the smallest ones taken place in Malabar, were.

While in Calicut, the factor of the farm, José Francisco do Amaral de Menezes, requested the Governor of the State to relieve him of his post as he wanted to return to Goa. This was accepted and the Governor appointed Fr. José da Soledade to administer the farm, by his letter of 3 January 1780. But as José Francisco do Amaral de Menezes was delayed in Calicut, Fr. José da Soledade was not able to take charge as manager and he returned to Goa in October 1780.

The reasons why Fr. José da Soledade came to Goa were because of the differences between the two dioceses. He came either to get necessary instructions or to make a report of his assignment, as reported by the Bishop of Cochin. It appears that initially, he leaned towards the Franciscans because when he returned a second time to Cochin, in April 1781, he carried a letter from the Governor of the State to the Dutch Governor of Cochin requesting him to keep Fr. Soledade under his patronage for the peace of Christianity, especially so, because the Dutch government had ordered that Frs. João da Silva and Ricardo da Silva be sent back to Goa, at the earliest opportunity, because, by their temperament, they only created more problems to the Christians. In that same letter the Portuguese Governor requested the Dutch to hand over to Fr. Soledade the church of St. Andrew, founded in a palmgrove belonging to the Dutch government, together with the people of that parish who were vassals of the king of Travancore.

The Governor also wrote to the king to issue orders that all churches in his kingdom should recognise the jurisdiction of the Bishop of Cochin who would be competent to expel the Carmelites of Propaganda from it; that the Christians should continue to contribute the same amount they were contributing at the time of the Jesuits and that the church of Angenga, which had been taken away without the consent of the said king, be returned to Fr. José da Soledade and not to allow the Jesuits of Propaganda to use his kingdom to usurp the jurisdiction of others. He, likewise, wrote to the Governor of Angenga requesting the same.

Fr. Caetano Victorino says that the Apostolic Vicar of Verapoly, on the pretext of differences among Christians, for which he blames Fr. José da Soledade, sent, in the absence of Fr. Soledade, his Vicar General to take over the bishopric, with residence in the church of Angenga cathedral, or in the expression of Fr. Caetano Victorino, the See of the archbishopric.

Letters regarding these developments were reaching Portugal via Rome and were shown to H. Majesty (doubtlessly by him). What must, however, be remembered is that the church of Angenga served as a Cathedral in olden times but this privilege had lately been transferred to the church of Mudacra in Ceylon, where the Bishop D. Clemente José lies buried, a circumstance that could not have been ignored by Fr. Caetano Francisco who was Fr. Caetano Victorino's informant.

These continued differences among the Christians of Malabar under Goan jurisdiction were a godsend to the Propaganda to extend their jurisdiction and, to our shame we must confess this time, they were to a certain point very right. In their reports to Rome they pictured the events here to their maximum advantage because Fr. José da Soledade had neither necessary backing to make truce among the intrepid friars and astute clerics nor sufficient force to halt the invasions of that common enemy, the Discalced Carmelites, both of Italian and French origin, who though wearing the same habit, had nevertherless been taught in different schools of hermitages in Bussaco.

The context of the notes of Fr. Caetano Victorino clearly indicates that the latest news from India was that of the monsoon of 1781, written when Fr. José da Soledade had arrived in Goa and before his return to Cochin in April 1781, which probably took place after the dispatch of the mail of that monsoon, as one can infer from the information of the Bishop, Governor of the archbishopric of Goa.

It is not known if the suspicion or conjecture of Fr. Caetano Victorino about the activities of Fr. José da Soledade was verified, but Fr. Soledade should not have returned to the bishopric, as all his efforts at peace proved fruitless and aggravated the differences into an open war between him, after he was confirmed as Bishop, and the Franciscans. The latter, assisted by the king, found all means to vex the Bishop who, not accustomed to the ways of the world committed plenty of indiscretions and excesses and he was very lucky to have the king help him leave Travancore safe and sound and reach Goa, whence he was soon sent back to the kingdom. But these events though very curious and important from a historical point of view of the bishopric have no value for the present purpose as they took place at a time much later to that referred to by Fr. Caetano Victorino.

Fr. Caetano Francisco do Couto did not stay long in Goa, after his return from Cochin. He left Goa in the monsoon of 1780 or in 1781 for Lisbon, where he was in the latter year, when Fr. Caetano Victorino de Faria wrote his notes. They lived together, trying to influence the mind of the ministry against the Bishop, Governor of the bishopric of Goa and trying his best to hasten his own promotion to any vacant bishopric in India. The Secretary of State, Martinho de Mello e Castro, did not give him and his colleague, Fr. José António Gonçalves that much attention as they expected, and in the monsoon of 1785, he sent them back to Goa promising to recommend their case to the Archbishop to employ them suitably. They, however, understood their suitability in a different way from that of the Secretary of State, and in frustration they plotted the revolt, which is already known.

Fr. Francisco Caetano do Couto, arrested in 1787 as the mastermind of the conspiracy, was the one who turned over most evidence against the others during the investigations and disclosed most of the details about the work of the conspirators. He was sent to Lisbon in 1789 with other priests, all of whom were lodged in the tower of St. Julião da Barra. After some days he was sent to the convent of St. Francis of the city to be examined if he was mentally sound, because while others behaved themselves naturally and with moderation, he was just the opposite, sometimes refusing to eat and at other times breaking the crockery.

We have narrated all this elsewhere and this is also recorded in the letter of the Secretary of State, dated 9 May 1790.

If his madness was real, and there are no reasons to believe otherwise, to what could it be attributed ? The normal causes of such a malady are so varied and unknown that it would be far fetched on our part to subscribe to the real one. But with due respect that such a delicate matter deserves, we dare propound the theory (as Gomes Eannes de Azurara would say) that those ample and many accusations that Fr. Couto made during the proceedings against his colleagues, not sparing his brothers and relatives and friends, would, after the appalling catastrophe of executions and punishments meted out to them, cause such remorse of conscience that it is not surprising that it could disturb the mind, especially if one adds, as is very probable, the unceasing invectives and censures that other priests, who travelled with him to Lisbon as prisoners heaped on him during so long a voyage, invectives and censures which would prick his conscience to the same extent as would the thought of them all suffering the same punishment as the civilians in Goa.

The letter of the Secretary of State dated 9 May, 1790, is the last document that deals with this priest. We do not know if his mental affliction increased or if he was cured of it. His name does not figure among those who died in prison nor among those who were pardoned and sent back to their homeland after their confiscated assets were released

This silence can give rise to various speculations and doubts. Was he set free and in Lisbon? In that case he would have been one of the beneficiaries of the restitution of the confiscated assets, but no such records exist. Did he die in the hospital or in prison before others were set free and, as mastermind of the plot, was he not considered deserving of any compassion, nor his heirs of being given the benefit of the release of his confiscated assets? Would the government have decided for that same reason to keep him under life confinement? All we can say to this is, that the silence of the documents is revealing.

In this respect we recall the testimony of the most respected Mr. Felippe Nery Xavier, a high official in the Secretariat of the government, and who died on 26 May 1875. He stated that Fr. Couto returned to his homeland and that he, as a young boy, knew him in Panjim. Confronted with the fact that there was no record of Fr. Couto's death in the death registry of the parish, his answer was that people of the parish had told him that Fr. Couto was buried in the church of St. Dominic at Old Goa. But this does not appear to us as sufficient proof to explain the lack of record in the death registry at Panjim.

But the testimony of Mr. Xavier is controverted by those of two other respectable persons, namely Mr. Diogo Felippe de Andrade, presently a high official in the Secretariat, who says that he knew well one Fr. Jorge Dias who came from Lisbon on his pardon and who died in Panjim on 5 July, 1819 and whose death is duly recorded in the death register of the parish. This Fr. Dias had no idea of even knowing Fr. Couto nor of having heard that he returned to Goa. The second person is Mr. João António de Saldanha, present *magistrate* of Panjim, who said that he knew the said Fr. Jorge Dias, already an octogenarian living in his house in Panjim till the end of his life, but of Fr. Couto he only heard that he had returned to Goa with that priest and had gone to the South of India where he died. This does not appear to us to be true.

With these testimonies, the youthful reminiscences of Mr. Xavier lose much of their force, justifying to a certain point the silence of the documents and corroborating our doubts on the fate of the priest.

Thus, it will remain in darkness, till some fresh and definite evidence surfaces to prove the real truth.

6

FR. JOSÉ ANTÓNIO GONÇALVES

The flight of Fr. José António Gonçalves, the liveliest, the most active and the most intelligent of all the conspirators whose fiery mind, haughtiness and unbridled ambition caused the uprising, making many a person unhappy as expressed by the Governor, caused him in particular, the greatest of grief and forced him to expend great efforts to trace and capture the elusive priest.

There are many versions in the country about how he escaped and these gave rise to diverse legends. From official documents it transpires that he had dined on 6 August at Bardez at the house of Fr. Vicente Alvares, brother of the Vicar of Pilerne, who resided within the limits of that village. While he was there, he received that same evening a warning on receipt of which he left the house and went to spend the night at Guirim where it appears he was given shelter by the Vicar, Fr. José Manoel de Menezes of Piedade and who was one of those who were arrested later. Because of this warning he was not found on the island of Piedade, at his brother's place where according to the warrant, a search was carried out, in the early hours of 7th. On receipt of this information, the Governor immediately issued orders mentioned earlier to keep a watch on the square and in other places where one could expect him to pass through in his bid to escape. He especially deployed a posse of soldiers to spread out in Bardez province, the last place he was seen at. All these efforts, however, proved useless because as is recorded by the government, every single person he sought, willingly rendered him all help and assistance and according to the investigations, this is how he escaped.

On the morning of 7th, as he got the news of the arrests of his colleagues and of his brothers, he left Guirim and made for the island of Chorao, through unused paths and in civilian clothes, accompanied by Manoel Silvestre, a student.

At Chorao, he went in search of Fr. Mathias Bernardo da Fonseca who sheltered him in the house of a neighbour of his, called Vicente de Abreu, a farmer, where Fr. Gonçalves remained in hiding for three days. This farmer contracted three labourers as guides who accompanied Fr. Gonçalves, leaving the island of Chorao, at the dead of night of 10-11 August, and avoiding the military and excise posts at Mayem, a village in Bicholim, they crossed the borders of the State, stopping in the village of Azarem belonging to the domain of the Marathas.

The legend says that the priest, feeling that he was being pursued by a posse of soldiers, who were after him, on reaching a spot where the road bifurcated, threw one of his slippers to one side and he escaped, carried on a palanquin, by the other. The soldiers, tricked by the slipper, went in the opposite direction from that taken by the priest.

This, however, is in contradiction of fact that the posse of soldiers was rounding in the areas in the province of Bardez and not that of Bicholim, and on the other hand, there is no indication that he was being carried in a palanquin. On the contrary, all evidence points out that he went on foot in the company of the three guides from Chorao, and possibly disguised in such a manner as to make recognition difficult, at first sight, dividing among themselves the little baggage he carried, and which was stolen on the way to Azarem at a spot called Zambotim.

As soon as the government was sure of his flight and realising that they could no longer hide the fact that he could not be listed as one of the co-conspirators and wanting to capture him, by any means, the government published on 21 August, an edict prohibiting all residents of the State from giving shelter and rendering any assistance or help which could enable the priest to evade capture and promising a reward of 5,000 *xerafins* to any person capturing him (Doc no. 26).

The government having learnt that the fugitive had crossed over to Azarem, both from the arrested labourers who acted as guides and from a letter from Fr. Miguel Delgado, a Goan missionary of the same village, sent some sepoys to trap him in the forest when he came out of his hiding to proceed on his journey and to capture him, bringing him immediately across the border to our State. Though Azarem was under the rule of Marathas, the Governor, aware of the lack of friendship the ministers of Pune had towards the Portuguese, thought it wiser to give later, if asked for, a satisfactory explanation of the event, indicating that the sepoys, dazzled by the reward of 5,000 *xerafins* had crossed the border without orders and carried out the deed to avoid entering into protracted negotiations with that court where, he knew, craftiness was the order of the day.

As a matter of fact the sepoys did manage to capture the priest when he was making his way out of Azarem, but on the way back to the border, they inadvertently passed by a spot where the priest called out for help and the Christians residing nearby came out to free him. However, the missionary of Azarem resolutely opposed the designs of his own parishioners who it seemed had more respect for the imprisoned priest than their own Vicar. The most the Vicar could manage, was to keep Fr. Gonçalves confined in the custody of a Brahmin called Babu Rao who was temporarily administering that village.

Fr. Miguel Delgado, missionary and Vicar of Azarem was Kshatriya by caste, belonging to the Delgado family of Pilerne, in Bardez, according to Mr. Agostinho Xavier Delgado, presently heir to that house and a second nephew of the said priest.

The Governor awarded through the Secretary of State, Sebastião José Ferreira Barroco, a commendation to Fr. Delgado and also entrusted him with the task of trying to persuade the Brahmin, Babu Rao, administrator of that village to hand over Fr. José António assuring him the sum of 5,000 *xerafins*, promised as reward in the edict and now confirmed in a special note (Doc. no. 27) and hinting that if the fugitive was not handed over, he would lose that pecuniary gain as arrangements would be made to have him returned, officially by the authorities in Pune.

The Secretary of State suggested that the best way out in this case would be for him, the Vicar of Azarem and the Brahmin, to pretend that the prisoner had run away and, surreptitiously send him to Goa.

This attempt, however, proved fruitless. The hopes that the Brahmin raised in the authorities, induced the Governor to depute not only corporal José Joaquim Mourão but also another Hindu corporal, a Brahmin, Dessai Sirpoti Rao in the expectations that their objectives would be more easily attained, and which in fact appeared almost accomplished. In this certainty, the payment of the reward of 5,000 *xerafins* was released in Goa in favour of the Brahmin of Azarem. The months of September and October went without any tangible results and after much dilly-dallying and continued hopes, the Brahmin decided that he would not hand over the prisoner without orders from the authorities of Pune.

By this time, the Secretary of State had written to our agent in Pune on 12 September to apply to that Court for the return of Fr. José António Gonçalves as a criminal charged with high treason as a mastermind of the attempted revolt against the State, and to place on record the way in which we had acted towards them when we graciously turned over to them a criminal, Tulagi Ponvar, in 1780, and ended his letter in this manner:

> "I, once again, repeat that you must conclude this matter without fail as this is of greatest importance to their Excellencies, by virtue of the circumstances underlying them. If the said Dessai Sirpoti, who carries this adds anything in it, you are to advise me and give me details of what is written. I would appreciate your best efforts in this connection, as its early execution is one of the most necessary things for its effectiveness."

Following this request, the agent informed by his letter of 11 December that he had obtained necessary orders for the return of the prisoner and enclosed a copy of the order issued by the ruler of Pune to Venkata Rao Narayan, Governor of that province. The original was being sent by the latter to the Brahmin, Babu Rao, his secretary who governed over Azarem and under whose custody the referred priest was. These orders were transmitted from Goa to Babu Rao at Azarem by Lt. Col. José Felix da Cunha on 26 December 1787. But a few days prior to the issuance of the order by the authorities in Pune for the return of the prisoner, the Governor of that province, Venkata Rao Narayan, issued another one shifting the priest to Ichalkaranji where the Governor resided and kept him under his personal custody. When our officer with the sepoys arrived at Azarem to receive the prisoner in accordance with the order, the Brahmin asked for two or three days to resolve the matter. He sent a letter to Venkata Rao and finally informed the officer that he had orders to say that he had made his best efforts to turn over the prisoner but was not able to do so.

It was evident that there was unwillingness on the part of the Court of Pune to return the prisoner and this compelled the Governor to ask the Secretary of State to order the agent by his letter of 9 January, 1788:

> "In this context it is imperative that you claim from the Sarkar the immediate return of the said priest, indicating that this non-adherence on the part of Venkata Rao is a shameful and reprehensible act towards the ministers and even towards the ruler of Pune. Subjects should dare disobey the orders of their superiors on matters of such great importance. If the fault lay with the Durbar who deals with this State, such behaviour is beyond all understanding and inconsistent with the action of this State as in a similar case when it promptly and

graciously returned Tulagi Ponvar to them. You must ask for an audience positively to discuss this matter which is of the greatest importance and you may inform in case of rejection that this State will keep in mind such a lack of co-operation. For your immediate information and guidance, I enclose originals of the letters received from Azarem. Please expedite the matter forcefully and with utmost urgency and at the first opportunity, I shall reply to the letters you have sent me."

The Governor also wrote to Peshwa Madhav Rao, ruler of Pune on 10 January 1788 on this matter reminding him of the good co-operation on the part of the State, the non-adherence of orders issued by that Sarkar to the Governor of Konkan, Venkata Rao Narayan, and requesting him to issue necessary orders for the release of Fr. José António Gonçalves (Doc. no. 28).

All efforts to this end were fruitless and the Governor of Goa feeling that it was no longer proper and decent on their part to proceed further before that Court on such a shady negotiation, asked the Secretary of State to put an end to it. By his letter of 4 March 1788, to our agent Narana Sinai Dumo, the Secretary of State wrote: "H. Excellency requests me to instruct you that in case you have not been able, upto now to get the order for the return of the said priest José António and the minister continues to delay the matter, do not bring it up again."

The Bhosale's emissary in Goa offered on 28 December 1788 to negotiate the capture of that priest who was supposed to be still at Azarem, but nothing came of this proposal nor do we know how the Bhosale or his emmissary could apprehend the priest in the Maratha land

It is said that the priest convinced certain people in the ministry of Pune that it would be to their advantage and benefit and that of their ruler if he was not handed over to the Portuguese and though he was not able to assure the fulfillment of his promises, he was helped to such an extent that eventually he disappeared.

What appears most probable is that he was saved due to the intervention of some of his compatriots of the same Brahmin caste of Bardez and the islands of Goa who at that time were in the Maratha army and had good acceptance at the Court of Pune.

Fr. José António Gonçalves who signed in this fashion was also known as José Felippe Gonçalves, because in India names are almost always arbitrary each one taking his own both among Hindus and the Catholics. He was born in the parish of Our Lady of Piedade, on the island of Divar in 1748. Gifted with talent, as is well known, he studied at the college of Chorao, qualifying with distinction and was ordained in 1772 when he was 25 years old. He was appointed Vicar of the church of St. Bartholomeu at Chorao, which at that time, boasted of the largest congregation of Christians.

After the expulsion of the Jesuits, two colleges or seminaries were established in Goa, one at Rachol and the other at Chorao, in houses belonging to ordinary residents. That of Rachol was abolished by a memorandum from the Finance Committee in 1774, and this fact was reported to the Royal Court, from where as is usual in all serious matters, no reply ever came.

The college of Chorao remained but of little use for the purpose for which it was instituted. For its restoration and education of the clergy, Queen D. Maria I sent in 1779 two priests of the mission of St. Vincent de Paul, Fr. António Luis dos Santos and Fr. Manoel Correa Valente and a lay brother, all Portuguese. During the same monsoon the new bishop of Cochin D. Fr. Manoel de St. Catharina, a Discalced Carmelite arrived. He was appointed Governor and Administrator of the archbishopric of Goa by a Pontifical Brief which also contained an order recalling to Portugal the Archbishop, D. Francisco da Assumpção e Brito.

The Bishop of Cochin reached Goa on 3 October 1779 and took charge of the governorship of the archbishopric on 5 February 1780, when Archbishop D. Francisco embarked for the kingdom. The Bishop of Cochin carried with him many and varied orders for the reformation of ecclesiastical matters in India. One of the most recommended was the teaching for priesthood. By a letter of 21 March 1779, the Secretary of State, Martinho de Mello e Castro ordered the Governor of Goa D. Frederico Guilherme de Sousa that in consultation with the said Bishop of Cochin one of the colleges either of Rachol or Chorao should be handed over to the missionaries of St. Vincent de Paul, deciding with the bishop, the yearly amount that should be apportioned, and that he, the Governor of the State should execute the interim orders mutually agreed with the bishop so as not to waste time and to report accordingly all that he had done.

After a meeting, they mutually agreed to hand over the college of Chorao to the priests and took necessary measures to provide proper maintenance until after a year's experience, they could find out what was most suitable and accordingly send their final proposals to H. Majesty. In fact after a year, in the beginning of 1781, the Governor and the Bishop agreed to apportion to the College a sum of 9,038 *xerafins* per year an amount which they did not think excessive for the useful objective for which it was meant namely the sustenance of the said missionaries and of fifteen collegians who would be educated and thoroughly trained for the priesthood.

However, the Finance Committee which by its order of 1774 had abolished the seminary of Rachol, noticing that the Royal Court had maintained a guarded silence on it now decided to refuse payment of the amount voted by the two persons of higher authority who had been entrusted with the task on the pretext that there was no need of collegians since H. Majesty had opened many public schools which taught subjects like grammar, rhetoric and philosophy, with the result that the bishop had to advance the amount. The Governor made a report to the Court about the conduct of the Finance Committee. Financiers and economists are, often a scourge of the republic with their savage and brutal stinginess. At that time, however, Portugal was more extravagant than the Finance Committee in India. Without grudging expenses, they sent, in subsequent years, many Italian priests of the same congregation of mission with whose assistance and that of the two Portuguese, already here, three seminaries were opened at Chorao, Rachol and Bom Jesus at Old Goa.

Coming back to Fr. José António Gonçalves, according to the notes of Fr. Caetano Victorino de Faria written in 1781, mention of which has already been made earlier, he was appointed professor of philosphy at the college of Chorao, by the bishop of Cochin and Governor of the archbishopric of Goa. (He is mentioned as Fr. José Felippe by Fr. Faria, an alias for which he was also known). He remained as professor for a short time, the reasons for giving up this position and proceeding to Europe in 1781, being obscure.

According to Mr. C. R. Ernesto Alvares of Margao, in an article on Fr. José António Gonçalves published in *Almanack Popular* of Mr. José Pedro da Silva Campos e Oliveira in 1867, one reads in the Italian periodical *Notizie del Mondo* of 12 October 1782, the following:

> "Having arrived in the city, Fr. D. José António Gonçalves, of Brahmin caste, and a Portuguese subject, parish priest of one of the most important churches in the neighbourhood of Goa, and royal professor of philosophy in the seminary of that capital, and after visiting and appreciating the stately pomp and rarities of this metropolis, appeared before the Congregation of the Most Reverend theologians, with authentic documents of his studies, completed in his country, and after a rigorous test by them on 11 July, and after having given

proof of his vast erudition, solving with precision, clarity and forcefulness all the problems presented, he came out with flying colours and earned accolades and general applause."

"Thereafter, he was awarded the doctorate of the faculty, on which occasion, Rev. Fr. Thomaz Mamachi, professor of the Sacred Palace, delivered an eloquent speech, from which all foreigners could emulate the examples he gave of the most famous saints of the Church who, at various times, came to the Holy City."

"Before returning to Lisbon, he had the unique honour of an audience with His Holiness the Pope, who received him with affection and covered him with special blessings."

We owe to Mr. Luis Xavier Correa da Graça the information that Fr. Thomaz Maria Mamachi, the speaker on the occasion of the awarding of the doctorate to Fr. Gonçalves, was a Greek and belonged to the Dominican Order. He was secretary of the Congregation of Index in 1779, and soon after that he was elevated to professor of the Sacred Palace, a position which he held upto July 1792 when he died at the age of seventy nine.

From the above it is evident that the new doctor returned to Lisbon from Rome in the beginning of October 1782. Therefore, in order to obtain his doctorate on 11 July 1782 he had perforce to be in Portugal at least in the previous year, that is 1781.

When in Lisbon, he associated with Fr. Caetano Francisco do Couto in whose company he travelled to Portugal with Fr. Caetano Victorino de Faria, who was there for the past ten years well entrenched with the nobility, and in the Royal Court and therefore a natural patron of the freshly arrived Goans in that capital, and with other compatriots who were already there or who had arrived after him, like Fr. Custodio de Santa Maria, an Augustinian, José António Pinto, son of Ignacio Pinto of Candolim, then a very young boy, and with other people, among whom we must especially mention the two Catanar priests of the Syro-Chaldean rite of Malabar, who must have been there around 1779, according to the notes of Fr. Caetano Victorino de Faria of 1781. Herein he mentions that the two Malabar priests had been there for the past two years and though he has not named them, they could not but have been those two, José Cariattil and Thomas Pariemakel both of whom had the protection of the Queen and lived at H. Majesty's expense. It was under her patronage that they went to Rome, the former having had the privilege of being appointed Archbishop by the Queen, and later confirmed by the Pope.

The main reason behind this appointment was the hope that H. Majesty and the Pope entertained that, with a native prelate of the same Syro-Chaldean rite in that diocese, they would be able to draw more efficaciously the entire congregation to the Roman church which, since the time of D. Fr. Aleixo de Menezes and despite their best efforts in this respect, they could not obtain.

To us it appeared that this would be possible because of the various and special favours that the Pope granted the Archbishop such as, a brief of indulgences at the hour of death to him and his relatives upto the third degree, another plenary indulgence to be devoted to the souls at the time of visits to any church after the sacrifice of mass, a personal, privileged and daily altar, authority from the Congregation of Propaganda of Faith to delegate powers to any two priests for a period of five years to administer the sacrament of confirmation in remote areas of his archbishopric. He was also given a brief to grant plenary indulgences at the time of death, another for a special altar for a period of fifteen years to the souls of the departed, another plenary indulgence in the Cathedral on the day of general communion which he (the archbishop) was free to declare each year, another plenary for the missions during the celebration of a first mass and a pontifical blessing, another papal blessing as if the recipients had visited churches in Rome, authority from the Congregation of the Propaganda of Faith to give papal blessing on Easter day and on any three other festivities in a year, and a brief of indulgence for the Church of Our Lady of Assumption at Malabar on certain days only. He was also granted another for those who visited the Cathedral at Cannanore on the first day of the Provincial Synod[1] and above all authority from the Congregation of Propagation of Faith to absolve people from censures and accept the new profession of orthodox faith of Mar Thomas or Mar Dionisio designated as Archbishop of Nernam of the Chaldean rite.

With these privileges and absolution of the schismatic Archbishop, both Rome and Lisbon hoped that the schism and the Nestorian heresy of that old Malabar Christianity would disappear, a task we feel was far superior to the capabilities of a Catanar archbishop as it proved to be earlier, with so many Europeans who were well conversant with the customs of those people and very fluent in their common language as well as in the Syrian language used in their rituals.

The Roman Curia did not forget their main interest, namely to recover what the Congregation of Propaganda had usurped. Though sanction to establish a Synod at Cannanore and the special faculties granted to the Archbishop for the absolution of the schismatics were a sort of public confession that Syrian Christians could not be reduced to subservience and obedience of the Roman Church by the mere expedient of appointing an Apostolic Vicar at Verapoly and sending the Discalced Carmelites, still to save them from a reprimand from the Bishop and to allay their fears that they would not be held accountable for the encroachments made by them, the Prelate carried an appeal to them from the Superior of the Carmelites.

Armed with these privileges and papal blessings, D. José Cariattil and his companion Fr. Thomas Periemakel returned to Lisbon en route to India. If Fr. José António Gonçalves and especially Fr. Caetano Francisco do Couto did not know the Archbishop of Cannanore and his companion in India, they became very good friends in Lisbon and as they were returning together on board the *Senhor Jesus Resuscitado, Santa Zeferina* and *Princeza do Brasil* in April 1785. They planned and decided to share the provisions during the long voyage. This daily social intercourse gradually developed into a friendship and mutual confidence among them and emboldened Fr. José António Gonçalves to borrow some money from the Archbishop.

A few days before the embarkation, Fr. Gonçalves found himself forced to approach the Archbishop again for a loan not only for himself but also for Fr. Couto, his travelling companion, and for Fr. Custodio de Santa Maria and José António Pinto, the last two residing in Europe, but who were presently in Rome or about to reach there.

The total amount of the loan that Fr. Gonçalves took from the Archbishop was 486 *xerafins,* 400 *reis* (Doc. no. 29). As the vessels set sail after the monsoon, the voyage was very rough and long. It docked at Galle in the island of Ceylon and reached Goa only in May 1786.

However, Fr. José António Gonçalves stayed back at Galle for reasons unknown to us and which were certainly not because of ill health.

The Archbishop of Cannanore carried orders from H. Majesty to proceed to Goa and discuss with the Archbishop Primate of Goa various matters concerning his new archbishopric, matters which from the documents mentioned were serious and of great importance. While in Goa, he was a guest of the Archbishop Primate, D. Fr. Manoel de Santa Catharina in his palace at Santa Inez (today in ruins) where he lived. But he was not able to take charge of his diocese because he died at the palace on 9 September 1786.

The judicial inventory of his few belongings, which were given to his heir and travelling companion, Fr. Thomas Periemakel, who was appointed provisional Governor of that archbishopric by order of Archbishop

Primate dated 21 September 1786 to fill the vacancy caused by the death of Bishop Cariattil, throws some more light on some peculiarities of Fr. José António Gonçalves. It was found that there was a box with books with the label of the Archbishop which Fr. Couto claimed as his, another belonging to Fr. Gonçalves, keys of which were in the custody of Fr. Couto, and a small cellaret said to belong to Manoel Francisco Gonçalves, physician, resident of Piedade and brother of Fr. José António Gonçalves.

It also transpired that two days before the embarkation in Lisbon, the Archbishop had given 50 half dobras to Fr. Gonçalves to be exchanged for Spanish patacas and that soon after they had embarked Fr. Gonçalves asked the Archbishop to keep the purse containing the change in his box and that he would give a detailed account soon after the vessel had set sail. This he never did, though the Archbishop reminded him. Since they were still very far away from their destination, the Archbishop did not insist and did not want to rush the priest because he was not well, and awaited a more opportune occasion.

In the meantime they reached Ceylon where Fr. Gonçalves disembarked. When they were about one and half nautical miles from Goa the Archbishop while checking his documents and papers noticed the shortage in cash. He had the change given by Fr. Gonçalves checked by others and found that there was a shortage of one and a half dobras and one *pataca.*

In addition to this, Fr. Pariemakel stated that when the Archbishop was boarding the vessel, Fr. José António Gonçalves had taken from him a walking stick with a gold-plated head and an episcopal ring.

Fr. José António Gonçalves had not reached Goa when the inventory of the personal effects of the Archbishop had been completed on 7 November 1786. He must have arrived somewhere between the end or beginning of the next year. We have no records to indicate if he came directly from Ceylon or if he disembarked at some port in Malabar, where at any rate he could not have stayed long because when the revolt was discovered in August 1787 he had already been in Goa for some time. His flight and efforts made to capture him have been narrated elsewhere.

Having taken refuge in the territory of Pune, we have no information regarding the length of time he remained there but it could not have been too long because his own protectors were well aware of how inconstant and unreliable that ministry was and the risk he was exposing himself to, of being handed over to the Portuguese any time the Government of Pune needed a favour.

He, therefore, left that territory and kept himself hidden. It is said that he found shelter in the land of Tipu Sultan, which may be true, and he remained there as long as the power of that Nawab lasted but after the Nawab was killed and his empire destroyed by the British in 1799, he had necessarily to find some other refuge. He went to Calcutta where he lived for many years supporting himself with the meagre income of his masses and the little derived from one of the English schools which he had opened with the help of his brother, Luis António Gonçalves, seminary student, who joined him after his return from Lisbon pardoned with other priests in 1807.

We owe to Mr. Luis Xavier Correa da Graça the favour of an original letter from Fr. Gonçalves, written from Calcutta on 31 January 1814 where he states that he was 66 years old (Doc. no. 30). This letter was in reply to another which Joaquim Xavier Correa da Graça, father of Mr. Luis Xavier had written to the priest recommending his cousin António Caetano de Menezes a naval lieutenant, when he was posted to Bengal.

In 1817, a certain João Pinto of Assagao, Bardez, published at Calcutta a booklet to teach Portuguese to the youth, entitled *Tutor Portuguez, ou primeiros elementos da instrucção portugueza reduzidos a methodo pratico para uso dos meninos da freguezia de Assagao* (Portuguese Tutor or The First Elements of Portuguese Language reduced to practical methods for the use children of Assagao by J. Pinto, Calcutta: J. De Souza & Co, 1817, 97 pages).

The front page of the book carried the Opinion by Prof. Fr. Manoel de Santa Theresa, ex-Provincial of the friars of St. Augustine, synodal examiner, provincial commissioner of the mission of Bengal and delegate of the Most Reverend Archmetropolitan of Goa, Primate of the East, and by Most Reverend Fr. José António Gonçalves, doctor in sacred theology and philosophy by the Papal and Imperial University of Arch-Gymnasium of Wisdom of Rome.

Availing of one of the chapters of the booklet dealing with the solar system, Fr. Gonçalves makes a dissertation in it on astronomy and because the book is very rare and totally unknown we transcribe (Doc. no. 31) that small dissertation so that one may study his style of writing and judge his knowledge in that field of science.

As informed by Mr. Luis Xavier Correa da Graça, the booklet *Tutor Portuguez* was of the authorship of Fr. Dr. José António Gonçalves and not of João Pinto, a businessman little versed in letters. He died in that same city of Calcutta where in the death register of the church of Moorgyhatta, today a cathedral, is the following annotation in Portuguese: "Fr. Dr. José António Gonçalves born in Goa, of 69 years, 8 months and

22 days of age, expired on 1 July 1818 at 3 a.m. and was buried at the foot of the altar of Our Lady of Conception, with decorum, gratis."

Of his brother, Luis António Gonçalves, says a respectable person of Calcutta who is now 70 years old, he died in 1827 or 1828.

Both died poor, Luis António reaching penury, as he had to close the school after the demise of his brother. This information was given by Rev. Francisco de Assis, presently Vicar General of Portuguese missions in Bengal in his letter of 6 April 1875.

Of the rest of his family, says the same Luis Xavier Correa da Graça, Manoel Francisco Gonçalves, elder brother, a well-known doctor, who was tried as an accomplice in the conspiracy but was found innocent and set free, had a daughter named Angelica Maria Victoria Gonçalves, married to João José Monteiro, who was in charge of the regulars of Bardez, between the end of the last and beginning of the present century. The eldest son of this couple, Domingos Wenceslau Gonçalves was professor of Latin grammar at Piedade and died in 1828.

A sister of Fr. José António married José Manoel de Albuquerque of Chorao. He was an official in the government and later auditor of the province of Bardez. Their son Caetano José de Albuquerque was also a senior official in the Secretariat and was dismissed in 1822 for political reasons and replaced by Capt. Luis Prates de Almeida e Albuquerque. (See Notes for the catalogue of senior officials by Miguel Vicente de Abreu in *Chronista de Tissuary*, no. 9, September 1866). It seems the male line of this family is extinct.

FOOTNOTE

1. The documents state Provincial Synod and not Diocesan Synod. This was done after due consideration because it was necessary to maintain before those from Malabar, at least a semblance of the eminence of the metropolitan church of Angamale now transferred to Cannanore with the title of archbishop.

7

FR. CAETANO VICTORINO DE FARIA

Caetano Victorino de Faria was born in Colvale, province of Bardez. As a young boy he went for ecclesiastical studies and after obtaining minor orders he left the Order and married Rosa de Souza of Candolim, the only daughter of Alexandre de Souza, commonly known as *Concro*, meaning a rich man.

It is customary for the bride to join and live with the family of the husband but in the present case since the daughter was the only child, Caetano Victorino went to live with his father-in-law. Perhaps this deviation from the custom gave rise to dissentions and unpleasantness that followed. Rosa as the only child and heiress apparent to the large fortune of her father because of which she turned pampered was (as stated by a relative of hers Mr. Genezano António João de Souza in the *Ultramar* of 18 May 1865) a haughty lady with a domineering temper and unable to adapt to married life and submission to marital domination. Because of this their married life was in constant domestic turmoil. The mental distress that her poor father suffered for six years without any remedy to restore peace in his troubled house, undermined his health and hastened his death. As he had neither heirs nor hopes of having any, he bequeathed one-third of his fortune to his nephews, children of his brother Manoel de Souza, whose male issues formed separate families, all commonly known as *Concros*.

Seven years after their marriage and precisely ten months after the death of her father, Rosa gave birth to a male child, who was named José Custodio, later known all over France as l'Abbe Faria and to whom we shall revert in a special chapter. The birth of the child did not bring any truce to the dissentions between the parents, who by mutual accord decided to separate and after due formalities, Caetano Victorino was ordained priest and Rosa de Souza entered the convent of St. Monica at Old Goa. After the dissolution of the conjugal ties and their son attaining the age of 15, Fr. Caetano Victorino decided to proceed to Europe taking his son with him.

They embarked on board the *S. José* on 21 or 22 February, reaching Lisbon on 23 November 1771, after a pleasant voyage during which he had as travelling companions, among others, Mr. Justice and ex-Secretary of State, Henrique José de Mendanha Benevides Cirne, who was going back, under arrest to Limoeiro on orders of H. Majesty, and charged with being responsible for the failure in the conquest of Piro in 1768. The friendship that he developed with him and the recommendation that he carried opened the gates of easy access to people that counted in the royal court. However, while in conversation with Prof. Fr. Francisco, the poet, who resided at Cruz dos Quatro Caminhos, he was advised to abstain from such activities and to take a different course of action. This was also approved by the said Mendanha, and accordingly he was directed to Fr. Master João Baptista of St. Cajetan, a Benedictine, with a request to the latter to listen to Fr. Faria. After a four-hour exchange of views at the Convent of Estrela, which apparently means that of S. Bento da Saude and today known as Palace of Courts, he decided to take Fr. Faria under his wings and help him in his plans.

In fact, he personally spoke to the Nuncio producing all documents of the priest and of his son, giving favourable information about them. What the plans of Fr. Caetano Victorino were in Lisbon and in Rome, are not recorded in any documents that exist today but it is true that in the letters he wrote to India during the first monsoon of 1772 addressed to the Pintos of Candolim, letters we owe to the courtesy of Mr. Julio Gonçalves, advocate of Panjim (Doc. no. 32). Fr. Victorino stated that he was about to proceed to Genoa en route to Rome with recommendation from the Nuncio to the Cardinal Secretary of State and to other dignitaries of that court and with personal requests to each of them.

The other source of his contacts with high people was through the house of the Counts of St. Vincent. Here is what he reports in this respect in a letter dated 1 February 1772 addressed to António João Pinto his friend and neighbour in Candolim:

> "As an opportunity to speak with the Counts of St. Vincent, where I was received with much affection and ready willingness on their part, to place at my disposal their good offices, and for which I thanked them, I had occasion to acquaint them through the Majordomo, João Evangelista Machado e Oliveira, the great affection and generosity that you bestowed upon Mr. Miguel Carlos da Cunha, mentioning that your house was at the disposal of the said gentleman and of his family, informing him distinctly how and when you helped him, for

which he was extremely grateful and awaited an opportunity to reciprocate your affection.[1] To discharge my obligation and satisfy you, I handed over to him a petition on behalf of Mr. Ignatio Pinto to be appointed as Treasurer-General of *Bulla da Cruzada*, which was drafted by Luis Manoel Tavares since I was not familiar with the system of this Court. In the alternative I would have had it written by Mr. Mendanha. I entrusted the subsequent task, in case the post was still unfilled to the said Luis Manoel Tavares asking him to post it to you, in case the Majordomo does not do so, who I hope will write to you and your brothers. I am sure you will reply through the same person who is like a door of this house and the best in this Court."

And to better understand the role of a Majordomo of a nobleman in Lisbon at that time, let us continue with Fr. Victorino's letter. "I found in João Evangelista Machado a similarity in temparament with that of yours, for he is serious, modest, solemn, affable, truthful and loyal. For this reason the entire household submits to him and His Eminence the Cardinal adores him. It was through his good offices that Miguel Carlos of Sinquerim was favoured with the annuity against the wishes of his own mother. He is heard and listened to in the ministry and it is he who controls the affairs of the house and, therefore, you and your brothers can direct your needs to that house through the same Luis Manoel Tavares. Even though the Majordomo is old and deaf, he loves this house very much."

The licentiate Luis Manoel Tavares, referred in that letter, was also a person who had good influence in the Court. Fr. Caetano Victorino had carried a letter of recommendation from Ignacio Pinto to Tavares who was his proxy and who negotiated the coat of arms on his behalf. In a letter from Ignacio Pinto to this proxy of his in the monsoon of 1771 there is the following paragraph:

"During this monsoon a priest by name Caetano Victorino de Faria and his son who were paying-guests in this house for over seven years went to that Court with intentions of proceeding to Rome. He was a real help to us and lived honourably. Though he goes against our wishes, considering that his intentions are honest and meritorious, we have eventually agreed with his decision. Since you have done so many favours to us in the past, we are certain that you will also extend your assistance and guidance to him so that he may achieve his objectives for which I shall remain ever grateful."

It was through the patronage of Fr. João Baptista of St. Cajetan, as already stated that Fr. Caetano Victorino also had personal contact with the Archbishop Nuncio of Tyro, in whose palace he dined many a times and was given an open invitation to come at any time with standing instructions, to the sacristy of Boa Morte, which was very close to the palace, to be given the vestments at any time he came. After the mass the breakfast tray was always ready and full.

But everything was not sweet in the dealings with the Nuncio. The bitter pill began with the Nuncio asking him for correct information on the missions in Goa and other bishoprics, on religion and the entire ecclesiastical state, and all this to be given in writing. Now, Fr. Caetano Victorino, a simple seminary student of Colvale in his youth, later married in Candolim, tormented with family dissentions, ordained priest in his middle age, had never given thought to the missions or religion nor even to the ecclesiastical state. But fortune came to him in the form of two men. One of them was the Bishop-elect of Halicarnasse, D. António José de Noronha[2] and the other Mr. Justice Mendanha. Though they were not experts on this subject, they certainly had more knowledge than Fr. Victorino. Mr. Mendanha had been the Secretary of State in India, and all reports on the missions were invariably routed through his office. Though these reports were full of exaggerations and with subtle pretences at truth, whatever little he could remember from what he had read was useful for the present purpose, and so from what one and the other said, Fr. Victorino managed to make and submit his report to the Nuncio.

In his letter of 2 February 1772 to Pascoal Pinto of Candolim, referring to this report, he wrote:

> "And this time I submitted a series on all missions, without mentioning their actual position, not to displease that person who would not listen to us, and offered it to the Nuncio who recognising the handwriting as that of my son, was very pleased and forced us to stay at his residence and to write the actual position which I did, in accordance with the dictates of my conscience giving as example the life of Venerable Fr. José Vaz on whose behalf I submitted a recommendation. He appreciated this very much and I stressed the point that the spread of Christianity and its preservation depended more on natives of the land than on foreigners, a rule followed by St. Paul and other apostles. I brought to his notice the deeds of our Fr. Joaquim de Miranda, the progress he made with the building of the Hospicio, for which purpose be brought materials from his own house, and did all that he could.

Similarly I spoke of Fr. João Francisco Gonçalves, founder of Vaddy church, of the progress of the Theatines and Filipinos, and of the missions in Bengal, Timor and of the coast. He had all this translated into Italian and dispatched it to the Secretariat at Rome, and recommended us to them of our arrival. He sent us to the Archbishop of Genoa who would in turn direct us to the court and give a letter of recommendation directing us to His Eminence the Cardinal Secretary where, God willing, I hope to receive his orders and execute his wishes."

When Fr. Caetano Victorino, full of pride submitted his papers to the Nuncio, he never expected that he would force him at that very moment to write down the actual position of the missions and not wanting to show any embarrassment, he wrote as he states, in accordance with his conscience. Now with so little preparation, as insinuated by him, the dictates of his conscience would have really been very limited and God alone knows what garbled information the Nuncio translated into Italian and sent to Rome. Even then the cunning of Fr. Caetano Victorino came to his rescue when he found himself in a tight corner. Digressing from the main points, he wrote at length on Fr. José Vaz, an old subject, on the singular case of the Hospicio of Fr. Joaquim de Miranda, on the foundation of the church of Vaddy or Varim and other trites, more or less antiquated.

The Nuncio gave him three strings of silver beads, one for his son, the other for the nun who had been his wife and the third for himself, all with plenary indulgences at the hour of death. They were free to offer it to any person they wished. He offered his to Fr. Pascoal Pinto. Upto now he had been receiving favours from the Nuncio. Things were, however, different with respect to the Nuncio's servants. In that same letter one reads: "There is a lay servant of the Nuncio who has requested me to arrange through my agents the import into India, of beads, crosses, bells from Loreto and other things which I am sending to you packed in a carton and addressed to Mr. Ignacio Pinto. I request you to dispose of these articles and with its proceeds send handkerchiefs, bedspreads and other things which he asks for in the list attached. He promises to pay for the excess, if any. I am also writing to Fr. José Ribeiro to see if he can make up the difference." This Fr. Ribeiro is probably the same one who at the time of the discovery of the revolt was found at Pune.

Before leaving for Rome, he wanted to do something for his compatriots which could make them grateful to him. He submitted a petition to H.

Majesty on behalf of Ignacio Pinto of Candolim praying for a decree allowing his daughters, granddaughters and nieces and also those of his brother, António João Pinto, to be allowed to become nuns of black veils at Santa Monica at Goa, with the same dowry and honours as those of white, and requesting that this facility should also be extended to cover all lay sisters, a petition which he expected to obtain easily and fast.

It is well-known in Goa that the first Goan lady to become a nun of black veil was none other than the one who had ceased to be the wife of Fr. Caetano Victorino. This at the time was a privilege and honour (we do not know if Fr. Caetano did manage to obtain the same on behalf of Pinto's family). Now it has become a general rule by virtue of the order issued by the Court and sent to the Bishop of Cochin, D. Fr. Manoel de St. Catharina when he came as Governor of the archbishopric of Goa in the monsoon of 1779 (Doc. no. 33).

Besides the mysterious business that took him to Rome, it was the intention of Fr. Caetano Victorino to obtain a doctorate, which he did and thereafter he returned to Lisbon where he established and went on building up his acceptance. From the influential people in the beginning he now extented to the Royal Palace, becoming a favourite of the King D. José and of the Queen D. Maria I and her consort D. Pedro III.

He acted as agent to promote business which his compatriots had in that Court. He obtained through the Nuncio or from Rome briefs of indulgences, chapels, etc. and all who came from Goa to make their fortune or conduct business in Lisbon would invariably approach him first. It is well established that he was not the confessor of the Queen as some assert (Doc. no. 34) but he used to be consulted in matters pertaining to India, especially ecclesiastical.

The reports or information on ecclesiastical matters sent by the Bishop of Cochin, D. Fr. Manoel de Santa Catharina, Governor of bishopric of Goa in the year 1780-81 were submitted to him for his comments. The opinion of Fr. Caetano Victorino on the first of those reports is not of public knowledge. However, the notes that he made public in 1781 were printed through the good offices of Mr. Jacinto Caetano Barreto de Miranda in the *Ultramar* of 30 May, and of 6 and 13 June 1867 and are reproduced in Doc. no. 35. These notes or annotations are noteworthy in more than one respect. Firstly, they clearly bare so much ill-will towards the Bishop that even the normal rules of decency and respect due to a prelate were given the go by, for he begins in this way: "When *that* Bishop of Cochin reached Goa, etc." in which, besides being grossly disrespectful, the author shows his ingratitude towards the Bishop who was instrumental in obtaining for him an audience with H. Majesty after he had failed in his many earlier attempts. In Goa the author would melt with pretended gratitude for this very favour.

This is told by Mr. Luis Xavier Correa da Graça in the "*Ultramar* of 20 April 1865 and we were personally assured by him that this information was given by his father as a true fact.

It also follows from his notes that the recent facts and details about the missions of those later years which he mentioned in his report could not have been known to him, as during that time, and in fact for the past ten years he was in Europe.

Thus, his animosity towards the Bishop as well as his alleged knowledge of recent successes in the missions, especially that of Malabar, derive from the same source which the very Fr. Caetano Victorino thoughtlessly reveals while transcribing the excerpts of para. 1 of his comments on the report of the Bishop. It is well known that Fr. Caetano Francisco do Couto, who had been the Governor of the bishopric of Cochin for three years, and had been discharged by the same Bishop D. Fr. Manoel de St. Catharina, immediately on his arrival in India was in Lisbon at the time when the notes were written. Fr. Couto had gone to Lisbon with complaints against the Bishop and we believe that Fr. José António Gonçalves or José Felippe Gonçalves was also there, at the same time with similar complaints against the same Bishop.

As Fr. Caetano Victorino was the first person any Goan arriving in Lisbon would approach and as he cherished the idea of being considered as a protector and patron of all his compatriots, it was very easy for the two smart and crafty priests to induce Fr. Caetano Victorino to develop the same rancour they had against the Bishop of Cochin. These same two priests and especially Fr. Couto who had worked in the missions of Malabar, briefed the author of the notes on the recent progress made by the missions, and this is very evident from the fact that the largest and minutest details in the notes not only refer to Fr. Couto himself but also contain such instructions as were given to him by the Bishop, something that Fr. Victorino could never have possibly known as they were not of public knowledge.

We now know how expert Fr. Caetano Victorino was in making reports on missions. With this we do not want to insinuate that Fr. Caetano Victorino has not reported events of his own knowledge especially those that took place in Goa, in his other notes.

The effect that these notes had on royal ministers was far from what

Fr. Caetano Victorino and his colleagues ever expected. Thus, in the notes at para 4 of the information from the Bishop, Fr. Caetano Victorino tries to show the unsuitability of Fr. António da Assumpção, an Augustinian, for the governorship of the bishopric of San Thomé of Mylapore and adds, with certain arrogance that he should be removed from such governorship. But the result was that in the monsoon of 1783 bulls confirming the elevation of Fr. António da Assumpção as Bishop were received with order that he be consecrated in Goa or any other place where this could be properly conducted, an order which unfortunately could not be carried out due to his untimely demise.

In the notes at para. 6, Fr. Caetano Victorino criticises the appointment of Fr. Amaro de St. Thomaz, a Dominican priest, as Governor of the prelacy of Mozambique. The result was that Fr. Amaro was appointed permanent prelate of Mozambique, and besides this, he was given the title of Bishop of Pentacomea, having been consecrated in Goa by the same D. Fr. Manoel de St. Catharina, already Archbishop, on 23 October 1785.

At para. 10 of his notes he challenges the proposal of the Bishop that a person from Portugal be appointed as Bishop of Cannanore and suggests that instead it should be an Indian priest, but educated in Europe so that assimilating the customs of those rude people he could more effectively tame and educate them. With this he meant one Latin Goan priest, but the government appointed a Syro-Chaldean Fr. José Cariattil from Malabar, who having come already consecrated in Europe, died in Goa before he could take up his assignment.

He gives vent to his feelings in many paragraphs to show the mismanagement of Fr. José da Soledade, a Discalced Carmelite, companion of the Bishop, during his governance of the bishopric of Cochin, but the result was that the same Fr. Soledade was appointed and confirmed Bishop of Cochin in the vacancy resulting from the promotion of the Bishop to Archbishop of Goa, and consecrated, in Goa by the new Archbishop on 21 November 1784.

We must confess and record that by his own actions, Fr. José da Soledade proved himself unsuitable for the position but the criticism in the notes about his governance of the bishopric took place much earlier.

He concludes with the innuendo that the Bishop of Cochin was incapable of governing, that he cheated H. Majesty, that he knew not what it was to be a Bishop, that he behaved in Goa with contempt towards the natives, both clerics and lay, and that he made himself very unpopular to

Christians in India. He levelled many other charges. The result was that the same Bishop was elevated to Archbishop of Goa, a charge he took up on 21 November 1784.

What Fr. Caetano Victorino states in para. 2 needs to be corrected. He says that Fr. Pedro de Figueiredo of the Congregation of the Oratory had been appointed Governor of the archbishopric of Cannanore and that having taken charge he had fixed his residence at Calicut in the house of the manager José de Amaral Carvalho and that he held that position till the end of his governance; that he was received by his flock with affection but that he had to suffer a lot because of the troubles created by the Jesuit Excerpentel who had joined forces with the Propagandists and was assisted by the Franciscans; and that he lived for two years amidst these troubles till he was recalled to Goa to take up the charge as Inquisitor.

It is correct that Fr. Pedro de Figueiredo went to the bishopric of Cannanore in the last months of 1778 and that he was in Calicut and took charge of the governance of the bishopric, but it is equally true that he did not leave Calicut and was not able to join, in the proper sense of the word, the archbishopric of Cannanore, despite the recommendations of the Governor and Captain General of India, D. José Pedro da Camara, to the manager, José Francisco do Amaral de Meṇezes (and not José de Amaral de Carvalho) and to the Governor of Cochin, Adriano Muns, and also to the Governor of Calicut, Budu Khan (Doc. nos. 36-42). The confusion and problems of those Christians, always restless, were now being fomented, as Fr. Victorino himself confesses, not so much by the Franciscans as by the Jesuits who remained there after their expulsion, and by the Propagandists. The Naval Captain, Nicolau Delgado Ferreira da Cunha d'Ega, Commander of the frigate in the port of Calicut, and Manuel Bernardes, a Portuguese established there, intervened as mediators, but against Fr. Pedro de Figueiredo, as one can judge from the concerned documents. (Doc. nos. 36-42).

It is not true, therefore, that Fr. Pedro de Figueiredo was received by his flock with affection, nor that he governed the archbishopric. On the other hand it is equally true that the Bishop of Cochin, Governor of the archbishopric of Goa sent Fr. José da Soledade there to appease the dissenters and in this respect we are in full agreement with Fr Caetano Victorino that Fr. José da Soledade did nothing.

The accusation that this priest handed over the governance to the Jesuit Excerpentel is unjust, though the fact that his forces were not sufficient enough to prevent the latter from claiming the governorship of the diocese and of his not being obeyed may be more credible.

It is also inadmissible that the Franciscans joined the Jesuits, as they represented a party diametrically opposed to both the Franciscans and to Fr. Pedro de Figueiredo.

Considered in its entirety what comes to the fore from the notes of Fr. Caetano Victorino *vis-a-vis* the information from the Bishop, is the prevalence of his desire to make accusations against the Bishop, among which he now includes that of the Bishop being partial to the friars and of his despising the native clerics, making according to Fr. Victorino, the former unworthy and the latter the only ones capable of governing the churches and missions properly. He further accuses the Bishop of being contradictory saying: "H. Majesty was informed by the same Bishop of the incapacity and uselessness of the regulars of Goa due to the general corruption in their customs," and adds "And this was confirmed by two missionaries of St. Vincent de Paul, wanting therefore their expulsion," and ends the paragraph in this way: "And besides this, H. Majesty, particularly inquired of persons of confidence from whom he learnt the truth. I do not know how the Bishop forgot his earlier information."

These people of royal confidence of H. Majesty from whom he particularly learnt the truth though expressed in plural, appear to us to refer to the very Fr. Caetano Victorino whose notes prior to this and the first information of the Bishop, remained hidden from the public.

From the second, however, which we learnt from the excerpts of Fr. Caetano Victorino and from other documents which we could refer, one can conclude, firstly that the Bishop was not contradictory in so far as the friars were concerned, as Fr. Victorino makes out, and, secondly, whatever he said about Goan clerics was duly confirmed by the Portuguese priests of St. Vincent de Paul who accompanied the Bishop to India.

Regarding the first point, perhaps Fr. Caetano Victorino failed to notice properly para. 10 of the information of the Bishop in which, according to the excerpts taken by himself, the prelate said "And I record that we made use of the best (friars) that were available in that State and there were no more left in the missions than the Provincial of Graça, who was a very sick man". If Fr. Caetano had noticed this paragraph, he would have convinced himself that the Bishop, after having made use of two or three friars, confessed that he had no more to make use of.

The words of the Bishop when he says "made use of the best that were available" seems to mean that though those whose services the Bishop availed of were not really capable, they were at best less incapable, and so the second information is in consonance with the first.

But in the midst of all this we can aver that the government of H.

Majesty did not need the information either from Fr. Caetano Victorino or from the Bishop of Cochin or even from the priests of St. Vincent de Paul in order to learn the extent of the capabilities of the friars. Before leaving for India, the prelate was given a good many instructions, in Lisbon, in which the government acquainted him of the pitiful condition of the regulars and asked him to evince his best efforts to cure the ills which seemed already incurable.

In the brief of 5 March 1779 (Doc. no. 43) the Queen said to the Bishop:

> "The management of the missions, established in various parts of the East, subjected or suffragan to the archbishopric of Goa, is an area which demands your pastoral care and vigilance, and the said missions are under the care of the Regular Orders, established in that capital and which they should have and actually have. If you deem it necessary you will start inspecting them and according to me should continue to be, I have so directed the Archbishop of Goa and the Governor and Captain General of that State by letters dated 20 April 1777 and dispatched by the Secretariat of Ministry of Navy and Overseas Dominions, to carry out my orders. The happiness and prosperity of the said missions consist essentially in sending of missionaries who not only by their religious tenets but with their examples and fervour ought to fortify the Christian people in the preserverance of their faith in the communion of Christianity within the confines of and obedience to the Catholic church. The downfall of the same missions springs mainly from missionaries who with laxity and lack of regular and monastic discipline instead of enlightening serve to scandalize the faithful and even pagans. In order that you may carry out this important mission with visible success, immediately on your arrival in Goa you must inform me of the state in which these missions are, of the number of missionaries that each of the Regular Orders ought to have, and actually have. If you deem it necessary, you will start inspecting them and sending inspectors to those different regions, as far as it is practical, using priests whom you may find worthy to substitute you in your pastoral care and who will faithfully, impartially, correctly and truthfully inform you of the behaviour, lives and ways of each and every missionary employed in the said missions. They ought to inquire minutely if they are correct and careful in the administration of sacraments, in preaching the gospel, in imparting to the people the

knowledge of catechism and other precepts of the church and, finally if they themselves abide by all the duties of true and exemplary shepherds or if on the contrary they are missionaries only in name and are more interested in hoarding riches through the disallowed means of business and commerce, oppressing and vexing people with extortions and practising other misdeeds diametrically opposed to the sacred ministry that was entrusted to them. As soon as you have all the information about this and you have ascertained all the facts (as you may be faced with sinister and incorrect information which is a normal and frequent behaviour in India), you shall commend the missionaries who conduct themselves with apostolic spirit, imitating those holy patriarchs, founders of the Religious Orders, and whose children they are in the virtue, holiness, religious zeal and the good of the souls. But you shall conduct yourself with all severity, permitted and ordained by the canons, against the perverse, the wicked and the incorrigible, not only expelling them from the missions where they only create scandals, but also putting them on trial and punishing them according to the gravity of their faults, the punishments awarded being duly executed. You shall order the prelates of Regular Orders to immediately replace missionaries where needed, and you shall be careful that each mission has the exact number of missionaries that they must have, not allowing under any circumstances that religious are sent unless you are personally satisfied with their exemplary behaviour, life and habits. After they are duly interviewed and approved by you, you may confirm them and authorise them to exercise their parochial ministries and the saving of the souls in their missions. In order that in the exercise of your episcopal jurisdiction of these tenets you should not find any hindrance, opposition and misunderstanding from the diocesan prelates and Regular Orders, because of their privileges and exemptions which in the past have caused so much damage to the church in my dominions, I have issued an order which you will receive together with this, where among other dispositions I have framed and determined the rules that will bestow power and authority upon bishops over the Regulars who are entrusted with the salvation of the souls. Everything that has been prescribed therein should be followed without any breach throughout all my conquests and, particularly in the State of India with regard to the missionaries of the Regulars."

In the letter dated 6 March 1779 from the Secretary of State, Martinho de Mello de Castro to the said Bishop (Doc. no. 44) we find, "With regard to the matter of missions I have to say that even if they are entrusted to the Regular Orders of St. Dominic, Graça, St. Francis and St. Felippe Neri and even though the august monarch, predecessors of the Queen, Our Lady, had neglected their zeal and care on those Orders to keep, increase and promote our holy Catholic faith in those missions through religious missionaries, graced with education and virtues and a truly apostolic spirit who could properly manage them, however, a very sad and serious experience has shown that everything is just the opposite." Further, "All the care with the said Orders is limited to maintain each mission that is entrusted, not allowing any other religious or priests to interfere in it. It is the duty, however to send to the said missions able and exemplary religious who may enlighten people instead of scandalizing them, who may spiritually teach the herd instead of shearing the wool, who may be true shepherds and not voracious wolves. All this has not upto now had proper care from the prelates or the concerned religious and the reports and information that exist in this Secretariat of State are constant reminders of the deplorable situation in which the said missions are and how much deserving they are of vigilance and pastoral care on your part."

The degradation of the friars was of long standing. Forty-five years ago the Viceroy, the Count of Sandomil wrote to H. Majesty the following letter: "Since there are many religious in this city, all coming from the kingdom as missionaries, I have not seen upto now, the spirit of missionaries in them. The bad example that the majority of them, normally give by their actions would not allow their words to bear fruit and given the free conscience with which one lives here, we are really in dire need of charitable ministers who, with understanding and example may correct the existing vices, for such ministry only those who are not familiar with the sinners are the most indicated. I feel that Your Majesty should make it a point to send some missionaries from Varatojo or Brancanes, who after working for two or three years in this State, should be sent back to the kingdom to be replaced by fresh ones.

May God keep and grant our highest and most powerful ruler happy years.

Goa, 19 January 1734.
(Sd. Viceroy)
(*Livro das Monções,* no. 102, fl. 697)

Varatojo and Brancanes were experimental reformation centres, in response to a permanent cry and public demand of some honest friars against the general licentiousness of some of their confreres. This reform of reforms signified that none of the previous attempts had produced any desired results, nor did the present one too. The Count of Sandomil was so convinced of the uselessness of this reformatory and that the very ascetics of Varatojo and Brancanes would get demoralised, once in contact with other friars, that he proposed that they should not remain amidst them for more than two or three years, after which they should be replaced by new ones. Varatojo was affiliated to the Observant Franciscans, the province of Algarve, and Brancanes appears to have been of the Capuchin Franciscans, the province of Arrabida. These were isolated houses and exceptions to general rule.

In addition to what the Count of Sandomil had to say of the community of friars, let us see what the earlier Viceroy, Vasco Fernandes Cezar de Menezes, thought of those who were elevated to bishopric positions to which the best were chosen. Writing to H. Majesty on 10 January 1714, while reporting the death of Archbishop D. Fr. Agostinho da Annunciação, he added, "Experience, Sir, has shown that bishops who came to Asia in this century were good religious men. But following them many bad prelates have come who blindly and inordinately strive and try to interfere with the political and military government of this State and when they fail, they create problems with intrigues." (*Livro das Monções*, no. 79, fl. 111).

In another letter of 11 January 1716 he said, "And at the same time (when reporting the death of the Archbishop) I would suggest that friars should not be selected for these appointments because due to the tendency they have of fomenting partisanships, they cannot abandon this habit. After assuming duties they practise it all the more because it gives them either more power or because business in India is something very strange to those in the cloisters who normally see no more than the walls of their dormitories and they satisfy their primary encumbrances and get more knowledge than one does in the choir. For this reason I once again repeat what I then felt that these friars should on no account be nominated for the archbishoprics to which the circumstances I mentioned above contribute in great measure."[3] (*Livro das Monções*, no. 81, p. 224).

But coming to the instructions given to the Archbishop of Cochin, in another letter of the same date, 6 March 1779 (Doc. no. 45), the Secretary of State writes, "Neither is it possible to establish the missions nor can we find the means as so much desired by H. Majesty unless the higher prelates seriously participate in this important task. You may please make them understand clearly that the religious piety of Our Lady, the Queen, when she decreed in her letters which this Secretariat dispatched on 20 April 1777 that religious Orders should be maintained in the missions which they had been previously entrusted with, was not to allow them to remain in a state of slackness in which they presently are, but that the same prelates should fully cooperate with you and endeavour to root out all vices and maintain virtue and propagate the holy words of the gospel not only with sermons but also with purity in their actions and examples."

In another letter of the Secretary of State of the same date, he begins (Doc. no. 46), "Since you are not only in charge by virtue of your inherent duty of pastoral ministry but more particularly as you have been entrusted by the religious godliness of Our Lady, the Queen, of working to the best of your abilities not sparing any effort to see that virtue flourishes and vices are rooted out in missions of Asia, it is necessary that I do not hide from you some facts which by their gravity deserve special attention. It has come to the knowledge of this Secretariat through various letters, complaints and representations, with documents and proofs attached, that generally in all missions entrusted to the regular Orders a sort of a business similar to those carried out in normal business establishments is openly carried out by some of the regulars and this is as much general as it is public. Therefore, the prelates cannot claim ignorance of what is going on. It is evident that this business is being carried out either with permission or it is being tolerated by the prelates. This being so, what spiritual fruits can one expect from such missionaries who instead of dedicating themselves to the service of the church and the good of the souls combine the sacred ministry with wordly gains? And, if the principle and doctrine of eternal life is that no one can serve God and mammon at the same time, how can the missionaries then be ministers of God and business people at the same time? What fruits can one expect from such mercenaries who have been entrusted with spreading to the people at large the law of the Gospel and the doctrine of Christ, of Christ who expelled them from the temple as defilers of the house of God? It is evident that as long as the prelates of the regular Orders do not restrain their subordinates efficaciously and not outwardly from this sordid business and they do not join you, you may expect no more than rocks and thorns for all your labours."

What, however seems very surprising is that the minister who wrote this in the monsoon of 1779 was the same who two years ago in the monsoon of 1777 had given specific orders to the Archbishop to return back to the friars the missions that had been taken away earlier, and to let things revert to what they were when he arrived in Goa and that the orders brought by him for the removal of the regular Orders from the missions should be announced as there were reasons to doubt their zeal in the propagation of the gospel and protection of the faith and religion that we profess.

The Archbishop complied with this order. However, when he returned to the metropolis he declared that both, according to the instructions given by H. Majesty in 1774 and in the edict of 7 April of the same year, it was clearly decreed that in the name of the same Lord secular priests should be appointed in all churches even in those which were earlier known as missions but were actually parishes in replacement of friars (Doc. no. 47).

This declaration should have alerted the forgetful minister who issued the above orders in 1779 and this seems to be a solemn act of contrition on the part of the government which showed its regret for having given way in the first days of the reign of D. Maria I to the current practice of reacting against anything which was the work of the Marquis of Pombal.

Regarding the second point, that of clerics: There are some curious explanations in a letter of the Secretary of State, Martinho de Mello e Castro, to the Governor D. Frederico Guilherme de Sousa, of 19th March 1781 (*Livro das Monções*, no. 162, fl. 85) regarding what the Bishop-Governor stated in his first information of 1780 and from the priests of St. Vincent de Paul where one reads: "The same Bishop-Governor states that there is a great need to train people for priesthood and therefore he sent to Chorao twenty clerics from the best he could find to teach morals and ceremonies and also to help the missions, even while the erection of the college was still under way and the seminary still incomplete."

Dealing on the lack of knowledge on the part of clerics, the prelate said that many examinations were held at the Palace, at St. Inez, while the priests of St. Vincent de Paul were still here. They made a mention of the great need to have capable priests or sufficiently intelligent ones but it was found that there was an almost entire lack of knowledge among them not that they were incapable but they were not properly trained. They knew nothing of morals and though there were teachers for other subjects there were no students, either because they were afraid of the diseases of the city or because they lacked sufficient funds. There were teachers who maintained some students, at their own cost, so that they could draw fat salaries that H. Majesty gave. The missions also confessed that there was a great need of teachers and that there was also a great lack of knowledge among the religious. The Bishop refrained from instituting inquiries on this for fear of having to close many churches even after being content with mediocres.

And he continues, "The priests of St. Vincent de Paul also mention that the task that the Queen, Our Lady, entrusted to their diligence, care and zeal, under the direction of the Governor of the archbishopric of Goa was the one that was most needed in the State so far as it concerned the spiritual side, and one could assert that this was necessary. As long as the clerics did not have adequate knowledge and virtue, the people could not be educated and shown the way to attain eternal happiness, much less of being imbued with enthusiasm to overcome the difficulties which the corrupted society presented.

Whatever might be the state of this clergy, says one of the priests, if I am to judge from what my companion and I have observed and from what has passed through our hands, I am forced to say that they are buried and submerged under a dark cloud of ignorance for after interviewing the priests sent by the prelate of this archdiocese I find them so devoid of basic knowledge that I cannot but form this opinion about them.

I have no doubts that there may be some priests with a passable education and perhaps with something much more as for instance the one who presently occupies the position of Vicar-General and who is educated. But if we compare these with those ignorant, the former form but a very small number. The measures that our Queen took in establishing a seminary is an action in the right direction. At the time when our founder St. Vincent de Paul lived the clergy of France was reduced to the lowest level of misery with their vices and ignorance. The bishops of France, wanting to eradicate this great evil consulted St. Vincent de Paul. The saint said: "There is nothing to expect from old people. You have to build up the young and therefore the need of a seminary is imperative". This project was put into execution and the wonderful results are there for all the world to see. I should also speak in the same way; "Do not expect anything from old people. Build up new and young men in the seminary, this is the only way. They have ingenuity, ability and perspicacity in judgement but they lack training. Therefore what I say should not come as a surprise. If the Queen, Our Lady, is prepared to defray the expenses of a great number of persons, in a short time you will find the results."

"This is substantially what the prelate of the metropolis and the two missionaries mentioned and stated about the very important aspects of the crass and deep ignorance to which the ministers of the church of this

State were reduced, and about the only means by which they could be educated, namely by the seminaries. In the light of these considerations, H Majesty has approved all that you suggested when you handed over the college of Chorao to the priests of St. Vincent de Paul with all its income and jewels."

If these priests who had come with the Archbishop-Governor to educate and teach the clergy found the friars incapable and unworthy as stated by Fr. Caetano Victorino and amply proved by documents, from the list of the same priests that was returned to India by the Secretary of the State, one can easily deduce that the secular priests were equal to the friars, if not in their habits, surely in their deep and crass ignorance. Now if the priests of St. Vincent de Paul were, in the opinion of Fr. Caetano Victorino, good judges of the friars one cannot deny their competence to equally judge the secular priests as they were their examiners too.

This state of the secular priests should not have caused surprise to the ministry because before the Bishop left Lisbon, he was cautioned that in Goa he would find many or perhaps a majority of secular priests unfit to be entrusted with any office, whatever it might be (Doc. no. 44). From all this, one can decide how much to believe the passionate notes in which Fr. Caetano Victorino commented on the information of the Bishop-Governor, and it also explains why the ministry did not attach much importance to his opinions despite the sententious and arrogant manner in which he elaborated them, confident perhaps of the favours of the courtesans who he thought were more powerful than they really were. We must add by way of information that even after years, the Secretary of State would mockingly and contemptuously call him 'famous' Fr. Caetano Victorino, as if he was unimportant.

In Lisbon the priest made his fortune either through his own efforts or through the munificence of the sovereigns D. José, D. Maria I and D. Pedro III, who protected and favoured him. When he reached Lisbon he wrote in the monsoon of 1772 to his friend, António João Pinto, of Candolim: "The poverty in which I live does not permit me a greater show of affection than this blue-beaded string with a wrought cross, a poor gift from a poor priest, but with great love, and filial trust. The rosary carries plenary indulgence at the hour of death."

In 1778 at the time when news of the conspiracy became known and the accomplices were in Lisbon, the Secretary of State replied that on inquiries about these accomplices, it transpired that José António Pinto, Joaquim António Vicente and with them a priest, called José, son of the famous Fr. Caetano Victorino, had left Lisbon helped by the same Fr. Caetano, bound for France en route to India.

He was at that time imprisoned in the convent of Paulists where he resided though it is not known for how long but he was not allowed to get any news upto 1799, the year in which we find a letter dated 4 April written by him, from Lisbon, to a Hindu friend called Rama Custam Naik (Doc. no. 48). In this letter, dealing with business and accounts that existed between the two, and after referring to a certain sum that he had kept to his credit in Lisbon over a transaction of cloth, he wrote: "You mention in your letter that you did not agree to any commission to me on this transaction, and I may excuse you for this because you do not profess that holy, true and only law of Jesus Christ which is the only one that opens our eyes to see and find the true path to our everlasting happiness, and whose foundation is charity and consists in loving God above everything and your neighbours as you love yourself, for the glory of God, our Creator and Redeemer. I have the good fortune of professing that holy law through the infinite mercy of our Creator, though unworthy of it. This law not only gives commissions with which one can help others, as I did on your behalf, but also enjoins that we do it in such a way as we would wish ourselves. If you had done the same for me as I have for you, I would not only have praised you but also would have been extremely grateful for the favour received, for the love and interest that you took without being duty bound or having any other interest than the affection towards a compatriot".

We are sure that neither Rama Custam Naik nor his partners would find the sermon of a Christian priest of great benefit nor of intense affection of a compatriot and would rather prefer more accurate accounts than these religious maxims. One can judge how tolerant Rama Custam Naik would have been and the others with the contents of that letter which proceeded in this style:

> "Now I assure you with the purity of my heart that I shall not content myself with only holding that amount on your behalf, which otherwise I do not consider worth, as it is very safe, even if you did not have your accounts books to confirm it, but I also want to assure you of a greater and incomparable happiness for which I am fighting for the past twenty years, in the whole of Europe, which exalts in your misfortunes and is happy to see your deplorable ruin. I, as a good and true compatriot take upon myself without being asked or commissioned,

and I do it willingly even at the risk of my very life, to bring those tidings so that my compatriots may really be happy, since our Creator has shown to me the misfortune of our motherland which is plunged in a pitiable blindness the likes of which does not exist in Europe." "I have worked to take away from the hands of Europeans, our archbishoprics of Goa and India, which our Creator and Redeemer gave us a thousand and eight hundred years ago, through his apostle St. Thomas and which Europe stole from us three hundred years ago for their worldly interests and to the detriment of our souls and salvation. I take it now, against the wishes of entire Europe and of this Court, not with my strength but with the omnipotent arm of our Creator and Redemptor, through the patronage of the Holiest and Immaculate Mother of the Redemptor, who shares in our misfortunes and helplessness, and wants to restore it to us. I am going to baptise all Hindus not only of Goa but of the whole of India and will give my life for them so that they may be happy for ever".

Had we not seen for ourselves these absurdities written in Fr. Caetano Victorino's own handwriting, we would have thought that it was the work of some of his enemies, but we cannot escape from the reality. It may be that old age might have disturbed his mental faculties which even before were not very sound but were at least sensible.

According to ecclesiastical history, which the insane Fr. Caetano Victorino believes, the bishoprics in India were given to the natives by Jesus Christ through his apostle St. Thomas one thousand and eight hundred years ago. The priest wrote this in 1779, but let us allow one more year to round up his account. Thus we come to the strange facts that the bishoprics were created in the year that Jesus Christ was born and also that St. Thomas was an Indian. A strange fact that the historian has not discovered. We do not question his contention that Christianity was introduced in India by the Apostle. What history however tells us since there are authentic documents, is that bishops came to the small church in Malabar, the only one that existed when Vasco da Gama landed, from Syria or Mesopotamia, regions which till now no geographer has placed in India. Therefore, the Syrians and the Chaldeans were as foreign to India as were later the Europeans and to whom the ancestors and compatriots of Fr. Caetano Victorino owe the light of faith and who did not steal bishoprics from any one for the simple reason that there were none to be stolen, but were created by them many years after they came.

With such arguments, it is no wonder that Fr. Caetano Victorino toiled in vain for twenty and odd years, to take over the bishopric in India from the hands of the Europeans.

It is not with ordinary but with supernatural power of the Omnipotent arm of our Creator and Redemptor and through the patronage of the Most Holy and Immaculate Mother that, Fr. Caetano Victorino says, he found himself invested against the wishes of entire Europe and of the Court of Portugal, with the jurisdiction we know not of which archdiocese, as if he was a Patriarch or a Pope of India, where he was all set to go and baptise all Hindus so that they may be for ever happy. Even at the risk of his life which in a task such as this, he thought would really be risky. What he wrote would be tolerable if it was for his confreres but to preach a senseless and unsolicited sermon to Hindus must have been a proof of his senility. Perhaps to save embarrassment and discredit to an old friend in the event of such news becoming public, the Pintos seized the letter and kept it hidden among their personal papers in their house, where one can still find it.

It is, however true that Fr. Caetano Victorino did not return to India and the letter of 1779 is the last he wrote. We do not know if he lived longer or what happened to him later.

FOOTNOTES

1. Miguel Carlos da Cunha, son of the Count of St. Vincent and brother of the present one came to India in 1756 as Miguel Carlos de Tavora, but took the surname of Cunha when that of Tavora was abolished. He married poor, but in compensation he was given the palmgrove of Sinquerim which belonged to the Jesuits and an annual annuity from the Royal Exchequer, in addition to his salary. But spendthrift and prodigal that he was, no money was enough for the honest maintenance of his family. Therefore, he was forced to receive some charity from the Pintos of Candolim, his neighbours, to meet his needs. The house of Sinquerim, built near the mouth of the cave of Fort Aguada, no longer exists. Miguel Carlos da Cunha died in the rank of Lt. Col. and as Governor of the fort of Cabo da Rama, in April 1813. Even today, there are legends of humorous and sarcastic anecdotes with which, in his moments of fantasy, he entertained society people. Carcomos Lobos of Goa are descendants of this family.
2. D. António José de Noronha was the son of D. Francisco de Noronha and of D. Cecilia Anna de Menezes. He received the holy oils in the parish of St. André of Goa Velha on 14th July 1720 and was baptized at home. When young he was sent to become a Friar at St. Francis (Goa) where he took the name of Friar Anthony of the Incarnation. He was sent to the mission of St. Thomas of Mylapore, where he discarded the habit, abandoned the religion and was expelled from the order. Being or pretending to be a relation of the wife of Marquis Dupleix, the famous Governor of Pondicherry, a French possession in India, he received a lot of patronage from him. He joined the French army as a corporal of native troops, was friendly towards the

French and always against the British. The latter surprised him, one day, in his house at Mylapore and sent him to England as a prisoner, from where he escaped to France. Here it appears, the king Christianissimo appointed him Bishop of Halicarnasse, and it is said the necessary bulls had been issued but they never reached his hands. Returning to Pondicherry he continued his military pursuits and obtained from the Grand Moghul the title of Nawab Delavargenga Shamasher Bahadur. When in January 1761 the British took Pondicherry, for the first time, fortune began to be less favourable to D. António José de Noronha and he returned to Goa and soon after he took a prominent part in the conquest of Ponda in 1763 and, perhaps, it was he who persuaded the Viceroy, Count of Ega, to embark on this enterprise. After the conquest, he was made a General of that province and its dependencies. He was removed from there by the succeeding government and accused of grave offences. He was sent as a prisoner to Portugal in 1770 but was able to justify his actions before the Marquis of Pombal and return, cleared of all blame and with commendations, in the monsoon of 1773. One day, after having dined with the Governor, D. José Pedro da Camara, in February 1776, he died of an apoplexy on reaching home.

This space is not sufficient to narrate the many successes of so adventurous a life as that of D. António José de Noronha. Perhaps, we may do so, elsewhere, and more in detail. In the meanwhile, one can read what Felippe Nery Xavier had to say about him in *Esboço de hum Dicionario Historico* (4th vol.) of *Gabinete Litterario.*

3. If anyone is interested in knowing the Franciscans, see *Ensai Historico de Lingua Concani,* for the Augustinians and the Capuchins, see *A Jurisdicção Diocesana do Bispado de S. Thome de Meliapor nas possessões Inglezas e francezas,* and for the priests together, *O Manifesta preventivo dos Propagandistas da India contra a Concordata* and *O Cronista de Tissuary.*

8

FR. JOSE CUSTODIO DE FARIA

Fr. José Custodio de Faria, son of Caetano Victorino de Faria, who later became a priest, and of Rosa Maria de Souza, who later became a nun at St. Monica Convent, was born in Candolim on 31 May 1756 and was baptized in the church of Our Lady of Hope, parish church of the same village on 7 June of the same year (Doc. no. 49). When he completed fifteen years of age his father took him with him to Europe and reached Lisbon on 23 November 1771.

Soon after, they went to Rome where it is presumed he obtained a doctorate from the College of Propaganda as is known from the theological thesis that he presented under the title: "Theologicae Propositiones De Existentia Dei, Deo Uno, et Divina Revelatione' and contains *De Existentia Dei* (20 chapters), *De Deo Uno* (20 chapters), and *De Divina Revelatione* (23 chapters). (Doc. no. 50).

In the dedication to Queen D. Maria I and to King D. Pedro III, he says that he owed his studies in the college of Propaganda solely to King D. José and in gratitude he decided that on concluding his studies he would dedicate the fruits thereof to the King. As he could not carry out this promise due to the demise of the same monarch, he therefore came to render his homage to his heiress and his son and to the royal consort, in gratitude for the everlasting benefits that such generous patrons had bestowed on him and his father.

After obtaining his doctorate, we believe he came to Lisbon together with his father, whom he always treated as such, and so did the father to the son, as there were no reasons why they should deny or abjure their natural relations as Genezano António João de Sousa, a relative of his mentioned in an article in the *Ultramar* of 18 May 1865. We do not know if he was a royal preacher, nor did we believe Genezano when he said so.

He was preaching for the first time in the royal chapel and seeing the distinguished audience and the intellectuals of the kingdom he became nervous. His father who had also come to listen to him and was hiding under the pulpit came to his rescue telling in a voice he could hear and in the local language of Goa that the people in the audience were all men of straw (*bhagi*). With these words of encouragement he recovered his calm and delivered a brilliant sermon which was very much appreciated. The bystanders tried later to find out what the father had said to him but in vain.

As he went to Europe at a very young age, he did not correspond with his relatives in India. Mr. Genezano says that the only time he wrote was once to António João de Sousa Concro, who we think was his cousin and the great grandfather of Genezano. In this letter, José Custodio requested his cousin to take care and to protect the companion of his youth, the adopted daughter of his mother called Catharina who after the departure of her foster-father to Europe lived with the family of the same António João. He availed of that occasion to offer him as a gift a golden crucifix with indulgences, a bell and a beautiful small oratory which had images of the Infant Jesus in a crib with various images of the Most Holy Mary, St. Anne, St. Joseph, all in ivory, with crowns of gold, and the Holy Spirit, also of ivory in the canopy of the oratory, and a relic of Our Saviour, all of which he had brought from Rome. The images still exist, though the oratory is much decayed.

The houses in which José Custodio was born became the home of the Concro family, and continues till today with a few repairs, and those at Colvale where Caetano Victorino was born are demolished and all that remains is a chapel.

When the news of the conspiracy reached Lisbon in 1788, José Custodio had already left for France, where he took up residence. What we know about him is from the *Diccionario Bibliographico* of Innocencio Francisco da Silva, who refers to the information conveyed to him by Dr. Levi Maria Jordão, later Viscount of Paiva Manso, and is as follows: "José Custodio de Faria, known in France as l'Abbe Faria, was born in Goa in 1755[1] and died at Paris on 20 September 1819, according to the death register of the second suburb of that capital. His life was of a perfect adventurer. Son of a native of Brahmin caste, he came very young to Lisbon where he received his first lessons in education and instruction and leaving later for Rome, he received there Sacred Orders, including those of priesthood.[2] As the French Revolution broke out in 1789, he returned immediately to that country,[3] and took a prominent part in the events of that time, marching at the head of a band of protestors against the Convention, at 10 Vindimaire. Leaving the capital after some time, he studied philosophy in the Lyceum of Marseilles, Nimes and other cities of the province. Returning again to Paris, he began to acquire some fame as a mesmerizer and illuminator, having given an exhibition on magnetism-manie, vaudeville, a variety theatre.

He died of a fulminating apoplexy. In the same year of his death a posthumous book of his was published under the title *De la cause du sommeil lucide*, ou *etude de nature de l'homme by l'Abbe Faria,* Brahmin, Doctor in theology, Paris, 1819, 8th ed. (About the cause of a lucid sleep or the study of the human nature). Only the first volume was published, the second and the third remained unedited.

Chateaubriand in *Memoires d'outre Tombe* and Alexander Dumas in his romance *The Count of Monte Cristo* speak of Abade Faria, the former using him in an extravagant act and the latter in a romantic one.

One can also find details about him in *Moniteur* of 1 and 5 October 1819; in the newspaper *L'Ordre* of 3 December 1851: *Les Archives du Magnetisme Animal* by H. de Cuvillers, vol. 1, p. 134; Hoffman in *Oeuvres Complets*, 1828, vol. 4, p. 384; Burdin & Ribois, *Historique Academie du Magnetisme*, Paris 1841; and in an article of Luis Lateur in *Nouvelle Biographic Generale*, etc

His work *De la Cause du Sommeil Lucide* gained fame and was quoted extensively by those who were abreast of the progress of science. In Goa, both the author and his book received special attention in the least likely place, a satirical paper *Gazeta de Goa* whose editor, Luis Prates, was inspired by the political trends of the day, and came out with an article entitled *Carapuçada* (hooded) in June 1822.

This was perhaps the first loose page from a printing press in Goa which had just been started. The article commented: "Fr. Faria, apostle of somnambulism who became a literary figure in Paris was born and educated at Malabar."

The education was in Europe, but the editor was not of Goa, and not particular about the details in his historical writings and, therefore, one can excuse his lapse or inexactitude of the incident of his discourse. But it goes to show how well-known the name of Fr. Faria was at that time.

FOOTNOTES

1. The right day of his birth is mentioned later.
2. His father was a Brahmin but a Christian. He left for Lisbon having completed 15 years. He went with his father to Rome in 1772 and studied there till he got his doctorate in 1780.
3. He went to France in 1788.

9

REFLECTIONS ON THE CONSPIRACY

It is an incontrovertible fact that the conspiracy with the intent of expelling the Portuguese from India, did take place as is amply established by the confessions of the accused, among whom the one who gave out most of the secrets, was Fr. Caetano Francisco do Couto. He did not spare himself, his brothers and his relatives, and this is also proved in the trial conducted impartially and in accordance with the laws of the land by judges most of whom were recent arrivals in India.

There are various doubts about the means which the conspirators relied on to carry out such a risky task. It is incredible that they relied solely on one movement inside the Legion.

In 1787, excluding the garrison in the North, Goa had the following armed forces:

1st Regiment	1,022 men
2nd Regiment	1,022 men
Artillery	546 men
Total	2,590 men
Legion of Ponda (Infantry)	1,120 men
Legion of Ponda (Cavalry)	87 men
Legion of Bardez	1,120 men
Total of the two legions	2,327 men
Corps of Sepoys	2,223 men
Total of all	7,140 men

Of these 7,140 in two regiments and artillery, in a total of 2,590 men, which comprised of European troops with their officers, other Europeans and those of mixed blood, were loyalists. The Legions, the major portion of which comprised of locals and having a good number of Europeans and of mixed blood too, and commanded by European officers, could not be said to be willing in their entirety to join forces with the rebels and under the orders of the two Goan lieutenants. The sepoys, totalling 2,223 Hindus of the New Conquests and accustomed to obey orders of Hindu corporals only and those of the corporals of their *sarkars* or headman of the region, could not be suspected of aligning with the native priests in the conspiracy. We will not consider the militia of auxiliaries because this did not in a proper sense exist, with the exception of few officers. The conspirators would be insane if they thought that with four lieutenants, one for each legion, some sergeants, a few corporals, a captain of auxiliaries and perhaps with some civilians under the leadership of clerics, they could safely face the onslaught of the entire troop who would rush to crush the revolt, even if it was necessary to slow the tempo of the skirmishes with the Bhosale against whose troops there was already a lull at that particular time in 1787.

No one better than the very conspirators knew that the upper classes or the high castes of the Christian population of Portuguese India had more than once sworn before the sovereign and the whole world, their horror to man arms and indicated their unwillingness to face any enemy that might challenge them. The monumental scolding that the Marquis of Pombal gave them on 28 February 1776 (Doc. no. 51) when to their utter surprise he brought to the fore their unmanly and cowardly attitude, seems to have been more than enough. There he said: "The petition of the Municipal Council of Salcete, dated 1 May 1775, was presented to H. Majesty, my Lord."

"In it he saw for the first time, a nation degrading itself so much before their sovereign, firstly in admitting the weakness of their bodies and souls and disgracing themselves before the world; secondly, in showing lack of patriotism and evading the obligation and principles of unity in civil society which enjoin a subject to give his life for his king, his country and for the lives and property of other citizens; thirdly in renouncing progress and a rise both in name and money to which those in military career rose and acquired fame for themselves and their families and in turn grew in the esteem and admiration of their monarchs and became members of the nobility of the nation; and fourthly in showing ignorance that a military career is not all-exhaustive of other professions, because in all monarchies where there are inevitably soldiers, there is a court that assists the sovereign, and there are many political tribunals, civil magistrates, and a great number of businessmen who fill the squares of this kingdom[1]. There are also an infinite number of farmers, agriculturists who till the lands, plenty of artisans and mechanics, and servants who serve. All this is compatible with military service because there are rules for recruitment and the enlistment of soldiers and if one compares the number of those who join the army with those who remain as civilians, the former is but an insignificant part of the latter." And further on one reads in the same letter: "H. Majesty expects that as soon as that Council realises the gravity of its absurdity it will raise itself from the despondency in which it is enveloped". Finally, he concluded with these flattering words, "The said Lord cannot believe that only the Portuguese are endowed with greater spirit and courage and are more capable of bringing honour than the Indians".

However, this did not have the desired result, for soon after and before the revolt was planned, the Council ratified and confirmed in a most emphatic and minute memorandum, full of malicious impudence their unwillingness to join military service, 'their utmost cowardice and weakness' (textual words) to fight the enemy, especially pointing out with inner satisfaction, to the occasions when they were routed, and ending with a pretence at rebuttal of the letter of Marquis of Pombal reiterated their request to be exempted from military service (Doc. no. 52). The government, however, this time peremptorily did not entertain the request (Doc. no. 53), and continued in encouraging natives of the State to join military service promoting those who were worthy and meritorious.

Would the rest of the Christian population which otherwise is not superior in martial valour to that caste, risk their lives to bring the Brahmins to power only with the hope that the victory of the rebels would mean their victory also? Did they think they were less tyrannical than the present rulers? Would the Hindus, among whom there are less martial castes, forsake their native chiefs, headmen and Dessais to follow Christian priests? All these questions invariably invite a negative answer. And experience showed that the lone Dessai that was arrested and tried initially was acquitted and set free. Of Muslims there is nothing to speak about as there were none in the Old Conquests and very few in the New and they were of so little importance that they would not tilt the balance either way whichever side they took.

It is, therefore, improbable that the rebels were relying on the internal movement only.

As soon as the conspiracy was discovered, the first suspicion one had, both in India and in Lisbon, was that the rebels were working in concert with some foreign powers, especially with Tipu Sultan. But during the course of the trial, it appears these suspicions were unfounded and ultimately in the final sentence we find the two masterminds, Fr. José António Gonçalves and Fr. Caetano Francisco do Couto "who pretended to have the assistance of foreign powers and of having thousands of arms and large sums of money." Eventually, it was found that they had nothing and that it was a ruse with which these seditious clerics and their partners tried to deceive those recruited and charmed into their party"

We also feel that they did not have those thousands of arms and the large sums of money they boasted of. But that they did not even have any promise of foreign help or any hopes of getting it, is beyond our understanding. The judges, basing themselves on the evidence on record duty bound as they were, and not finding any tangible evidence about help or support from any foreign power, could not conclude that there was any, though some of the replies given by some of the accused seemed to imply this, and there was no concrete evidence to support this view. Hence it was concluded that it was a figment of their imagination and merely a strategy — a conclusion which somehow would have been corroborated by the attitude of some of the accused who were ignorant of the vital secrets involved. The masterminds and their righthand men had all the interest in hiding these ploys. Since this was known only by a few, it seems there is some truth about its existence and the silence on the part of the accused. One would not be far from truth, if one maintains that those who knew the secret kept it well and only those who had a vague idea about it or heard some whispers about it, touched on the subject.

Following the conclusion of the sentence, the Governor wrote to the Secretary of State, in a letter dated 18 March 1789: "There were no foundations to all the otherwise credible suspicions that these seditious clerics had asked for assistance either from Tipu Sultan or the Marathas or even from Bhosale or from the support they found in the King of Sunda. It is quite probable that they might have given their help knowing how weak and ill-equipped they were and ignorant of the real intentions of the rebel priests of becoming bishops (we do not know how), of establishing universities, forming a parliament and other such absurdities, which Your Excellency must have read about in the depositions of witnesses and confessions of the accused. We only wonder that there are heads that can store such rubbish.

History can however leaving aside the 'alleged and probable' of law, question all sources, investigate facts, re-examine all circumstances that were recorded in the evidence, study and verify other details, though extra-judicial. It can come to a different conclusion from that of the

Governor, who had to abide by the sentence given by the Court and was limited by certain constraints of the moment, and its findings which might have been rejected earlier.

The promises of creation of universities were not something new in the circle of Brahmins. In 1772, Fr. Caetano Victorino de Faria wrote from Lisbon to Fr. Pascoal Pinto of Candolim: "The Neri priests did me a great favour offering all their help, but I had no occasion to avail of that. I firmly believe that the universities will be established in that city and province both for Latin, Greek, French and Hebrew as well as for science, philosophy, theology, and even canonical law, and any one can obtain his doctorate in any of the faculties. I propose *Arte Franceza* by Lima. It would be of great help if you can send the work, yet to be published, of Luis Caetano de Lima and of Menezes, addressed to the same Reverend and with a gift copy to the ministry, as I have already advised them about it". (Doc. no. 32).

The parliament was a new and recent addition so that with one or the other offer they could attract more adepts to the revolt.

The Governor could not believe that the main objective of the masterminds was to become bishops and even that native military officers expected to get higher ranks with Asian rulers, but this was true, as we shall see. The native officers, perhaps felt that they were given lower positions than they merited, that is why a petition was submitted to the court asking that the number of posts for officers should be increased to accomodate more persons. Among the petitioners was Manoel Caetano Pinto, later one of the rebels. The Queen, in the monsoon of 1782, in a letter through Marinho de Mello dated 9 February to Governor D. Frederico Guilherme de Sousa asked him to give his opinion regarding the merits and ability of each of the officers, and in case he found anyone worthy of being considered, he, the Governor could promote him to the rank he deserved bearing in mind however that in consequence of the system adopted by the court of encouraging natives to join the royal service they should not forget that while merit would be rewarded with promotions the same would not apply to those found unworthy (*Livro das Monções*, no. 169, fl. 639).

A very just rule, but one which would not satisfy all and would make them wish for a less scrupulous ruler. Manoel Caetano Pinto was not one of these. Born on 21 October 1758, he enlisted at the age of 17, on 1 March 1775 in the regiment of Brig. Gen. Henrique Carlos Henriques and was soon promoted to Ensign-Bearer on 25 March 1775, to 2nd Lt. in the Legion of Volunteers on 1 April 1777 and to full Lt. in 1780 or 1781, when, with others, he submitted to H. Majesty the petition mentioned earlier.

The discovery of the conspiracy did not make the court at Lisbon change the system of considering natives of India equal to the Portuguese of Europe in their access to military posts, for though the brief of 28 April 1773, which created the regiment of artillery in Goa, determined that no one who was not born in the kingdom or at Algarve should be enlisted as officer or soldier in the three companies of fire brigade, miners and artificers, under pain of severe punishment, the Queen, however, considering the representations made by Governor Francisco da Cunha e Menezes, through her royal letter of 5 October 1792, ordered the cancellation and deletion of that clause, removing this obstacle so that it should not retard the progress of the studies and inclinations of natives (Doc. no. 54)

Let us now consider the position of the neighbouring rulers and see which of them could favour the conspirators in their goal.

The young King of Sunda, son of the one deposed from the throne and being sheltered by the Portuguese, was certainly not a person, despite his royal posture, to extend any support to so risky a plan.

Bhosale, though a perennial enemy of the Portuguese State, presently under check by the latter and even threatened and invaded by the Raja of Kolhapur, was so weak that to obtain our help against that neighbour, he had signed a treaty on 29 January 1788, returning to us the possessions of the provinces of Bicholim, Sanquelim and part of Pernem and the other parts of Pernem which were not in our possession. He too was not in a position to offer any better assistance to the conspirators.

The Maratha, being more powerful, and if he could free himself from the war against Tipu Sultan and from other difficulties that beset him, could if he so wished decide to attack us and extend a helping hand to those inside, who would cooperate with him. It is true that when the conspiracy was discovered there was a rumour that armed people were ready to join the rebels and were stationed at Pune. But, immediately thereafter it was found that there was no truth in this. It was only a priest from Goa, Fr. José Ribeiro by name, residing at Pune, his brother who was in the Maratha army and serving as a soldier in the company of D. Manoel de Noronha then stationed at Kittur, and another Goan, Lazaro de Souza, a very smart man and a friend of the priest and who also served there, who were all aware of what was happening in Goa. These and perhaps other Goans who resided there and who knew of the conspiracy were the ones who would help the movement at some opportune moment. Our agent at

Pune offered to carry a search of the papers of Fr. José Ribeiro, but the Governor refused, as it was not convenient to alarm the court of Pune, unnecessarily, because of something that was suppposed to be known only within Goa. We do not think that there was any connivance on the part of D. Manoel de Noronha who was a Captain in the Maratha army and later promoted to General and a favourite of Peshwa Baji Rao, given his lineage and nobility.

We can eliminate the Maratha also.

There remained only Tipu Sultan, and here it was that we struck dirt, so to say. Let us study the documents that we have and let us, then, judge accordingly.

Tipu Sultan was day by day expanding his conquests in meridional India. He had annexed the kingdom of Kanara, had taken the provinces of Sunda upto our borders, thus becoming our next door neighbour. He threatened each day to attack the State. The war that took place between him and the Maratha gave some respite to the government of Goa, but while it was expected that this war would drag on, our Governor received a letter from Monsieur de Montigni, who resided at the court of Pune, through S. M. Christianissimo, dated 25 February 1787, in which he informed that a peace treaty had just been concluded between the ruler of Pune and Nawab Tipu Sultan, and this was confirmed by other sources also. The Governor advised the court, by his letter of 14 March of the same year, saying: "I am back with the same problems that the court and my predecessor faced before the war between those powers broke out. The aversion that Tipu Sultan has for us is very manifest and he does not even try to hide it. His forces cannot be compared to ours and the finances of the State are barely adequate for its own sustenance, even in peace time. Therefore, I beseech you to place this matter before H. Majesty, so that she may be pleased to take measures that she may find adequate and necessary."

This news and the natural surprise that such a peace treaty caused in all, a treaty which, by the way, was very expensive to Tipu Sultan, as he had to pay lakhs of rupees to the Marathas and which he would not have done unless for some hidden motives as there were no reasons of public interest which could have forced him to do so, compelled the Governor to dispatch to our agent at Pune, Narana Sinai Dumo, who had come to Goa and carried, among other instructions, the following two, dated 5 April 1787:

"You must, particularly, advise me, with utmost urgency possible, about the peace treaty which is said to have been concluded between the ruler of Pune and Tipu Sultan enclosing the treaty signed between the two, if it is public, or to inform what you feel is pertinent. You must inquire, carefully, what are the real reasons behind this treaty and what led Tipu Sultan to ask for it, as it is rumoured, at a very great expense of lakhs of rupees and the return of the lands conquered by him; if Tipu Sultan and the ruler of Pune have divided the troops and disbanded the army and where they have been sent. The same information is needed about Nizam Ali and additionally find out if he also agrees or not with the treaty and what is the strength of the forces that each of the three powers has. Since you will not be able to get all the information at one time, keep me informed as the details keep trickling in. Be very careful, and find out what transpires in the *Sarkar* of Pune in respect of the English and the French with regard to Tipu Sultan."

The agent completed this task by 8 June 1787. Regarding the forces of Tipu Sultan he wrote that, barring the garrison of the lands and forts he could dispose of 80 armed men, 20 to 25 horses and 125 artillery pieces. With this information and others from various sources, the Governor wrote again to the court on 18 June 1787 maintaining insistently, the same serious apprehensions on the intentions of Tipu Sultan.

On 15 October 1787 the agent wrote: "Nana Phadnavis (Prime Minister in the court of Pune) told me that he had correct information that Tipu Sultan sent more than 15,000 men, some cavalry and artillery against the dominion of Goa and that they had already crossed the river Tungabhadra; that he was sure of this and advised me to inform you immediately so that you have enough time to be forewarned and prepared."

Despite the protestations of friendship, our Governor feared that an alliance between the Maratha and Tipu Sultan, and prejudicial to our interests, might be hatched; that the peace treaty between the two was fictitious because Kittur was to be taken by Tipu after the treaty and the fort was provided with Maratha troops without the court of Pune showing any reaction or being scandalized at such an action. Therefore, the Governor urged the agent at Pune by letter of 20 October 1787 to watch carefully the movements in that court and to endeavour by all means to make them desist from this alliance with Tipu. This alliance did not materialise at all.

A greater trouble came from the alliance Tipu had with the French who even at that time, tried to maintain their power in India. Our agent at Pune, Narana Sinai Dumo, is his letter of 30 September 1787 to the Secretary of State in Goa, advised him that a pact had been entered into between Tipu and the French to conquer Goa. This secret reached him through a friar called Fr. Joaquim de St. António who had gone from Chaul to Pune and had said that while he was in the house of a Frenchman *Mutro* (this is how the agent wrote) who was in the service of the Maratha, another Frenchman, called Ferrat, who had recently returned from Goa, was also there. They were talking about the recent discovery of the conspiracy in Goa and mentioned that there was an understanding between Tipu and the French to take Goa by land and sea on condition that Goa would be turned over to the French; that this would have been carried out some time back but was kept in abeyance because of the war with the Maratha. When the agent asked the friar how they talked so openly in his presence, he said they were boisterous, then realising their error, they changed the subject. In the same letter the agent wrote that he had come to know from the people at the court that Tipu had sent his ambassador to France.

In his letter of 15 October, he adds, that an ordinary man who served in the house of the French envoy, Montigni, said that the latter had received a letter from Kittur written by Lally, French General, saying that he had orders from Tipu that after conquering Kittur he should send the army to Goa, and that more troops would follow. This confidence from a simple and ordinary man, not interested with political and military plans, appears to us to be of great value and worthy of credit.

The Secretary of State of Goa urged the agent Dumo to investigate the details of the talks that the two Frenchmen had before Fr. Joaquim de St. António, because nothing of such nature should, at first, be neglected. In his reply, dated 20 January 1788, he said that through his investigations in this respect he found that the very Montigni had said that in the conference between the Governor of Pondicherry and Tipu Sultan, among other subjects, Tipu Sultan had, on his part, demanded that the French place 25,000 white men at his service, but the French agreed to place only 12,000 men, on condition that Tipu Sultan should conquer Goa and hand it over to the French, to which Tipu Sultan agreed but on the proviso that the French would help him in the conquest after which he would hand over only the port, keeping the rest of jurisdiction to himself. The port of Goa obviously, meant the province of Ilhas, Salcete and Bardez, whose extremities form the port.

The agent adds that to confirm the said understanding between Tipu and the Governor of Pondicherry, Tipu Sultan had sent three ambassadors to France, to assist one another, and the Governor, on his part, had already advised his court of the matter before the ambassadors left for France.

He further says that the conquest of Kittur was undertaken as a ploy, while his real intentions were of descending further down. This could not be executed because of the discovery of the conspiracy which thwarted his plans of collusion; that the troops that came to Kittur had not yet collected at Seringapatnam, the capital of Tipu and that they were spread in four parts, namely Copol, Jazendragoddo, Badarbanda and Dharwad, which was also a strategy as he had not given up the idea; that Tipu was at Seringapatnam with his troops quartered there and in the neighbourhood. The agent gave us to understand that all this information he obtained from the same person mentioned in the other letter and that gives this information the same degree of credence.

Writing to the court on 1 February 1788, the Governor, Francisco da Cunha e Menezes, shows himself calm and thanks divine providence that Tipu Sultan did not carry out his designs, which our agent at Bombay said were exaggerated. The agent learns that Tipu Sultan, after having taken Kittur and its jurisdiction and demolished the square, did not march on Belgaum as he intended and Montigni informed him that most of the forces were in the Ghats over Madras, a smaller Corps at Adoni and a still smaller one in the neigbourhood of Tamandara. It appeared to our Governor that the reason for such positioning of the troops of the Nawab was because of his fear of the heavy armaments and a big army that the British maintained at Madras, as confirmed by the letter dated 21 June of the previous year of José Ribeiro de Macedo, a smart Portuguese businessman, residing in that city, and partner of some big business houses in Bombay; that Tipu suspected that the British had some designs against him and were preparing to attack him before he could be helped by the French, with whom Tipu had strengthened, more and more, his friendship, bestowing on the French king a generosity unbecoming of Asian customs, as not receiving payment for supplies made to the French nation in India during the entire war period, which it is said, amounted to two million rupees. The Governor confirms in his letter that Tipu had sent three ambassadors to France.

If this news had alleviated the fears that had gripped the Governor, they were not totally over, for on 11 February 1788, he ordered our troops stationed outside the territory where they had been sent in aid of Bhosale and against the Rajah of Kolhapur back to the State, aware that despite the armaments of the British and the presence of Tipu at Patane, the latter could suddenly decide to avail of the opportunity and attempt some usurption of our provinces, especially that of Ponda.

The Secretary of State, Martinho de Mello e Castro found the fears of the Governor justified and replying to his letter of 1 February 1788, in his letter of 28 January 1789, he said: "The information that you give in your letter of 1 February of last year, of the steps and movements of Tipu Sultan and particularly the contents of the letter from Pune to the Secretary of State of Goa, should make us careful that there really are between the ruler and the French some projects against us. The ambassadors that Tipu Sultan sent to France, the good reception they had there and the novelty of such ambassadors, indicate that there is some important business which increase our fears. The only way we have to avoid the danger that threatens us is to keep the dominions in a better defence position to the extent that the finances of the State may permit."

"With this objective in view, we sent in the last sailing a good number of men and officers by the vessel Campelos which left from here last July and those that have embarked on the vessel are mentioned in the list that I shall send in the next letter, and if it is possible to have another sailing this year, then more men shall be recruited and sent."

It is not that the limited help sent by the Portuguese would save us from any invasion by Tipu Sultan alone or with French help.

In our quest to find out how much truth there was in the rumours about the alliance between the French and Tipu Sultan to conquer Goa, we took the assistance of the curator of the Public Library of Pondicherry, where the archives of the old French government are kept, and to our good fortune we met there Mr. de Gacon, our acquaintance in Goa, where he had been in 1862 and who did the favour of turning on to us very curious notes regarding the negotiations of that time. Mr. de Gacon, to be helpful to us, took the trouble to refer to the official correspondence of that time between the French government in India and the court of Versailles, and found no written mention of any treaty between Tipu and the French regarding Portuguese possessions. But he found a draft of a commercial treaty made in that same year of 1787 with Tipu, a project that gave him the pretext of sending his ambassadors to France. It is incredible to us that a simple commercial treaty should have compelled that Nawab to such an extravagant diplomatic show. There must have been, doubtlessly, some other proposals which could not be rendered in writing and those ambassadors had to deal in person. That these proposals referred to a conquest of Goa, is evident from the wide publication given which the

French spread in India and which those in Pondicherry were wont to announce.

This commercial treaty remained dormant and there was no proposal agreed on at Versailles, on the conquest of Goa. But Mr. de Gacon informs us that there are detailed instructions from Marshal de Castries to Mr. de Souillac, Governor of Pondicherry that same year wherein he sets the conduct of the government towards Indian princes, especially, with Tipu, where he recommends that they should be treated with deference and should be humoured with vague projects. This is in consonance with the alleged conquest of Goa, over which the French in India dreamt — a vague project to humour Tipu and which, to avoid any committment on their part, was not put to writing.

If the conquest of Goa was not given any serious thought by the government of Versailles, it was by the government of Pondicherry, from Dupleix onwards, and it became an everlasting obsession among the French adventurers in India and in the very government of Pondicherry. The quotation which Mr. de Gacon transcribes from a piece of *Histoire de l'Inde ancienne et moderne* by Collin de Bar, "Il est vrai que la Compagnie ne devait jouir des quatre Circars qu'autant qu'elle entretiendrait au service du Souba un nombre de troupes determine, mais un tel engagement ne pouvait borner l'ambition de Dupleix, ni arreter l'execution de ses vastes projets de conquete; il meditait de se faire ceder Goa, capitale des possessions portugaises et de s'emparer ensuite de cet immense triangle qui est entre cette ville Muzilapatan et le Cap Comorin; mais ce n'etait la que de brillantes chimeres; le cabinet de Versailles et la Direction de la Compagnie n'etaient pas capables d'adopter de si grands vues, ni de suivre une determination ferme et invariable. La cour de France d'abord charmee des succes de Dupleix l'avait recompense et encourage en le creant Marquis, et en le decorant du cordon rouge mais elle fut effrayée ensuite des vastes projets de ce gouverneur general d'l'Inde, elle le laissa incertain, elle ne lui envoya aucun nouveau secours, elle lui prescrit meme de renoncer a la nababie du Carnatic."

The fears of the government of Goa about the plans of the French seem to be justified as the French were notorious and such plans also helped the conspirators to regulate some events of their own. But the cordial correspondence which the Portuguese exchanged with the French envoy at Pune, who also congratulated them on the discovery of the conspiracy in time, should have been sufficient to allay these fears (Doc. no. 55). But diplomacy, sometimes forces one to such ploys. On the other hand the Governor was not aware of what we know today from the documents found at Pondicherry and Mr. de Gacon informs us that the correspondence of 1786 and 1787, between the government of Versailles and that of Pondicherry speaks of various obstacles that Tipu, secretly stirred among the French, in his commercial transactions from which one can clearly notice the acrimony between Tipu and the cabinet at Versailles.

But the lack of co-operation by the French was not sufficient for Tipu to desist from the invasion and conquest of Goa. It was, in fact, a new order of business in India that forced him to search the continuance of his power in regions remote from our dominions and drew him away and stopped him from thinking of conquests.

The English had negotiated with the small Rajah of Cherika on the Malabar Coast, who paid tribute to Tipu Sultan, to take on lease the customs duty of Tellicherry, a port in the State of the Rajah. A big confusion of accounts ensued between them because of this contract and because of many other loans and subsidies given by the British to the Rajah. The British approached Tipu to force his vassal to clear the dues and the Nawab, either because of his inability or unwillingness did nothing in the matter and this was left in an impasse for quite some time. In the meantime, Tipu came at the head of an army down the Ghats ostensibly to visit his dominions on the Malabar Coast.

Before marching from Calicut to Palacatcherry on 8 May, he addressed a letter to the British commander at Tellicherry informing him that the Rajah of Cherika had paid all his dues. He wrote simultaneously to the Rajah to say that the British still owed him rupees one lakh.

The Rajah of Travancore too, became anxious with the coming of Tipu with his army. The Rajah was the only potentate who was a neighbour of the dominions of Tipu and on this side of the Ghats was the only one that had escaped being absorbed and annexed by Tipu. He was also the only one who opposed and prevented Tipu from extending his dominions continuously all along from the Maratha frontiers to the Cape Comorin to join Tinevelly, the farthermost and least defended part of the British possessions in Coromandel.

The Rajah of Cochin found himself in the same, if not greater predicament than that of Travancore though he paid homage to Tipu as his vassal, but presently in 1788 no hostilities broke out. (*The History of British India* by James Mill, vol. V, pp. 230ff).

Our Governor was well aware of all this; and writing to the court on 28 November 1788, he wrote: "Tipu Sultan, by May more or less came down to Calicut, visited his possessions by the sea and tried to declare war against the king of Travancore, but returned defeated, they say. He is presently at Patane and has recruited some men at Kittur. The British, fearing he might attack Tellicherry when he visited his forts, fortified the place and kept its defence in a state of readiness but the Nawab returned without declaring any hostilities."

In the following year 1789, Tipu Sultan did not rest until he had invaded the territories of Cochin and Travancore and had laid a siege on Tellicherry, and in 1790 he formally declared a war against the British which lasted till 1792 (Mill, *loc. cit.*). It was only then that the fear of invasion of Goa by Tipu ceased as he could no longer rely on the help of the French because the new Revolution did not permit the French to divert their power for such adventurous enterprises.

But, with or without the French help, it is true that the conquest of Goa was one of the ambitions of Tipu at that time, because the conspirators wanted to avail of his help to expel the Portuguese either joining him in the invasion that they thought was near and imminent or raising the first cry themselves and later calling Tipu to their help. It appears that the latter option, though riskier, was the one preferred by them because from the proceedings it transpired that 10 August had already been fixed for revolt. This bigger risk would be compensated with the hope that Tipu would be considered an ally but not a ruler and conqueror. But it seems unbelievable that the rebels would place their future on so unreal hopes because irrespective of how Tipu helped, one had to forcibly recognise in him the supreme arbiter.

Everything goes to confirm the conclusion that Tipu had intentions of intervening in this revolt. Besides the information that came from Pune and Bombay and from various other sources on his plans of conquest, we must also remember the information that came from Lisbon about Joaquim António Vicente, who recruited for the revolt, was in hurry to return to India to join in the service of Tipu. He decided to come via France where he would contact the ambassadors of Tipu who were there at the time. We must also recall that this same Joaquim António Vicente lived with Eloy José Correa Peixoto who while in India served Hyder Ali Khan, father of Tipu and as such must have had dealings with corporals and other influential people of that Nawab to whom he could recommend the said Joaquim António Vicente. We also recall that Fr. Caetano Francisco do Couto, one of the masterminds of the conspiracy was Governor of the archbishopric of Cochin and in that capacity he must have had many occasions to exchange views with corporals and other influential people of Tipu. Also to be remembered is the fact Fr. José António Gonçalves, another mastermind, remained in Ceylon when he returned from Lisbon, and it was easy, while passing through Malabar, on his way to Goa, to exchange views with Tipu, and that is, perhaps, how he used the episcopal ring of the Archbishop of Cannanore, taken by him at Galle, to add to his stature while holding discussions with distinguished Malabaris. We must also consider that the earlier Bishop of Cochin, Fr. José da Soledade, had asserted that the Archbishop of Cannanore, D. José Cariattil (then already dead) and his companion Fr. Thomas Pariemakel, then Governor of that archbishopric and a declared enemy of the Portuguese, came to know of the plot during the voyage that they made together with the masterminds and, as residents of Malabar they could be of good help before Tipu. The latter would also be happy to find contacts within the state, that could favour him in his designs though it was not the discovery of the conspiracy and the consequent uselessness of that contact that made him desist from his plans but as mentioned earlier, it was due to the need to hold on to what he had won and to other various successes he had gained.

The governance by Tipu, the Marathas or any other potentate was not repugnant to the local Christians of Goa, especially to Brahmins, it being very common to find Portuguese, born in Portugal or in India, in the service of those potentates. If Tipu had annexed the Portuguese State to his conquests the local military officers then in our service, would have been immediately absorbed in that of the new ruler with scope of getting higher ranks and increments and at par with other compatriots already in the service of the Marathas. From a note given by Mr. Luis Xavier Correa da Graça one finds, a few years after the events we have dealt with, i.e. at the end of eighteenth century, that the following served as officers with the Marathas:

1. Joaquim Luis António Vaz, General, native of St. Matias of the Goa Islands, ganvkar of Navelim, in Piedade. He married the sister of the Pintos of Candolim.
2. José António Pinto, Major, and Francisco Caetano Pinto, Major. Both were of Candolim and were brothers of the Pintos implicated in the conspiracy.
3. José Joaquim Pinto, their cousin.
4. António Felippe Gomes, of St. Matias, brother-in-law of José António Pinto.

5. Marcos António Gonçalves, Captain, nephew of Fr. José António Gonçalves.
6. Marinonio Gonçalves, his brother, died of small pox on 28 July 1799.
7. Vicente Felippe de Frias, Lieutenant, of Arpora, brother of Lourenço Lino de Frias, brother-in-law of the Pintos.
8. António Vicente Cabral, Lieutenant, from Piedade, cousin of Caetano António Mathias Cabral, brother-in-law of the Pintos. He died at Piedade in May 1828.
9. Francisco Luis Vaz, nephew of General Vaz of St. Matias.
10. Cosme Damião de Noronha, son of José Felippe Fernandes de Noronha, Captain-Auditor of the 2nd Regiment of Infantry, of St. Matias. He died of small pox in 1795.
11. Gilvito Felippe de Sa, of Piedade, brother of advocate Marcos Ignacio de Sa.

Correa da Graça is right when he says that all these Goan officers with the Marathas were so closely related among themselves, that they almost constituted a family, which goes to prove that the inclination among Goans for military career was limited to a small circle.

Regarding the clerics, it is more difficult to explain if they would find the rule of Tipu more advantageous, but since this ruler tolerated the Christian religion, those who headed the parishes and missions would remain in their previous positions while the masterminds who aspired bishoprics would present their cases to Rome and would receive titles of Bishops or Apostolic Vicars in districts to be created anew. Considering the risky and precarious maintenance of the Portuguese bishops in India, the appointment of local Apostolic Vicars would be a welcome expedient to Rome than it earlier was.

Assuming on the other hand, that after the conquest, Goa would be shared with the French and Tipu, as indicated in the information from Pune, the right of benefice would pass from that of Portugal to the French Crown. Would that Crown be so ungrateful as not to bestow episcopal honour to the priests who showed them the way to the conquest or to whom they offered their services? At least, that is what we believe they would hope for, not reckoning as no one did with the French Revolution at their door.

And finally, we can safely state that Tipu was the axis around which the plans of the conspirators gravitated, so fragile an axis as the events showed, and our dissertation if dispassionate, will show to those who thoughtlessly and without consideration plotted this adventure, which but for a collection of miraculous occurences, could have had the desired results.

FOOTNOTE

1. We have lost the Memorial of the Marquis of Pombal. If we analyse gramatically the discourse, it will appear that he affirms that in all monarchies there is a large number of businessmen who fill the squares of the kingdom.

10

AN ANALYSIS OF THE COMMENTS ON THE CONSPIRACY

For nearly a century, the success of the conspiracy was a guarded secret among Goan families, none daring to make public such a delicate subject neither admitting nor denying it.

But at the end of that period, when freedom of the press was ushered in, which gave each one the liberty to express freely his honest or seemingly honest opinion, one could notice from then on two different historical versions from the sons of India regarding the said conspiracy

Some deny, without solid foundations, its very existence maintaining that the accusation was slanderous, the punishments and prison sentences tyrannical and those condemned and jailed, innocent martyrs of despotism.

The first version, as far as we can see, came out in bold print in *Refutação Analytica do Manifesto do Governo Provisional* (Analytical Rebuttal), printed in Bombay in 1835. This was written by António Semeão Pereira of S. Pedro, Panelim, editor of *Pregoeiro da Liberdade* (The Crier of Freedom) at Bombay, assisted somewhat by Luis Caetano de Menezes of Divar or Piedade, later editor of *Abelha de Bombaim* (The Bombay Bee), though the judge José Joaquim Duraes, in a letter published in the *Boletim do Governo* of the State of India, no. 21, 12 April 1839, tried to take the authorship from the *Pregoeiro* and give it to Luis Caetano de Menezes. This was doubtlessly with a view to belittle that editor whom he disliked intensely which probably led him to write: "Some say that *Refutação Analytica* is the work of *Pregoeiro*. It is, however, hard to believe that a dull-witted person could write such a piece. I am inclined to believe the opinion of others that maintain that it is the work of Luis Caetano de Menezes whom, I find, is capable of that and of much more while the *Pregoeiro* is a zero before him."

Irrespective of who was the author of *Refutação Analytica* in para. 8, speaking of the sentence of 9 December 1788, there is an annotation which reads: "The Court at Lisbon found passion, rancour and hatred so patently clear in the sentence pronounced that not only was the Governor severely reprimanded by a decree but equally was the Archbishop, who assuming that some clerics were implicated in that imaginary revolt and in concurrence with the Governor, sent them to Lisbon to be tried and punished there. They, however, returned victorious and with specific recommendations to be granted the best benefits and appointments in existing vacancies in addition to being favoured with life pension, as one can find in the ordinance that follows, where the notice on behalf of Fr. Manoel da Expectação is published and who, as all know was one of the clerics mentioned above" (Doc. no. 9).

The reader will now be able to decide how incorrect was the information and conclusion of the author of the earlier annotation. The Governor was not reprimanded for having ordered the trial of those innocent accused. Assuming that he was reprimanded, it could not certainly have been by a decree as stated but through a note or memo from the ministry on behalf of the ruler. The Governor on receipt of numerous complaints of the conspiracy ordered their arrest and immediately committed them to the court whose duty it was to decide on the innocence or guilt of the accused. The other duty he had and which he duly discharged was to advise the court of the happenings and to expedite the dispatch of whatever details of the investigation were available in the first monsoon. This was carried out by him so expeditiously that orders from H. Majesty to try the accused, after following all due processes of law and other legal formalities, were received on the return voyage. The government of Lisbon did more. They sent the details that indicated that the idea of the revolt was old and that some sons of India residing in Lisbon knew about it. Their arrest was ordered but since all could not be found, only Fr. Caetano Victorino de Faria was arrested.

As for the Archbishop, since he was the first person to receive the complaint, he discharged his duty rendering the complaint in writing and submitting it to the Governor. He did no more. The clerics that were arrested were not handed over to him, not only because of the decision of the High Court but because orders had been received from Portugal to send them to Lisbon together with their charge-sheets. These orders were addressed to the Governor, and the Archbishop was not asked for his assent nor could he oppose the course of law. He was neither reprimanded nor was there anything reprehensible in his actions.

The judges who passed the sentence could not be suspect in the eyes of the court of Lisbon nor could they have held any passion, rancour or hatred against the accused because they were all recent arrivals in India, and it is surprising that while the author maintains that the court at Lisbon realised that the judges were prejudiced against the accused who, he says, were innocent he should, at the same time, admit that the judges were not punished nor even reprimanded. The reprehensions, severe as they were, were solely directed at the Governor who ordered the trial which he could not avoid, and at the Archbishop who received the first complaint which he could not conceal.

If innocents were tried and sentenced the fault lies with the judges and not with the Governor, though in his capacity as Magistrate of all courts in the land, he was duty-bound to be present at the High Court while sentence was being delivered.

To order a trial is an unavoidable duty of a government, especially when specific accusations are presented, irrespective of the gravity of the offence.

We refrain from commenting on the assertion of the author that clerics that were arrested and sent to Lisbon returned victorious with specific recommendations to be granted the best benefits and given vacant posts.

The documents mentioned earlier show what a sad victory the poor priests won, beseeching and humbly obtaining pardon for all offences that were levelled against them. Regarding Fr. Manoel da Expectação, who was found innocent, because of the information that the same Archbishop, who has been accused of being a tyrant or an abetter of a tyrant, had sent, he was sent back to his homeland five years before the others with the same pension of 400 *reis* per day with which H. Majesty favoured him in Lisbon. The author has generalised the events. It is not correct, not even with regard to this priest that they were asked to be given the best benefits and vacant posts. What was recommended was that the Archbishop should reinstate them in jobs they previously held or should employ them in the service of the church according to their merits and aptitude. The declaration of innocence of Fr. Manoel da Expectação, not being conferred on any other is in itself sufficient proof that others were in less favourable conditions and though no documents exist, they were pardoned of all charges that might have been levelled against them, which is very different from saying that they were found innocent and returned victorious.

This annotation in *Refutação Analytica* was accepted as gospel truth, without considering its real implications and served as a topic, on which various articles were written, each more discordant from the testimony of documents and logical explanations.

In *Noticia* which Genezano António João de Sousa of Candolim published in the *Ultramar* of 18 May 1865 on Fr. Caetano Victorino de Faria and on his son, l'Abbe de Faria, one reads that Queen D. Maria I favoured Fr. Caetano Victorino with a blind patronage making him her confessor and privy councillor; that because of this patronage he turned his heart to Goa, his motherland; that he succeeded in a short time to obtain the dismissal of Governor, D. Francisco because of his fierce persecution of the Pintos of Candolim for an imaginary sedition; that he helped many sons of Goa who were sent to the metropolis to be punished as accomplices in that sedition; and finally, that he sent some briefs and indulgences to Goa even against the wishes of a certain Archbishop whose name Genezano could not trace.

Genezano perhaps thought that he was praising the Queen when he was actually insulting her, when he stated that she should blindly favour him or any one for that matter with patronage, though he might have been supposedly her personal confessor and privy counsellor. He further states that a reprimand to a Governor is inconsequential, and that the Governor was dismissed at the instance of Fr. Victorino who, poor fellow, did not have enough powers to set himself free from prison of the Paulists. It is not surprising that Genezano should have convinced himself of such a strange case since he did not know the name of the Governor and readily accepted the first false information or version that he obtained.

As we all know the Governor Francisco da Cunha e Menezes having taken charge on 3 November 1786, governed till 22 May 1794 for nearly eight years though the normal period of office is three years. Since the conspiracy was discovered in the first year of his office it becomes evident that the action he took did not shorten but increased the period of his governance. On 15 February 1788 he requested the Secretary of State to relieve him of his post on the plea of continued ill-health, which he suffered since he landed in Goa, because the hot climate did not agree with him. He stated that he was advancing his request so that it might be favourably granted on completion of his tenure of service. On 5 March 1789 he reminded them again to send his replacement as his health had deteriorated further in this climate. It was after this reminder that the Secretary of State, Martinho de Mello e Castro replied in his letter of 8 May 1790, stating that presently it was not possible to take any decision in this regard and that H. Majesty was in the know of his request. He replied on 5 April 1791 insisting on a replacement as his health did not allow him to do justice to his office. The Secretary of State replied on 26 Ferbuary 1792 that he would convey to him the royal orders by the next sailing which was due in July or August of the same year, orders which limited to the Secretary of State saying, in his letter of 1 October 1792 that because of some problems that had cropped up they had to forcibly postpone this decision for the monsoon of next year, but that he would see to it and use his best efforts that there was no delay in the appointment of his successor.

Before the receipt of this letter, the Governor had insisted twice on being replaced on 16 March and 28 September 1792 but it was only on 24 August 1793 that by a royal decree the charge of the government of the State was handed over to Lt. General, Francisco António da Veiga Cabral, the Commander of the army of that State and to whom Francisco da Cunha e Menezes gave over the charge on 22 May 1794. The locals owe to him the privilege of their being considered equal to Europeans in the admissions to the company of graduates and in the regiment of artillery (Doc. no. 54).

In an introduction that Mr. Jacinto Caetano Barreto e Miranda wrote in the *Noticia* of Genezano (same number of *Ultramar*) accepting as true what he found in the annotations of *Refutação Analytica* he finds it hard to believe in miracles, which Fr. Caetano Victorino de Faria is supposed to have worked in favour of the accused in the sedition of 1787. However, drawn by the current opinion since the *Refutação Analytica* and now romanticised since as the poet Virgil says a *fama crescit eundo,* he seems convinced that the priests sent to Lisbon to be tried as accused in the conspiracy were well-treated there; that their arrival in Goa was triumphant; that the government was urged to grant them those benefits and jobs; that the Governor, Francisco da Cunha e Menezes and the Archbishop D. Fr. Manoel de Santa Catharina, had fallen from grace in the metropolis and that both were severely reprimanded, the former for having ordered the trial of the poor accused and the latter for having concurred in the prosecution of the nefarious trial in which innocent blood was spilt. We have shown above that all this took place in an entirely different way.

The victorious return and the reprimand of the Governor and of the Archbishop are also recorded in an article of C. R. Ernesto Alvares which was published in *Almanack Popular* of José Pedro da Silva Campos e Oliveira for the year 1867, giving information of Fr. José António Gonçalves. The same must have been repeated in many other publications, with lesser foundation and confirmation than in *Refutação Analytica* and with the same ease with which historical events are copied from one author to another.

The second version is more modern. It was created as an election propaganda and consists, as we said, in accepting the conspiracy of 1787 as proved and deriving from it the maximum leverage to excite the pseudo-patriotism of the motley crowds, obviously against the government and especially during election time.

It is found disguised in speeches and in newspaper articles of which we give but two examples. There was an election in the province of Bardez in 1861. An election meeting of the opposition party was convened at Guirim on 7 June, in which the main speaker was the Vicar of Parra who among other things, said: "And you, distinguished gentlemen, descendants of brave and always honoured people of Bardez! If you just cast your minds to old times, you will find that your ancestors have left you an honourable legacy in the Town Hall with their deeds; you will remember that they were martyrs for the sake of our freedom, some having been hanged from the gallows, others having had to eat the bitter bread of anguish in the most squalid dungeons and squares, still others having had to go in exile to foreign countries and many others shot with muskets[1] offering their heads to be staked, in the villages. And tell me, after all this, which province can lay claim to this honour and heroism? Is it not Bardez? So, since it is more than shameful in our present times of literacy that we should live and exist to tarnish those great names won with their blood, I decided to call you." This speech was published in periodicals of that time.

In an autobiographical article on Francisco Luis Gomes, one reads that his candidature having been rejected in his home constituency in Salcete, was welcomed in Bardez: "Bardez, liberal and patriotic, the province of Bardez which has given a galaxy of heroes, allow us the expression, to safeguard our legitimate rights and honour of the country during various crisis; Bardez, which has given enough proofs of its civic dedication and fought so much to plant the sacred tree of freedom and had to shed the blood of its sons to attain that objective, Bardez always fearful sacred tree of freedom and had to shed the blood of its sons to attain that objective, Bardez always fearful when goaded, because when goaded it rises as one man, with one wish, one thought, one strength, and patriotic as it is, it felt deeply the ingratitude of its sister, Salcete, and under the circumstances, could not but right the wrong and wash the stain that future generations would reproach, perhaps with scorn, and there it rushes, enthusiastically and honourably to save the national honour." (*Album Litterario,* no. 1, 1875). The national honour, in the opinion of the album, is of little consequence.[2]

Another version, but contradictory, originates from the same principle i.e. of an exaggerated and, therefore, false love of the motherland. The authors of the former, backing on the legitimacy of the people in power want to save their compatriots from the label of traitors and rebels feeling that that label will somehow attach to them also forgetting that a crime committed by some people does not necessarily reflect on all the others.

The authors of the latter starting from the legitimacy of the resistance to the occupation of his country by a foreign race find the attempt at revolt glorious and heroic, even though foiled. They forget that there is no heroism in going from one illusion to another and do not know how to balance means and ends. They are ignorant that irrespective of how much fortune may favour, in the first moments of the fantasy of a Goan republic or on the invasion by Tipu (alone or with the help of the French, who at any rate were on their decline in India), the Portuguese would not delay in reacting and would give their lives to recover their possessions. If unsuccessful, there were the British ever eager to expand their dominions in India, who would not loose the opportunity to seize the much coveted port of Goa.

But considering the origins and effects of the two opposite versions, one notices that they are purely speculative opinions, serving only as pathetic figures of rhetoric to capture applauses of the crowds on opportune occasions, after which both, the authors and the crowds, once again become as good Portuguese citizens as they were before.

ADDENDUM TO CHAPTER VII

When we came to know, from the *Catalogo dos Manuscriptos* (Catalogue of manuscripts) of the Public Library of Evora, that there were two letters from Fr. Caetano Victorino de Faria to D. Fr. Manoel de Cenaculo, Bishop of Beja, later Archbishop of Evora, and founder of that library, we tried to get their copies to see if they could be of any use in our historical records. The librarian,. our nephew and friend, Dr. Thomaz Fiel Gomes Ramalho, after securing the necessary permission promptly sent us the copies we asked for and which reached us after the text had been printed, hence we record them now.

The first of the said letters (Doc. no. 56) begins by informing that Fr. Dr. José António Gonçalves, returning from Rome to Lisbon, passed through Beja and was a guest of the Bishop who received him with cordial hospitality which the remarkable Prelate extended to all, especially to those dedicated to the letters. Availing of the excuse of thanking the Bishop for the favour extended to his compatriot and friend, Fr. Caetano Victorino began a correspondence, with the main aim of obtaining his concurrence to his plans of withdrawing the nuns of Santa Clara of Beja from the jurisdiction of Franciscan Provincials of Algarve, and bringing them to his (Bishop's) jurisdiction, and in order that the Bishop should not find it strange that he should interfere in these affairs, he apprises him that he had been entrusted with this task by the Marchioness of Angeja, in the interests of peace and tranquility of the nuns. As a secondary purpose, he requests the Bishop's good offices to convince a person from Beja, who had complained to the Crown that two estates administered by the nuns were vacant, to desist from the plaint. The wise prelate replied (Doc. no. 56) that he would give his reply on the matter of the jurisdiction of the nuns when approached officially and, if his earthly superiors agreed, he would act as circumstances demanded as he knew how to discharge the duties of his office. With regard to the estates, he was more condescending. He spoke to the person concerned but finding that he was not prepared to forego whatever he might get out of this legal action, respecting the freedom of others, he let the matter be decided by the court.

This letter from Fr. Caetano Victorino is not dated and the draft reply by the Bishop, annexed to it, clearly mentions the date and month though the year is illegible. However, as we know that Fr. Dr. José António Gonçalves left for Rome from Lisbon in October 1782 (p. 57) and the reply is dated 27 December, we can safely assume that they referred to the same year.

If we need a counter-proof, we would say that the second letter from the priest to the Bishop (Doc. no. 56) was written much after the first, not only because this is the substance of the preamble to the letter but also because sufficient time elapsed between the two letters to give Fr. Caetano Victorino time to apply to Rome for a brief exempting the nuns, to receive it and to allow him to complain about the slackness of the ministry in issuing the consent letter. All this could not have been done in less than the full year 1783 till 3 August 1784, the date of the second letter.

In this letter Fr. Caetano Victorino reports what he has done in respect with the claim of the nuns, the wrath of the friars, their chicanery and intrigues to block the transfer of jurisdiction which the priest said he would retribute in equal measure. He was ready to accompany the afflicted Abbess even to Calvary not afraid to die for her and with her because he knew she was dear to Our Lord notwithstanding the fact that when things began to go wrong he sent a note drafted by him to the Bishop with request that if approved by him to have the Abbess sign it and to post it, without delay (he meant without fail). It appears to us that the contents of this letter could have caused some disgust to the Prelate but a great master in questions of method and style that he was he could not but laugh at the writings of the priest and be scandalized when he read the recommendation that the Abbess should not send any note to the Queen without first being seen by him because the two earlier ones were just contrary to what he had drafted.

No one could find the reply to his second letter though there must have been one. Judging from the first letter and the known seriousness of the Bishop, it must have left Fr. Caetano Victorino well-convinced that the Prelate of Beja devoted his great spirit and great wisdom to more serious problems than to useless and unedifying fights between friars and nuns.

It may be surprising that Fr. Caetano Victorino did never, personally, know the Bishop of Beja who was the master of the Prince, D. José, and the President of the Board of Censors and in the year 1777, (or may be 1778) after the death of King D. José and the dismissal of Marquis of Pombal, he went to his bishopric. Considering that Fr. Caetano Victorino left for Rome in 1772 soon after arriving in Lisbon and obtained his doctorate in Rome, he must have necessarily stayed there some years and returned to Lisbon a little after the Bishop had left for Beja, that being the probable reason why he did not have an opportunity of knowing him personally.

FOOTNOTES

1. It is the imagination of the speaker.
2. Among the Chardos there is a variant in the manner of capturing the action of the conspirators. If one puts the people of India in the European class, it runs as the editors of the *Album,* but it fights through the excellency of his caste over the Brahmins. Then the raising of the Pintos is distasteful and the Brahmins were justified, killed for infidelities of the Portuguese crown, a conclusion that involves the protest of the infidelity of the Chardos.

SECTION II

DOCUMENTS

DOCUMENTS

Document No. 1

Letter of the Governor to the Chief Justice of the State, José Joaquim de Sequeira Magalhães e Lanções.

Whereas on the 5th of the current month in the morning, António Eugenio Toscano, clerkat Aldona came to complain that Fr. Dr. José António Gonçalves or José Felippe Gonçalves and Fr. Caetano da Silva, Vicar of St. Lourenço of Linhares had plotted an uprisingagainst the State with a view to expelthe whites from here, a complaint, later confirmed with the information brought the same night by the Governor of Alorna, Col. Manoel Godinho de Mira and Lt.of the Legion of Bardez, Nicolau Luiz da Costa.He on the morning of 6th, made his deposition before Mr. Justice and Secretary of State (which goes attached), all of this being later fully corroborated by the depositions on oath of three priests and submitted to me in the morning of 6th by His Grace Archbishop Primate, which also go attached herewith. Therefore, after duly considering the gravity of the offence, and as it amounts to a formal revolt and is consequently a heinous crime of high treason of the first degree and having in the meanwhile, ordered the arrests of all those who may be implicated in it or of those from whom we may be able to obtain necessary information and whose names figure in the list attached, and having also ordered the seizure of all documents thatwere found with them and which are sent herewith, I order you to proceed with the necessary investigations and inquiries in this matter, having as Secretary, Justice Sebastião José Ferreira Barroco.You are to keep me informed of the persons whom you may find, as the investigations proceed, are involved, so that these daring persons who have foolishly abused the honour and favours bestowed on them by H. Majesty, may receive their due and justpunishments.

God protect Your Excellency.
Panjim, 9 August 1787.
s/d Francisco da Cunha e Menezes.

Livro de Portarias (Book of Ordinances), Letters & Orders. fl. 21.

Document No. 2

Letter from the Governor D. José Pedro da Camara to the Secretary of State, Martinho deMello e Castro.

Most Respected Sir,

We are sending back to the Court on the ship *Madre de Deus*, Eloy José Peixoto who has retired from the service in this State.He is the same official who for many years served Nawab Hyder Ali and the King of Tanjore, and who on his return to this State in 1776, was appointed by me as Captainof the Legion of Royal Volunteers, as has already been told to that Court, in the monsoon of that year.

I presume that he is going to rest in his house at Azeitão, after all the problems he has faced through his long and continuous pilgrimages in Asia.It is possible that he may not be able to adjust himself to the lifestyle that he will find in his homeland, which will be very different from that he was accustomed to, a very licentious one.

With this knowledge, I am inclined to believe that it will not be long before he returns in search of that same life again. I am given to understand, here, that he goes with the intentions of proposing to Your Excellency big projects which at first sight may seem very advantageous to the establishments and dominions of H. Majesty and I am certain that he will embellish them with attractive offers but which are without solid foundations and which you will soon perceive.

I only wish to advise Your Excellency from what I have learnt of this official that his fickleness made him lose the very best of fortunes he had earned through no merit of his own than that of being a European and a Portuguese and that he is of no use, so far as we are concerned, as he is not amenable to reason and is very unruly.

God protect Your Excellency.

Goa, 29 December 1778.

Livro das Monções, no. 160, fl. 65.

Document No. 3

Sentence

Gaspar Elpideo Soares da Torre, clerk of the court of the second level of this province of the State of India:I certify that the Superintendent of the said Court produced before me some documents, with annexures, regarding the proceedings of the events that took place in 1787, against the Europeans residing in this State, some pages of which, due to the long passage of time, are completely worn out.In accordance with the orders from the provincial government of this State of India, on behalf of the requested Queen (the copy of which goes attached), I issued as a certified copy ofthe Sentence, recordingas much of its contents aswas possible, considering the defacement of the pages, details of which follow:

Decree, fls. 195-207v.

*Decree from the High Court:*Having gone through these documents and after obtaining endorsement from the Magistrate of Courts, a summary, together with articles, pleadings and the charge-sheets listed in the decree at fl. 151, were given to the accused.It was found that an abominable offence of revolt and high treason was hatched in Ilhas and other provinces of Goa and that the charge-sheetedpersons and other priests, who figure in the investigations and interrogations, had all conspired to withdraw this State from the subjection, obedience and governance of the said Lady, Our Queen, and overthrow this government, implanting a new republic, where the so-called natives would govern through a representative council and would be sovereign over the entire and mixed empire.This conspiracy could not, in itself subsist and was incapable of producing the desired results as is amply demonstrated from the details of their plans recorded in the proceedings but sufficient enough to cause very serious and damaging consequences.Anyone conceiving such an abominable offence of high treason ... upto now the mostfortunate government of the saidLady, whose kings always governed their people and subjects with fondest and paternal love, making no difference between those born in the kingdom of Portugal and in the conquered lands but, on the contrary, choosing and preferring the latter in the service of the churches, in benefices, positions, employments, honours and other public services in the provinces and in places of their birth, as is evident from so many and repeated royal orders which are recorded in the archives of the State and from so many other and useful actions and honourable occupations given to many natives.

It was also found that after leaving Lisbon in 1785, the two priests Fr. José António Gonçalves and Fr. Caetano Francisco do Couto, dissatisfied because they were not elevated to the high position of bishops to which they were foundunsuitable because of their lack of virtue and knowledge ... people of all nations, because despite various provisions of law against scoundrels, and many penalties which are given as punishments for their excesses, there will always be a great many number of these perverse people who will disturb the peace of the public and of individuals who live under the protection of the authorities,theirmonarch, bodyguardsand magistrates.

With special reference to this State, it was found that many of these scoundrels were natives and that neither they nor the so-called Portuguese wereeverallowed to gowithout punishment commensurate with the gravity of their offences and proof thereof. It was such people that, out of hatred and a spirit of revolt with which they were imbued, perversely and maliciously, imputed these injustices on us and coaxed other natives, friends and acquaintances and forced them to join the revolt.

They first appraised their colleagues in ecclesiastical profession of their aim and influenced them as well as the vicars, whom they suggested that, as parish priests, theycould easily mix the poison of dissatisfaction and sedition with religion, for which purpose they held meetings in the house of the mastermind, Fr. Couto and in other houses ... ecclesiastics, so that each one devoted to the revolt should make this business a common and own cause, enticingother friends and acquaintances.They also managed to enticemany military officers to the seditious group so that they in turn might corrupt the rest of the troops of the Queen.

As a means of persuasion they had recourse to most horrible lies and coercion, assuring that therevoltwas not a sin but the will of God and that they had the blessings of the High Pontiff, by virtue of an express precept.They pretended to have the assistance of foreign powers, of having thousands ofarms and a large sum of money, when on the contrary they had nothing, because it was all a ploy which those seditious priests and their partners made use of to deceive those they had recruited to their side, even taking advantage of the boorishness of some to influencethem with their braggadocio.

It was also held that this revolt and hightreason did not consist of vague and verbose speeches and wild thoughts, but that the masterminds, their partners and sympathisers had already worked out minute details of the shape and way of operations deploying the corps of rebels ... to surprise persons in high positions and of respect, to herald the so-called freedom simultaneously from various places, threatening to kill anyone who opposed the revolt and fixing the date of the execution of their plans for the 10th of August of the preceeding year and in case of any contingency, any other date but before the arrival of the vessel which, in accordance with the orders of the Queen, made yearly trips from thekingdom to this State.

The revolt was discovered when it was inan advanced stage and the traitors were arrestedin the early morning of 7th of August of the preceeding year.All these facts and many others which aggravated their heinous crime are fully established by the depositions of 41 witnesses, bycomplaints and confessions especially at fls. 5, 8-16v, 30, 34, 41, 44v, 52, and 55 of theinvestigations, and at fls. 27v, 40, 52, 61v, 81-160 of the first annexure ....

Pedro Luiz Gonzaga and Manoel Caetano Pinto were found to be agent-provocateurs and instigators of this rebellion and high treason and being invited by the masterminds they associatedwith them and undertook to ... Legion of Ponda where they were ... Francisco Pereira, helper of thesurgeon, according to the confessions made during the investigations at fls. 81, 85, 88, 40 of the 1st annexure and at fl. 37v and finally, his own confession at fls. 103, 110 of the 3rd annexure ratified at fls. 107 and 185 of the same annexure.These accused, like theother leaders, carried out their assignments in their respective Legions which, they boasted were totally suborned.They informed the masterminds of the additional enrollment of rebels made in the party through emissaries.

The accused Pedro Luiz Gonzaga went to Mandur to discuss with Ignacio Caetano Lopes, who also belonged to the same party, the confinement of Sebastião Dias, Corporal in his company, because they were aware of his disloyalty and his capacity to oppose the revolt and to examine the help that his Company of Auxiliaries, with whoseassistance andthat ofhis Legion, alreadysuborned, could extend to attacksome fortsasthe co-accused confessed at fl. 137 of 1st annexure and the said Gonzaga at fl. 115of the 3rd annexure and further that thisaccused was involved in the revolt with his colleague Pinto and it was further still found from the confession of bothofthemthatthey were partners in this revoltandtogetherdecided to influence the said Legion.

In the same .... Manoel Ferrão, João Vaz, David Francisco Viegas, Francisco Pereira and António Fernandes, Corporal, were aware of the conspiracy and had been invited to join it bythe said two Lieutenants and

David Francisco Viegas. They were duty bound to denounce the traitors without loss oftime, insteadthey not only did not carry out their bounden duty, inherent in a subject and more so in the accused, by virtue of their honourable military profession and the oath that they took pledging to defend the flags of the Queen, but also consented and joined the rebels, as is evident from their confessions at fls. 40, 81, 85, 88, 109v of 1st annexure ratified at fls. 34, 36v, 38 , 45v, and 55 of the 3rd annexure and from the confessions of the said seducers at fls. 103 and 110v of the 3rdannexure.

The accused Francisco Pereira, helper to the surgeon thought belatedly of his duty and went to obtain advice fromFr. FranciscoJosé de JesusMaria, ex-chaplain of the said Legion, according to his confession at fl. 3 of the inquiry. This irregular action does not exonerate him of his culpability because this crime was such ...may create doubt.

The persistent denials of the accused David Francisco Viegas cannot exonerate him (fl. 117 of the 1st, fls. 12 and 117 of the 3rd annexures) because, besides the proofs which surfaced from the confession of the accused António Fernandes at fl. 88, sustained at fl. 161 of the 1st annexure and fl. 56v of the 3rd annexure, and of Pedro Luiz Gonzaga at fl. 110, ratified at fl. 185 of the 3rd annexureandmaintainedin the confrontation at fl. 120 of the 3rd annexure, his guilt was established when he became nonplussed forsometimewhenGonzaga pointed out to two conversations he had had with the accused and muttered that he could remember no such meeting and was not aware of any such exchange. These replies were given before he was subjected to torture and after the confrontation. Ifwe acceptthe confessions of the said two accused, the declaration of the mastermind Fr. Couto at fl. 63 and his own at fl. 37v of the investigations in which he admits having beencalled by Gonzaga to go, are more than ample proofs of his guilt ....

Noronha at fl. 103 of inquiries, from which it is revealed that he asked Corporal António Fernandes notto tell anyone about that thing, as stated by him. This strange business to which that messageallegedly referred cannot serve without prejudice to the earlier proofs as an excuse notwithstanding his continued denials, even after torture (his protest at fl. 110 of the 3rd annexure).

Similarly, the following were called and joined the rebels: Caetano Xavier da Costa, Corporal, his brother Miguel António da Costaand Sebastião Paulo de Noronha. The last, when informed by the leaders of their final aim, not only joined them but, making the cause his own worked as much as the leaders themselves and tookupon himself toarrange armed people which he asked a Muslim to supply, assuring the party that he would have about 100 men ready.This is according to the confession of Fr. Couto at fl. 67 of the 1st annexure.He also recruited more people and went to Ponda to ascertain the progress of the revolt in that Legion as if ...atfl.159, of Miguel António da Costa and finally from his own confession at fl. 122v of the 1st annexure ratified at fl. 130v of the 3rd annexure, though minimal and full of denials in order to reducehis guilt, (which is found in confessions of almost all of the accused) still, one cannot but conclude that this accused did as much work as a person of his poorstaturecould.This is found in the confession of Fr. Couto at fls. 63, 64, 67 and 68v of the 1st annexure, confession which appear to be sincere and truthful by its contents and the way in which it was said.All this was earlier corroborated by other witnesses and, thereforebecomes more credible.

Regarding the accused Miguel António da Costa it is revealed not only by his confessions at fl. 150 of the 1st annexure ratified at fl. 41 of the 3rd annexure but also from the confessions of Fr. Couto at fl. 64 of the 1st annexure and of Sebastião Paulo de Noronha, his companion, at fl. 122v, that he had full knowledge of the conspiracy, that he associated with them and volunteered to take to the house of Fr. Couto to ... against whom it is also proved that he knew and approved of the revolt, as he confessed at fl. 155 and ratified at fl. 68of the 1stand the 3rd annexures and from the confessions of the accused Sebastião Paulo de Noronha at fl. 122 of the 1st annexure and of Lt. Luiz Gonzaga at fl. 110 of the 3rd annexure and of Fr. Couto at fl. 64 of the 1st annexure, where it is stated that hehad gone to the house of the accused with his brother, already aware of the conspiracy, and that, after holding discussions with them, he expressed his desire to join the rebels, accepted the duty to detain the Field Marshal, promised to do whatever he could and acted as a messenger of Lt. Gonzaga to carry his messages to other leaders, via Sebastião Paulo de Noronha, that this commission was turning out to be very expensive, as recordedat fl. 110 of his confession.

Though one notices studied modesty in the declarations of the accused and of Lt. Gonzaga .... and Salvador Alvares da Costa, as is revealed that the said Ignacio Caetano Lopes, having been asked by the leader Fr. Couto and his brother, joined the revolt and promised the help ofhis Company of Auxiliaries to attack the forts of the Queen and to confine Corporal Sebastião Dias, of whom Lt. Gonzaga was afraid, in his house.This is found in his confessions at fl. 137 of the 1st annexure repeated at fl. 70 of the 3rd annexure and from the confessions of Lt.

Gonzaga at fl. 110 of the 3rd annnexure and of Fr. Couto at fl. 68 of the 1st annexure.

Of Bernardo Mesquita, it is found that, having been called by Sebastião Paulo deNoronha, he joined the rebels and introduced himself to Fr. Couto ... his house twice, as he deposed at fl. 68v of the1st annexure and in the confession of Sebastião Paulo at fls. 122, 133vof the 1st annexure, ratifiedatfl. 57 of the 3rd annexure.

Of José Monteiro it is found that being called by the leader Fr. José António .... Couto, and he confessed at fl. 68 ofthe 1st annexure and the accused at fl. 130 ratified at fl. 60 of the 3rd annexure.And against SalvadorAlvares da Costa it is proved that he was called to join the rebels in the month of May of the same year and that after joining them, revealed to them the number of Portuguese soldiers that were in the 1st Regiment, where he was a private soldier, and also revealed the state of fortifications of the fortress of Rachol, as is evidentfrom his own confession at fl. 101 of the 1st annexure ratified at fl. 40 of the 3rd annexure and this tallies with what Fr. Couto said at fl. 63v of the 1st annexure. He was so imbued with the spirit of revolt, that when he was arrested, he dared state before the Lieutenant and thesoldier who was handcuffing him that what he, the soldier, was presently doing to him, they would do to them all, and he repeated this twice, as is found in his deposition at fls. 60 and 70v of the inquiries.

Similarly, Nicolau Luiz da Costa and Ignacio Caetano Toscano took part in this abominable crime of revolt, and when invited ... party of the rebels.They promised their efforts in enticing friends and acquaintances and there are reasons to believe that they were entrusted with suborning the Legion of Bardez, where they held the rank of Lieutenants, because the leaders were confident of the support of that Legionas well as that of Ponda, since both comprised of native soldiers, and there were no other indications to the effect that such a mission was entrusted to any other member, therefore the inescapable conclusion one draws is that these two officers were entrusted with this mission of suborning and enticing the Legion to their fold, while that of Ponda was entrusted to Lts. Gonzaga and Pinto. That is why in their confessions they stated that they were being asked by others what kind of people they had recruited for their party.All this is established by their confessions at fls. 28 and 52 of the 1st annexure, ratified at fls. 66 & 68 of the 3rd annexure, and through the testimony at fl. 44v, 50v, 52 of the inquiries and by the confession of Fr. Couto at fl. 67v of the 1st annexure where he mentions the absurd and cruel scheme that the accused had allegedlythought of poisoning the bread supplied to the troops ...thecomplaints that the accusedNicolau Luiz da Costa made atfl. 5 and the accused Ignacio Caetano, through his brother António Eugenio Toscano, at fl. 34 of the inquiries, was of no avail because, being aware for quite some time of the details and the stage at which it had reached, they made their complaints only on 5 and 6 of August of the same year, when the conspiracy was not only being discovered but had already been discovered and proved by a number of witnesses who were questioned on the 3 of August of the same yearbythe Vicar-General ofthearchbishopricwhowas at the same time Archbishop-Primateand to whom, on 31 July of the same year, Fr. Pedro Caetano José Lobo, then Vicar of Tivim, who refused to be influenced by the masterminds and dissuaded the rebels from suchunpatriotic deeds, madehis formalcomplaintas is recorded in every page of the inquiries and in the trustworthy testimony of the Archbishop Primate at fl. 1 of the 6th annexure, who satisfied that the revolt wasrealandwas far advanced ... zeal of a faithful subject ...person ...of ... said Lady ...of thishorrible crime José Luiz Guineti of Milan, Sebastião de Noronha, shore corporal of Bardez and Manoel Luiz of Candolim.Regarding the accused José Luiz, the leader, Fr. Couto, declared at fl. 66 of the 1st annexure, that Guineti was awareofthe conspiracy as they travelled together from Lisbon to this State in the same vessel and it was further revealed that this accused knew the Archbishop of Cannanore in Goa as he was his servant.Healso associated with the leaders,especially Fr. José António Gonçalves, whom he would accompany and follow in all his travels, meetingsandfunctions, andthough he stoutly denied, despite being tortured, the full knowledge ofthe attempted conspiracy, at fl. 100, it ishard to believe that he was not, personally aware of the conspiracy, when theleaders were expected to make use of his expertise inagriculture and manufacture of paper and glass, after their freedom.The accused confessed that in his presence they would curse the Portuguese and would show their resentmentto have to live under their subjection and obedience in this State .... of revolt of ... envying his fate and uttering ... seditious propositions ... annexed where he affirms that he was convinced that the leaders were intending something and had some plans which he was not sure, if it was to ask for assistance from one or the other potentate to cause a revolt or to secede to some foreign neighbouring power.

One may well conclude from his confessions that he was aware of the enmity and ill-will and perverse intentions of the masterminds and since he resided and lived in this State he should have, despite being a foreigner, upheld that loyalty which, even natural law, teaches everyone and binds every person who stays, even while in transit, as a guest in any house, under the protection and benevolence of its master loyalty that imposes the obligation of revealing and warning him of any harm or loss that, you may perceive, is about to befall on him when other members of the family plot against himand a duty which, in respect of a monarch, is much greater as they aredivine ...of head of families.

Added to this is the declaration of the said leader at fl. 62, repeated at p. 1 of the 1st annexure, the deposition of Fr. Couto at fl. ... discoveredtheconspiracy, that this accused was one of the conspiratorsand aggravated by the fact that the accused remained a fugitive, soon after the arrests of other accused.

Against Sebastião de Noronha, shore corporal, it is proved, by his confession at fl. 108, ratified at fl. 116 of the 3rd annexure, and by the confessions of Lt. Toscano at fl. 28 ratified at fl. 62 and maintained during the confrontation at fl. 88 of the 3rd annexure, that everything he said tallies with what Lt. Nicolau Luiz da Costa stated, no. 14, article[1] of his alleged complaint at fl. 5 of the inquiry and fl. 52 of the 1st annexure, that this accused was aware of the revolt before 26 July of the said year and that he failed to make a report. Though he now tries to excuse himself with the plea that he did not know what type of revolt it was and did not have sufficient details to make a proper report, so much so that Lt. Toscano promised to explain again the details, as he had not understood it the first time. This is corroborated by the same Toscano and it becomes evident that he was not informed ... and the manner of enticing andattracting to the party, still from his own confession it is clear that hehadenough details to understand that it was a revolt against the State and this same and simple information was sufficient to enable him to make his report .... should be considered the proper and true opinion and the other should be condemned as seditious, rash and erroneous; that not being able to distinguish a formal judicial complaint from a simple report or amemo, tries to repudiate what cannot be proved; a duty which not even the Roman law dared excuse the children and serfs from, with regard to their parents and masters and crimes of lesser gravity and importance.

Regarding Manoel Luiz, though one cannot prove his direct knowledge of the conspiracy except from the confession, at fl. 62, of the leader Fr. Couto, which legally, being theonly evidence, is no concrete proof, however, considering the circumstances underlying the case where the leader is the brother-in-law of the accused and that there were no dissentions between them, in an offence of this nature, they are sufficient proof to sentence the accused, although he might have stoutly, denied the charges at fl. 113 of the 1st annexure and fls. 17 & 102 of the 3rd annexure.

It is finally revealed that Vicente de Abreu, Lourenço Fernandes, farmers, Felippe Fernandes, Victorino Vaz, and Vicente Gomes also participated in this heinous crime of high treason ... witnesses fls. 74, 75v, 77 & 78 and from confessions at fl. 70, 143, 144v, 146 & 150 of the 1st annexure that Fr. José António Gonçalves, mastermind of the revolt, who was evading arrest which he expected after his confederatesandbrother were arrested, was sheltered and hidden by Fr. Mathias Bernardo da Fonseca in the house of the accused where Fr. Gonçalves remained for three days and the accused, having so confessed at fl. 1 of the 1st annexure ratifiedat fl. 43 of the 3rd annexure, itbecomesunbelievable that he did not know the reasons why the leader was trying to escape and hide, when the arrests of so many others, though carried with great secrecy, caused sensation in the State. The accused was aware of the blockades placed on the roads and paths leading to the borders and of the arrest of his brother.The accused further admits knowing all this, as the major part of the arrests was made ... in which ... outside the State.

His crime is aggravated by the many tasksheundertook in the cause of the revolt, arranging labourers to act as guides of the leader to take him to the frontiers of the State and forced ... provedby the confessions of the three labourers at fls. 116v, 143 & 150 of the 1st annexure sustained in the confrontation at fl. 44v of the 3rd annexure andthe accused cannot now resile, alleging that his confession was made under duress and torture, and be exonerated of hisguilt as stated at fl. 123 of the 3rd annexure.

Against Lourenço Fernandes, servant of Fr. Mathias Bernardo da Fonseca, it is proved, by his confession at fl. 144v of the 1st annexure, ratified at fl. 52 of the 3rd annexure and by the confessions at fls. 1, 71 of the 1st annexure, that under orders from the priest, he called the accused Vicente Abreu to empty the house next to his where the fugitive priest spent the first night on the 7th, that he accompanied this accused to the said house and that he was aware that the priest had stayed there up to the 11th, after which he escaped from the State.The accused could not have ignored, at that stage, the reason of the flight of Fr. Gonçalves, who was the mastermind of the revolt, a fact which was already of public knowledge.This is established at fl. 86 and in the inquiry.

The same .... it is presumed that the three accused Felippe Fernandes and ... 1st annexure ratified at fls. 47v, 49 and 51 of the 3rd annexure, who guided the said leader, leaving at the dead of night, from the island of

Chorao to Mayem, through Azarem, territory of Pune, and viaunused and circuitous routes.This very unobtrusive, suspicious and hidden manner was sufficient to raise doubts on any one that the priest wasone of the traitors who was attempting a revolt against the State and which was already of public knowledge on the 11th, as also were the arrests of many clerics and civilians.

It is also true that they could not have ignored that in assisting and guiding persons to escape from the State across the frontiers they were committing an illegal and criminal act for which they would be liable to be punished.

The same conclusion holds trueregarding the accused Michael Silvestre, student, for having accompanied the said leader from Guirim to the island of Chorao on 7 August, who to evade arrest, went in disguise and through unused routes.This behaviour would immediately indicate that he was a criminal and more so because the accused admitted that he knew that a search was on for the priest, that he obtained this information from the priest himself and from what hewitnessed at Pilerne.Knowing that efforts were being made ... he could not presume that the arrest ... order from the prelate, in addition ... he confessed that on 8th and 9th he had gone to the house ... and that the said priest was the mastermind.His candid and frank replies cannot mitigate the gravity of his crime because from these same replies one can infer that he was sufficiently intelligent to reason and understand the implications and gravity of such a heinous crime.All this is established in his confessions at fl. 79, ratified at fl. 92, and of the accused at fl. 1, 70,and 144 of the 1st and 4th annexures.

Regarding João de Souza of Honavar, as confessed by the accused Sebastião Paulo de Noronha, he was asked to arrange 25 to 50 seamen, ostensibly, for his crafts, which may be probable because the said Sebatião was in this trade as evidenced at fl. 2 of the 4th annexure.Hence there is no proof against the accused that he was aware of the revolt.

After duly considering all the evidence of the proceedings on record, the accused Pedro Luiz Gonzaga and Manoel Caetano Pinto are condemned that to the accompaniment of the town crier and bound with ropes they be dragged by the tails of horses through the streets of the city to the gallows which will be erected, and there they would be let to die anaturaldeath.While still alive their hands would be severed and after death their heads in each .... disintegrate and their bodies quartered and staked on high poles be exposed in public places on the islands of Goa and provinces of Salcete and Bardez and especially in the villages of

Candolim and Nerul, their birth-places, and in the villages of Pilerne, Piedade, Mandur andNagoa till they decay with time.

The accused Nicolau Luiz da Costa, Ignacio Caetano Toscano, Salvador Alvares da Costa, Ignacio Caetano Lopes, Bernardode Mesquita, José Monteiro, BalthazarCaeiro, ManoelFerrão, António Fernandes, João Vaz, Miguel António da Costa, Caetano Xavier da Costa and David Francisco Viegas are condemned and to the accompaniment of the town-crier and bound with ropes, they are to be taken to the same gallows and let to die there a natural death, after which they would be beheaded and their heads staked on poles erected in places of their birth.The two accused David Francisco Viegas and Caetano Xavier da Costa would in addition have their hands severed and staked on the same poles with their heads until they decayed with time.

All of the accused are further sentenced to confiscation of their properties and assets to ... head, their memory their children and grand-children be branded, for life, as infamous.

The accused José Luiz Guineti of Milan is condemned that to theaccompanimentof the town-crier andboundwithropes, he befloggedthrough the streets andbanished for life to serve in the galleys of Angola.

The accused Sebastião de Noronha is condemned to be bound with ropes and accompanied by the town crier, be flogged through public streets and banished for life to Bengal.

The same punishment as above and banishment for ten years to Rios de Senna and Mozambique is awarded to accused Vicente de Abreu and FranciscoPereira, respectively

All the accused condemned to banishment are also sentenced to confiscation of their properties to the Exchequer and Royal Council.Should any of them be seen in any square, island, province orplaceofthe Stateand captaincy general of Goa, theywould be liable fordeath.All the accused are to sign the sentence.

The accused Felippe Fernandes, Victorino Vaz and ... are also condemned ... be bound with ropesandwith the town crier be dragged through the streets ... transportation for ... galleys of Goa, and to the same sentence ... prison .... and galleys .... Lourenço Fernandes and each one of them ... 100 *xerafins* as costs ... High Court.

The accused João de Sousa of Honavar is absolved of all guilt, with costs.

Regarding the accused Sebastião Paulo de Noronha who died in prison, after a brief summary of charges were read and his defence advocate had pleaded on facts and law, is declared a traitor and guilty of the crime of high treason of first class and his memory, his children and grandchildren should be branded as infamous throughout their lives and all their assets revert to the Exchequer and Royal Council.

It is also ordered that all those accused not sentenced to death be taken to the gallows and to the scaffolds where they would witnessthe execution.

And with regard to the accused who died in prison and those who were absent, they should be proceeded with in accordance with the existing law.

Goa, 9 December 1788
Signed by Rocha, Amaral, Tavares, Teixeira.
In my presence— Barroco.

This is the complete text of the sentence which I copied faithfully with the exception of what I could not understand, either becausethe words were illegible orthepages torn, and the omissions I have rendered with dots.I confirm this to be a true copy.

Panjim, 10 April 1835.
Written and signed by me, clerk of the Court,
Gaspar Elpidio Soares da Torre.

No. 90. Since the government requires an authenticated copy of the sentence delivered on the events which took place against the Europeans in 1787, you are hereby required to obtain two copies of the said sentence and submit it with utmost urgency.

God protect you.

Palace of the Governor,
31 March 1835.

João Casimiro Pereira da Rocha de Vasconcellos, President. Manoel José Ribeiro,Fr. Constantino de Santa Rita, Manoel Felicissimo Louzada de Araujo de Azevedo,Chief Justice of the High Court of the State.

The Superintendent has to obtain a copy as ordered.
Ribandar, 31 March1835.
s/dLouzadade Araujo.

Confirmed, Panjim, 31 March 1835.
s/dAntónio Feliciano de Faria Picão.

N.B. The sentence referring to Sebastião de Noronha (p. 12) says he is ShoreCorporalofBardez, butthe order of the Governor, dated 7 August 1787 to the Field Marshal, Francisco António da Veiga Cabral, Commander of the province of Salcete says,"As among the indicted in the same crime is one Sebastião de Noronha, married, resident of Nagoa, who left that province yesterday or the day before. I order his arrest with minimum delay immediately on receipt of this order either in that village or that square dependingon the information you may have of his whereabouts, etc."That is the reason why we mentioned in the textSebastião de Noronha as Shore Corporal of Salcete. We are not sure, however, if this man from Salcete was Sebastião de Noronha or Sebastião Paulo de Noronha, as the sentence makes a distinction between thetwo in the proceedings and in thepunishment. Ifthereisan error, it is of little orno consequence to the revolt.

Document No. 4

Letter of the Governor Francisco da Cunha eMenezes to H. Majesty.

Lady,

I place before Your Royal Majesty a report of annual happenings and of moreremarkable and noteworthy eventswhichtheSenate of the Councils of this city and of the province of Bardez submitted to me in accordance with Your Majesty's order of 20 July 1782.

God guard and grant Your Highest and Most Powerful Majesty for many happy years.

Goa, 24 March 1789.

Livro das Monções, No. 170, fl. 21.

Resolutions and Minutes of the Senate and Council of Goa.

On 28 February 1789, having the President, Councillors and officials of the Senate assembled with me, José Pereira de Macedo, as clerk of the Council, itwas proposed by the President to place on record the event which goes transcribed in the annexure as themost remarkable and noteworthy which after being read and understood by all present was unanimously confirmed as the true copy of the sentence and as such duly recorded alongwith as true and correct.

This is, accordingly, recorded and signed by me, José Pereira de Macedo, clerk of the Senate of the Council.

The President, Vasco Luis Carneiro de Sousa e Faro, José da Costa de Attaide Teive, Cypriano José de Mattos e Goes, Pedro de Moraes Correa, Miguel Caetano Nunes de Mello, José Agostinho de Baamonde, Felicio José Monroe, Manoel de Mesquita, and Felippe Caetano Pereira.

A most heinous and abominable crime of revolt and high treason was hatched in the islands and provinces of this State of Goa in 1786, wherein some natives of the State attempted to withdraw from the subjection of and obedience to the government of H. Majesty, the Most Faithful, and implant a new republic which the same natives would govern by a General Council or Assembly and would become sovereign throughout the empire.

The masterminds of this abominable crime were two priests, Fr. José António Gonçalves who obtained his doctorate in the University of the College of Propaganda, and Fr. Caetano Francisco do Couto, both of whom had returned from Lisbon in 1785, where they were for many years. Both were very much disappointed that they had not been elevated to the position of bishops (which was due to the fact that they did not possess the necessary qualities for that high position) and in retaliation, they were the first to conceive this rebellious idea, which they discussed between them and others, during their long voyage to India, and on arrival began to sow the seeds of their dissatisfaction, denouncing the bad treatment they were given by the Portuguese, the contemptuous way in which the Portuguese treated all Goans, so that with these imaginary stories, maliciously distorted with hatred and a spirit of revolt, they might subvert other natives, their friends and relatives and entice them to their cause, as in fact they did, suborning many parish priests, clerics, four Lieutenants of two Legions of Royal Volunteers of the provinces of Ponda and Bardez.

This revolt and high treason that the two priests and their confederates and sympathisers attempted did not stop at vague and verbose speeches but, as revealed in the inquiries conducted, the same masterminds and their collaborators had already decided among themselves the manner and way of the execution of the revolt, the deployment of the corps of rebels who would attack the squares, places, guards and important houses, the crafty attempt to detain people of high positions and on signals, to herald simultaneously from various places theso-called freedom,the proposal to kill anyonewho dared oppose them, and fixing the date of the execution for the 10 of August 1787.

Accordingly, as this treachery was discoveredby another priest who had alsobeen urged to join them but resisted, His Excellency the Governor and Captain General of this State ordered the arrest of one ofthe masterminds, Fr. CaetanoFranciscodo Couto in the early hours of 7 August together with some parish priests, clerics, four Lieutenants and many civilians with the exception of the other leader, Fr. José António Gonçalves who had escaped to the territory of the Marathas.It was not possible to capture him despite the best efforts of many people and in many places as ordered by H. E. the Governor and Captain-General.It later transpired that the priest had taken shelter in the territory of Tipu Sultan.

Of the arrested civilians, by the judgement delivered on 9 December 1788, 15 were sentenced todeathon the 13th of the same month on the gallows, two of which were freshly erected in addition to the existing one, in the fields of Mandovi in the city; the four Lieutenants and the Captain ofthe Auxiliaries were among those sentenced to death.The two Lieutenants who were found to be agent-provocateurs were, in addition, dragged to the gallows. Nine were flogged and fined and are undergoing banishment in various places to which they were sentenced.Eight were set free as they were found innocent, two of these being membersof the Congregation of Oratory of the Miraculous Holy Cross, one parish priest and another priest.Other clerics were held in prisons and recluse houses which were especially built for them and for the other accused of this heinous crime of revolt and high treason.

Written and signed by me,
José Pereira de Macedo.

This is a true copy of the original at fl. 2 of the Book of Annals of this Senate, which I have transcribed.
Goa, 4 March 1789.

Livro das Monções, no. 170, fl. 23.

Minutes of the Senate of Bardez

On 29 December 1788, the Senate of the Council of Bardez, having assembled in the Town Hall, the second councillor, Felippe Nery Pinto, presented a report of more notable historical events that took place in the province from January to the present date and having collated it in the form of a letter of H.E. the GovernorandCaptain-General of this State, Francisco da Cunha e Menezes dated 25 October 1788, and on its perusal by the officials and on hávíng been found true and correct, it was decided that it be recorded for posterity in the annals of this Senate.

Item: Being Governor of this State, H. E. Captain General Francisco da Cunha e Menezes, and Secretary of State, Justice Sebastião José FerreiraBarroco, the RajaKhem Sawant Bhosale signed on 1 February 1788, a treaty with this majestic state under terms of which he ceded forever to H. Most Faithful Majesty, the province of Pernem, for which purpose on the same day, the Adjutant General and Colonel of the Legion of Bardez, Joaquim Vicente Godinho de Mira, with the Legion under his command and 8 pieces of artillery, was dispatched to that province. They were joined by 300 men from the Legion of Ponda, commanded by Lt. Col. of the said Legion, Manoel Freitas, 900 sepoys commanded by Lt. Col. and their Commandant Rodrigo Homem de Quadros, 2 cavalry companies commanded, one by Sergeant-Major Henrique Claudio de Tonnelet, and the other by Captain and A.D.C. of H. E. the Governor and Captain-General, José Joaquim da Costa, under overall command of the ColonelandAdjutant General to take over chargefrom Raja Khem SawantBhosale, on behalf of this majestic state.The Colonel and Adjutant-General was given charge of that province in the presence of the troops and dignitaries of that province in the temple of Pernem on 4 February, the anniversary of the defeat the Portuguese had suffered in the same province andtemple of Pernem in 1759, under the governorship of H. E. Count of Ega, Viceroy and Captain-General.

After the celebrations of the takeover, H. E. the Governor and Captain-General of the Stateordered the Field Marshal and Commander of the troops, Francisco António da Veiga Cabral da Camara, to go to the province of Pernem with the 1st Infantry Regiment of Goa, under his command, and 8 pieces of artillery.He also ordered Brig. and chief of the Legion of Ponda, António de Assa Castelo Branco, with the legion under his command and 8 pieces of artillery and the 2nd Cavalry Company of the same Legion, commanded by S.M. Miguel Carlos da Cunha, legitimate son of the Count of St. Vincent, to proceed there.

On 7th of the same month, the Field Marshal and Commander ordered the Colonel and Adjutant-General to proceed with the Corps under his command, with the exclusion of the Corps of Legion of Ponda, to the province of S. Torda (sic) located at Aquerim, to protect the territories of the said Raja Khem Sawant Bhosale which the Raja of Kolhapur intended to attack. For this purpose and to give support to our troops which had advanced to Aquerim, where they were stationed till 27 April, the Field Marshal and Commandant shifted his troops to the same province located at Mandrem, withdrawing thereafter to their barracks as the said Raja of Kolhapur had desisted from the invasion and had withdrawn his troops from the borders of Raja Khem Sawant Bhosale because the court of Pune had taken upon itself to intervene and settle the differences between the two Rajas over whether the latter could or could not use the title of Raja, which was granted to him by the court of Delhi, and also if he could or could not use the distinctive of two marshals identical to the one used by the Raja of Kolhapur since ancient times, which were the real reasons of the controversy between the two.

Item: On 13 December 1788, during the Governorship of H. E. Francisco da Cunha e Menezes, Pedro Luis Gonzaga, Manoel Caetano Pinto, David Francisco Viegas, Caetano Xavier da Costa, Ignacio Caetano Toscano, Nicolau Luis da Costa, Ignacio Caetano Lopes, Salvador Alves da Costa, Balthazar Caeiro, Manoel Ferrão, António Fernandes, João Vaz, José Monteiro, Miguel António da Costa, and Bernardo Mesquita, all born and residing in the provinces of Bardez, Salcete and Ilhas of Goa were sentenced to death on the gallows.José Luis,Vicente de Abreu, Sebastião de Noronha, Francisco Pereira, Felippe Fernandes, Victorino Vaz, Vicente Gomes, Lourenço Fernandes, Michael Silvestre, and Manoel Luis, also residing in the same provincesand islands, to transportation to various terms and João de Sousa of Kanara was set free.In execution of the judgement delivered by the Supreme Senate of the High Court of Goa, State of India and welcomed by the people at large, by the nobility andby theSenate of this Council of the province of Bardez, which found the accused guilty of the heinous crime of revolt and high treason against the Crown of H. Majesty, the most faithful, Godguard her, the Senate, the nobility and officials, all assembled in the Town Hall together with the troops of the said province that had lined in formation in front of the Town Hall, while the execution was taking place.

Item: On 17 December of the same year, the birthday of the Queen our lady, Manoel Pinto of Saligao, of the province of Bardez, Manoel Francisco Gonçalves of Piedade, Narba Naik, Dessaiof Ponda, Thomaz do Rosario, customs guard, the reverend Vicar of Moira of the Bardez province, Rev. Frs. Pedro Delgado and Sebastião Baptista of the

Congregation of Oratory of Goa were set free from prison as they were found innocent.

The minutes of this report are being duly recorded in the Book of Annals of this Senate and signed by the Councillors signifying the correctness thereof.

Signed by Thomaz Felippe Ribeiro,de Tonnelet,Pinto, Noronha, Cardozo.

This is a true copy oftheoriginalwhich,written at page of the *Book of Annals of the Senate of the province of Bardez*, isbeing transcribed today.

14 March 1789.
Signed by Thomaz Felippe Ribeiro.

Livro das Monções, no. 170, fl. 25.

Document No. 5

Decision of the High Court

On 15 December 1788 in this HighCourt, in the presence of H. E. Francisco da Cunha e Menezes, Governor and Captain-General of India and Magistrate of all courts, the Chief Justice, José da Rocha Dantas e Mendonça, presiding officer of the inquiry proceedingsinto the revolt and hightreason plotted against the State, proposed the release of the priests who were arrested on suspicion, at the time of discovery of the conspiracy, and against whom no evidence was found during the investigations carried out.Since the inquiries have been concluded after examination and cross-examination of the witnesses, even under torture, and since the final sentence has been delivered against all civilians accused of the plot and there are no further proofs or additional evidence against the said priests, their further detention, though initially justified and necessary, is nolonger justified and is against the spirit of the decision taken on 20 July this year, which requires the detentions of only those clerics who are directly involved in the said crime, which is not true with regard, especially to Frs. Pedro Delgado, Sebastião Baptista,both of the Congregation of Oratory, and António Felipe Vaz, Vicar of Moira.Regarding Fr. António Felipe Vaz, the fact that he had lodged one of the two leaders and his partners in the revolt in his house, is not sufficient evidence to indict him.Besides there are no witnesses to corroborate that the priest knew what was being discussed among them or that he had participated indiscussions heldwith the lieutenants.On the contrary, they stated in their confessions that this priest was not present or aware of the subject of their discussions and further, the leader Fr. Couto, who did not even spare his brothers and relatives, made no mention that this priest was aware or was a member of the conspiracy.

Nor is the evidenceof Fr. Pedro Caetano José Loboregarding what the mastermind Fr. José António Gonçalves had told him, sufficient proof against the two priests of the Congregation.There were no other witnesses to corroborate him, not even the leader Fr. Couto, who seemed to know everything (he was being kept abreast of everything that occured) and no further evidencewas unearthed against them.On the contrary, one could see their innocence in the way they behaved during their detention.One may assume that what Fr. José António Gonçalves stated was one of his generalisations or falsehood which he used to entice people of good and exemplary conduct into the party.

Put to vote, it was unanimously agreed that the said priests Pedro Delgado, Sebastião Baptista and António Felipe Vaz should be set free, since in accordance with the law, they could notbe held guilty or suspect in the crime of revolt, and there are no valid or necessary reasons for the State to keep them in detention any longer.In accordance with the decision of 20 July of this year they are forthwith set free.

This is duly recorded and signed by us.

Signed by H. E. Francisco da Cunha e Menezes, Governor and Captain-General of India, Rocha, Amaral, Tavares, Teixeira.

Signed in my presence,
Barroco.

Livro das Monções, no. 170, fl. 426v.

Document No. 6

Decision of the High Court

On 20 July 1788, in the High Court of Goa in the presence of H. E. FranciscodaCunha e Menezes, Governor and Captain-General of India and Magistrate of all Courts, theChief Justice, José da Rocha Dantas e Mendonça, presiding officer of the inquiry and proceedings on the revolt and hightreason plotted against this State, raised his doubts on the correct interpretation of the *Ordinances* at Bk. 2, Sec. 1,para.21 to the end, and whether they covered all or any crime committed byecclesiastical persons.

Whereas some priests were found involved in the heinous crime of revolt and high treason, and whereas there were reasons to believe that they were the first and principal masterminds, we are of the learned opinion that they cannot be committed to ecclesiastical courts in accordance with the said ordinances, as crimes of high treason, by their very nature are outside the purview of ecclesiastical courts.

Since their privileges emanate from a jurisdiction granted or conceded and approved in this kingdom through a favour from the kings of old, it does not follow that such a favour could be granted against oneself or against everything that H. Majesty holds as most sacred and precious, as the complete obedience and respect of her sacred person, the preservation of her reign and dominions, their defence and that of her vassals, the maintenance of peace and order, the sovereignty and the supreme power of punishment which holdsthis order and the reign through bonds of obedience and fear of punishments; all these duties would become impracticable if H. Majesty did not have the required power to punish all or any person who attempted against the said maintenance, defence and order.

It was, unanimously, decided that they could not question the supreme power that H. Majesty has to punish any or all persons, civilians or ecclesiastical who commitany offence within her kingdom, in particular, that of high treason, and order that the law should take its own course, even with regard to ecclesiastics whenever it is found to be just and necessary to maintain those important duties, because this authority is inseparable from sovereignty and supreme power which, in this world is derived directly from God.However, the jurisdiction of the courts should cover ecclesiastics involved incommoncrimes andall the legal formalitiesandprovisions of law and ordinances applied to them.In very grave crimes, like those of high treason, the right and jurisdiction rest on H. Majesty, as these have not been delegated to common courts or High Courts as a matter of policy and which, lacking in authority and ordinary jurisdiction, cannot proceed against the ecclesiastics except if so determined by law and ordinances.The ecclesiastics, guilty of crimes of high treason, are not covered by provisions of the ordinance (Bk. 2, Sec. 1) whichstipulate the committal of ecclesiastics to their ecclesiastical courts, because it is against the very nature of such crimes that are exceptional and of royal authority.In such cases and specifically in the present one, we should observe the provisions of the law of October 24,

1764, para. 4 which cover the said ordinances and in conformity with the same law and practice followed in this and other Catholic kingdoms, all those ecclesiastics who are really guilty of that crime should be confined to the prisons of H. Majesty, where they presently are till H. Majesty makes known her desire, for which she has been duly advised.However, regarding the civilians accused of the crime, they should be proceeded with expeditiously till the final sentence.And so that there should not be anydoubt in future and in this case, we record and signify our decision by signing this.

Signed by H. E. Francisco da Cunha e Menezes, Governor and Captain-General, Rocha, Amaral, Tavares, Teixeira, Figueiredo.

Signed before me,
Barroco.

Livro das Monções, no. 170, fl. 425.

Document No. 7

Notice from the Secretary of State, Viscount of Anadia to thè Governor, Francisco Antonio da Veiga Cabral. No. 73.

Your Excellency,

Consequent upon the information that the Archbishop of Goa submitted regarding the innocence of Fr. Manoel da Expectação, who was sent from India in detention with other priests, the Prince Regent, Our Lord, is pleased to order his freedom and to permit his return to his homeland, where he will proceed to, in the same vessel, with recommendation to the same Archbishop to reinstate him in the service he held prior tohis arrest or to employ him inthe service of the churchaccordingtohismerit and aptitude.

This is for your information.
God protect you.

Palace of Queluz, 12 March 1802.
Viscount of Anadia

c.c. Mr. Francisco António da Veiga Cabral.

Livro das Monções, no. 183, fl. 139.

Document No. 8

No. 97

Your Excellency,

After advising you in my note of the 12th of this month of the freedom of Manoel da Expectação, secular priest, who was sent under detention from that State and who should travel in the next sailing, the Prince, Our Lord, is pleased to order that he be paid, for life, from the royal coffers, 400 *reis* per day, a grant he was receiving in this Court by virtue of the royal mercy of the Prince.

God protect you.

Palace of Queluz, 30 March 1802.
Viscount of Anadia.

c.c. Mr. Francisco António da Veiga Cabral.

Livro das Monções, no. 183, fl. 140.

Document No. 9

Reply from the Governor

Your Excellency,

In execution of the order of H. R. Highness, the Prince Regent, Our Lord, contained in your office note no. 97, dated 30 March 1802, I have directed that secular priest Manoel da Expectação be given from the royal coffers a grant of 400 *reis* per day for life.

God keep Your Excellency for many years.

Goa, 24 March 1804.
Viscount of Anadia.
Seal of the Governor.

Livro das Monções, no. 183, fl. 143.

Order

In conformity with the note dated 30 May 1802 of the Secretary of State and Affairs of the Navy and Overseas Possessions, sent to the Governor of that State, an account on behalf of Manoel da Expectação, secular priest, is to be maintained in the Accountant-General's office and he is to be paid from the Royal Exchequer for life a sum of 400 *reis* daily from the date of the above note.

Goa, 16 November, 1802.
Signed byCabral, Tavares, Loureiro, Silva, Pereira.

RefutaçãoAnalytica, p. 23.

Document No. 10

Notice of the Secretary of State, Viscount of Anadia, to Viceroy Count of Sarzedas. No. 10.

Your Excellency,

The Prince Regent, Our Lord, considering the pleadings of Jorge Dias and Caetano Francisco da Silva, secular priests, born in that State of India, and in detention here, for several years now, on account of the charges levelled against them, H. Royal Highness is pleased to pardon them and permit them to return to their homeland in the sailing due next monsoon and H. Highness further orders the release of any property of the two priests that might have been confiscated and its return to them so that they may administer it as their own.

God keep you.

Mafra, 3 December 1806.

c.c Count of Sarzedas.
Livro das Monções no. 187, p. 286.

Document No. 11

No. 15

Excellency,

The Prince Regent considering the pleadings of Miguel Alvares, Vicente Alvares, Mathias Bernardo da Fonseca, Diogo Benedicto Lobo, João Baptista Pinto and Luis António Gonçalves, the first five being secular priests, and the last a cleric with minor orders, all of the State of India, who have been in detention here for several years now, on account of the charges levelled against them writes:

H. Highness is pleased to pardon them from any and all charges that might have been levelled against them and to permit them to return to their homeland in the sailing next monsoon and H. Royal Highness, further, orders the release of any property of those clerics that might have been confiscated and their return to them so that they may administer them as their own.

God protect you.

Mafra, 5 February 1807.
Viscount of Anadia

c.c. Count of Sarzedas.

Livro das Monções, no. 187, fl. 287.

Document No. 12

No. 34

Excellency,

The Prince Regent, Our Lord, considers the representation made by the heirs and agents of the secular priests João Alvares de Sousa, José António Vaz, Luis Caetano de Sousa and José Manoel de Menezes, born in that State of India, who died when they were being brought to this kingdom.

H. Royal Highness is pleased to order the return of all the assets and properties belonging to the deceased priests to the petitioners in the same way he ordered the return of the properties of others, with the exception of any income derived from these properties in the past and reverted to the Exchequer.

God protect you.

Mafra, 23 March 1807.
Viscount of Anadia.

c.c. Count of Sarzedas.

Livro das Monções, no. 187, fl. 289.

Document No. 13

No. 24

Excellency,

The Prince Regent, Our Lord, considers the representation made by Ignacio de Noronha secular priest, his brother Xavier dos Remedios de Noronha and Josefa de Noronha, residing at Bombay, where they ran away to.

H. Royal Highness is pleased to pardon the crime they were accused of and to permit them to return to Goa, their homeland, and also orders the release of their confiscated properties which will be duly returned to them.

God keep you.

Mafra, 13 March 1807.
Viscount of Anadia.

c.c. Count of Sarzedas.

Livro das Monções, no. 187, fl. 288.

Document No. 14

Reply from the Viceroy, No. 18

Excellency,

In compliance with your notes nos. 10, 15, 24, and 34 of various dates, regarding the rebel priests Jorge Dias, Caetano Francisco da Silva and others to give effect to the beneficial measures and royal benevolence of H. Royal Highness, I have issued the necessary orders to the Chief Justice of the State, who is hearing the conspiracy case, to restore to the said priests or their heirs all properties which are still unsold and the income of which has not yet been reverted to the Exchequer.

God keep you.

Goa, 25 February 1808.
s/d Viceroy.

c.c. Viscount of Anandia

Livro das Monções, no. 187, fl. 290.

Document No. 15

Transcript of the Letter of Representation which the Christians from the bishopric of Cochin addressed to the Archbishop of Goa. Written on a palm leaf, duly translated from Tamil into Portuguese, it substantially reads as follows:

Twelve years have elapsed since the Franciscan priests were sent here from Goa to propagate the faith. They halted, instead, its propagation giving rise to and bringing disrepute to us, with their reprehensible behaviour. They forcibly took our wives and daughters as their concubines as if they were their husbands and placed on our shoulders the onus of bringing up and supporting their children, and not content with that, if we happened to complain, they would themselves punish us or ask the subjects of the King already suborned by them, to do so.

After tolerating all this injustice, we raised our eyes to heaven so that God Almighty might deign to listen to our prayers. God Our Lord, fortunately, did hear them and cast His merciful eyes on us enlightening Your Lordship to send a Governor of the Order of St. Peter and with him some priests of the same Order. With their arrival our miseries are over, all the complaints, grief, injustice and everything that we suffered is over, because, ever since these priests have come they treat us like humans, impart good advice, teach us the gospel and the way to the kingdom.

We have brought to the notice of our Governor all the injustices done to us by the Franciscans, and we are confident that he will inform Your Lordship. In fact, he must have already done so, and Your Honour, for the love of God, please do not recall these priests that you have sent us because they are a treasure.

This favour you must do and on bended knees we beseech Your Lordship and humbly ask for your holy blessings.

Your Secretary will convey the contents of this letter to you.

Livro das Monções, no. 168, fl. 134.

This letter with other documents were sent to the Secretary of State, Martinho de Mello e Castro, to the Bishop of Cochin and to the Governor of the archbishopric of Goa, Dr. Fr. Manoel de Santa Catharina in the monsoon of 1779 and later to the Governor Francisco da Cunha e Menezes in the letter dated 25 February 1786.

Document No. 16

Letter from the Governor of State to the Dutch Governor of Cochin, Adriano Muns.

Goa, 9 November 1779.

Having taken charge as Governor of the State of India and of Portuguese Asia, I wish to convey to Your Excellency that I have been informed of the attentions and favours that Your Excellency has kindly extended to all the vassals of this majestic State and assisted them in their needs and, whilst expressing my recognition and gratitude, I wish to confirm that I shall reciprocate it in equal measure.

Now, the Queen of Portugal, the most faithful, and my Lady, by virtue of the royal patronage she holds in Christianity in Asia, appointed the Bishop of Cochin to administer that archbishopric and also appointed as

Governor of the same archbishopric a religious, who is proceeding to Cochin to exercise his ecclesiastical jurisdiction over that bishopric. He is a person endowed with foresight, circumspection and other virtues worthy of his ministry.

I pray, Your Excellency, to extend to him your assistance and to take him under your protection and favour so that he may be obeyed by other priests and Christians and be able to discharge, peacefully and properly, his ministries, without any hindrance, and I shall await the earliest opportunity to reciprocate the favour. In the meantime, I reiterate to Your Excellency and the people of the States united in your dominions, the protestations of my high consideration.

I have been told ... Naval Captain Nicolau Delgado Ferreira e Cunha d'Eça that Your Excellency kindly ordered that all help sought by the vessel *Madre de Deus* be given through the frigate that açcompanied it from Macau.

God keep Your Excellency many years.

Yours obligingly,
D. Federico Guilherme de Souza.

Livro de Reis Vizinhos, fl. 142.

Document No. 17

In his letter of 9 November 1779 to the Governor of Calicut, Budu Khan, the Governor, D. Federico Guilherme de Souza, requests him to extend his assistance and protection to the Governor of the archbishopric of Cochin who leaves, in this vessel, to take charge of his diocese, for which he possesses the best qualities of a good religious.

Livro de Reis Vizinhos, fl. 143.

Document No. 18

On the same date, in a letter to the manager of the farm at Calicut, Mr. José Francisco de Amaral de Menezes, he suggests to him to extend all assistance to the new Governor of the bishopric of Cochin, who will disembark at that port in transit to his diocese.

Livro de Reis Vizinhos, fl. 143v.

Document No. 19

To the Governor of Tellicherry Ricardo Churchu.

On the same date he recommends to him the Governor of the bishopric of Cochin who now goes to that diocese, and hopes he will extend to him his assistance whenever he approaches him for any help, not only because he is deserving of such attentions by virtue of his good qualities but also because he, the Governor of India, will always remember and reward his favour, most willingly.

Livro de Reis Vizinhos, fl. 144v.

Document No. 20

Letter to the manager of the farm, Mr. José Francisco de Amaral de Menezes, dated 3 January 1780, granting him permission to retire and return to Goa, after giving charge to Fr. José da Soledade, Governor of the bishopric of Cochin.

Livro de Reis Vizinhos, fl. 159.

Document No. 21

Letter of credentials to Fr. José da Soledade, appointing him administrator of the farm at Calicut.

3 January 1780.

Livro de Reis Vizinhos, fl. 158v.

Document No. 22

Letter from the Governor of the State to the Governor of Cochin.

For sometime now, I had wanted to write to Your Excellency, and I avail of this opportunity that is offered to me, with the reporting to you of Fr. José da Soledade, Governor of the archbishopric of Cochin, to reiterate the protestations of my high consideration to Your Excellency and my desire to be of service to you.

The said Governor of the bishopric, while appreciating the particular attention with which Your Excellency favours him, desires for the better peace and propagation of Christianity, that Your Excellency continue this favour and requests that you be pleased to repatriate Frs. João da Silva of Pucota and Ricardo da Silva, who with their temperaments create only more problems for the Christians there. I do hope Your Excellency will take the necessary action in this regard, and at the same time order the return of the church of St. André, which was founded by the Company, to the same Governor of the bishopric though the parishioners are vassals of the King of Travancore and to whom I am writing separately in this connection.

I shall be pleased to be of any service, should Your Excellency need anything from this end.

God keep Your Excellency.

Goa, 8 April 1781.
D. Federico Guilherme de Souza.

Livro de Reis Vizinhos, fl. 73.

Document No. 23

Letter from the Governor of the State to the King of Travancore.

Please accept, Your Excellency, the salutations of the one who values your friendship and correspondence and who wishes Your Excellency the best prosperity.

I wish to recall to Your Excellency the fact that all the churches in your vast kingdom, through the privilege given by your illustrious ancestors, were founded by the prelates and missionaries of my nation and it is not just that strangers should now try to dispossess them of the fruits of the seeds they have sown with so much labour and sweat of their brows, for so many centuries. It stands to reason that Your Excellency should order that all the referred churches should recognise the jurisdiction of the Bishop of Cochin, who is authorised to exclude from them the Carmelites of Propaganda and that all Christians should contribute to their parishes the same tithe and in the same way that they were doing at the time of the Jesuits; that all books pertaining to the church of Angenga be returned to Fr. José da Soledade, the Governor of the bishopric of Cochin together with the church which was taken with the consent of Your Excellency and to endow him with privileges and freedom to discipline the Christians which the bishop of that diocese always enjoyed, not permitting that the Carmelites of Propaganda return to the kingdom of Your Excellency with the sole intention of usurping their jurisdiction.

I am confident that Your Excellency, with the usual benevolence, will accede to my request, for which I shall remain very grateful, and I shall have the pleasure to convey this favour to the Most Serene Queen, my most august leader.

God keep Your Excellency in his divine grace.

Goa, 8 April 1781.
D. Federico Guilherme de Souza.

Livro de Reis Vizinhos, fl. 73.

Document No. 24

Letter from the Governor of the State to the Governor of Angengu.

I am very pleased to avail of this opportunity to present my respects to you and offer my services in this State should you need and desire them.

I am sure that you are well aware that while the Church in that port of Angenga was earlier the cathedral of the bishopric of Cochin and always under the jurisdiction of the royal rights of benefice, your predecessors decided, without the least consideration for the prerogative of H. Most Faithful Majesty, to hand it over to the Bishop and Apostolic Vicar who presently has it under his jurisdiction thus depriving the royal rights of benefice of its due.

Since it behoves me to endeavour the due restitution to the rightful owners, I take this occasion to request you to use your best judgement in this matter so that I may have the pleasure to be thankful for your attention and to convey the same to the Most Faithful Majesty, my most august leader.

God protect Your Excellecy.

Goa, 8 April 1781.
D. Federico Guilherme de Souza.
Livro de Reis Vizinhos, fl. 173v.

Document No. 25

Letter from the Governor of the State to the Governor of Calicut, Sardar Khan.

In consideration of the representation made by Rev. Fr. José da Conceição who works as manager of the farm at that port, I authorise that he may return to this Court to help his family, ordering at the same time, that he should keep a person to substitute him until I am able to send a replacement to look after the farm.

I hope my good friend will have no objection to the said priest leaving and that you will extend the same attention to the person who substitutes him.

I wish my good friend all happiness and may God enlighten you with His divine grace.

Goa, 7 September 1781.
D. Federico Guilherme de Souza

Livro de Reis Vizinhos, fl. 112v.

Document No. 26

Proclamation

Francisco da Cunha e Menezes, member of the Council of the Most Faithful Majesty, Governor and Captain-General of India etc.. Let all people who read this proclamation know that, whereas there have been some people who forgetting their duties as subjects, and the goodness and kindness with which all of them are treated within the dominion of H. Majesty, the most faithful, have plotted contemptuously a revolt in this State to expel all Portuguese from it, claiming ostensibly that there exists a difference, which the same Lady has always reproved of, in the appointments of natives to high places, positions, honours and pre-eminence which they deserve; and whereas the mastermind of this abominable conspiracy of Fr. José António Gonçalves or José Felipe Gonçalves of Piedade, therefore, I order all residents of this State not to shelter or in any way help the said mastermind of such a despicable crime to evade arrest or to foil any efforts that are being made to arrest him, on pain of any one found doing otherwise, being charged as co-conspirator of this despicable crime and in the name of H. Majesty, I promise a reward of 5,000 *xerafins* to any one who captures the said priest Fr. José António Gonçalves.

And that all may know of this proclamation, this will be announced with the beating of drums in all public and customary places of the city and in the provinces of Bardez, Salcete, Ponda, Zambaulim, Bicholim and Sanquelim, and will be displayed in the market place of Margao.

Goa, 21 August 1787.
Francisco da Cunha e Menezes

Livro de Portarias (Cartas e Ordens), fl. 16.

Document No. 27

Note

Francisco da Cunha e Menezes etc.

In the name of H. Majesty, the most faithful, I promise 5,000 *xerafins* to any person from this dominion or from outside it, who captures and hands over to the State, Fr. José António Gonçalves.

And to give effect to this schedule it carries the seal and the Court of Royal Arms of the Crown of Portugal.

Given at Goa, on this day the 12 September 1787.

Francisco da Cunha e Menezes

Livro de Portarias (Cartas e Ordens), fl. 24.

Document No. 28

Letter from the Governor of the State to Madhu Rao Narayan Pradhan.

Most illustrious and distinguished Madhu Rao Narayan Pradhan.

On the envoy of this State, Narayan Rao Vithal, having requested the return of Fr. José António Gonçalves, accused of high treason, and who has taken refuge to Azarem, he obtained the issuance of an order to that effect, in reciprocation of the good relations that always existed between us, specially with our returning to you, the criminal Tulaji Ponvar.

However, as the order that Sarkar issued to the Governor of Konkan, Venkatrao Narayan did not yield the desired result, as our envoy will explain to you. I expect that my distinguished friend after hearing the honourable Narayan Rao will issue the necessary orders for the return of the above mentioned with the minimum possible delay.

May God enlighten you, my great friend with His divine grace.

Goa, 10 January 1788.
Francisco da Cunha e Menezes

Livro dos Reis Vizinhos, fl. 85.

Document No. 29

Letter from Fr. José António Gonçalves to the Archbishop of Cannanore.

Your Lordship,

Please tell Joaquim not to prepare today more than one casket of meat which holds six dozen sausages and many layers of small ham needed to fill it, and not to buy anything more. This is what I feel but you may decide according to your wishes.

Though I am aware that Your Lordship is always willing to be helpful to me, I do not dare be more impertinent. I will state my needs, but on one condition that my request should not in any way be detrimental to your interests and if so, I do not want it.

For my sustenance and that of Fr. José António Pinto, Fr. Couto and Fr. Custodio, I need some money. If I borrow elsewhere I will suffer two losses. The difficulty of not having a civilian guarantor and having to pay 30 percent, is too much for me.

Now if Your Lordship loans me, I save the 30 percent and regarding the surety both Fr. Couto and I will guarantee with our lives till our death.

The total amount I need is 400,000 *reis*, and you may also include in it the 18 coins that I owe you.

I want, however, that you do not trouble yourself or bother about it, because I prize more being your true friend and servant and I do not want those things that cannot be had. I only want to know if you will be able to loan this amount before we set sail, so that I may, alternatively, try to find it elsewhere — and if I am unable to — God will help me.

Your thankful servant,

José António.

P.S. Very soon I will send the receipt of the silver.

Declaration in the same letter.

I confirm having received from the Archbishop, today, the 20 March, 19 and 1/2 coins for his expenses. In addition, I have received as a loan from him 62 notes of 6,400 each and 1 more coin which I received earlier, 83 coins and 16 *tostões*, all of which total 400 *reis* which His Lordship kindly loaned me. In addition to the above, the 16 *tostões* which remain to make up the total of 400 *reis* are already included in the 19 and 1/2 coins of his expenses. In all I owe His Lordship, in addition to the above 18 coins which is equal to 86$400 *reis*.

Today, 20 March 1785
José António Gonçalves.

Livro das Monções, no. 166.

Declaration in the Inventory of Archbishop of Cannanore.

Remembrance — Money that Fr. José António Gonçalves owes the Archbishop of Cannanore — 19 and 1\2 coins, 1 and 1\2 coins and 82 half *dobras*. Two days before our departure from Lisbon to Goa, the Archbishop of Cannanore gave Fr. Gonçalves 50, half *dobras* to exchange into Spanish *patacas.* However, after boarding and when the Archbishop opened the box to take out a corkscrew, the said priest asked the Archbishop to keep his bag with loose change in and told that after the boat would set sail, he would give the full account of the money. This he never did, though he was reminded by the Archbishop. The Archbishop did not want to press the matter because they were still very far away from Goa and he thought that if it was not this day or the next, at least after the priest had recovered from his fever, he would submit the full account. But he disappeared when they reached Ceylon.

While we were about one and half degrees away from Goa, the Archbishop went to check his recommendation letters and the list of his effects and was surprised to find nothing, not even the copy of his appointment which Mesquita (sic) issued. The Archbishop then asked that the Spanish *patacas* that were kept in the box and which Fr. Gonçalves had to account for, he counted and checked. They found the bag to contain 99 *patacas*, 12 half *dobras*, one note of 24,000 *reis* and two smaller ones and nothing more. Consequently there was a shortage of 13 half (sic) and one *pataca*.

The amount that Fr. Gonçalves owes the Archbishop of Cannanore is 19 and 1/2 Dobras and 1 and 1\2 which mean 2 coins (sic).

Of the 82 half *dobras* and 13 *dobras* which make (sic) 93 and 8 *tostões* he would return to the Archbishop, on their arrival in Goa, 82 half *dobras* and 21 coins loaned, because that was the agreement reached at and this would not have been difficult for him to return because Fr. Couto and Fr. António Pinto would each return 25 *dobras* and Fr. Custodio 15 and all that Fr. Gonçalves had to return were the remaining 17 half *dobras* and 8 *tostões* which were found short. This is the extent of loss suffered by the Archbishop.

Fr. Thomas Pariemakel declared that Fr. José António Gonçalves, while embarking at Point Galle, had taken from the Archbishop his walking stick with its gold-plated head and an episcopal ring.

All the inventoried effects were handed to Fr. Thomas Pariemakel on 7 November 1786.

Livro das Monções, no. 166.

Document No. 30

Letter from Fr. José António Gonçalves written from Calcutta.

Mr. Joaquim Xavier Correa da Graça.

Dearest friend,

I was immensely pleased to receive your kind letter of 10 May 1812 on the 4 January of the present year. I was happy to learn of your good health which together with your happiness is and continues to be my permanent wish.

I was glad to receive news about you through A. C. de Menezes and was happier to know this young man is not only talented but very prudent, courteous and honest and above all honourable. I wish to God that I had the consolation to know here that Goa has many more such young men as Mr. Menezes.

He did not wish to burden me with anything probably because he realised I could not be of such help though I wish I could.

My brother and I are in good health, though poor in finances, as we are not businessmen, and maintain ourselves with my masses and an English school which in this place is little.

If you wish to know more about me, you may approach the same person from whom I got your news, and at 66 years of age, I cannot write much and only say that I am yours etc.

May God keep you for many years.

Calcutta, 31 January 1814.
Your affectionate friend,
José António

Envelope

To
Mr. Joaquim Xavier Correa da Graça,
c/o Dr. António Caetano de Menezes,
Piedade, Goa.

Document No. 31

Portuguese Tutor or First steps of Portuguese. Language Practical Methods for use of children from Assagao Village by J. Pinto, Calcutta, printed by J. de Souza & Co., 1817, 97p.

Opinion of Rev. Joseph António Gonsalves, doctor of sacred theology and philosophy of Papal and Royal University of Archigymnasio of Wisdom, Rome.

At your request I read, very carefully, your book *Tutor Portuguez* (a work of your untiring efforts) and studied the brief but complete information on the solar system. This book will go a long way to provide your compatriots easy means to develop their intellectual abilities. Your endless and devoted affection to the children have given you the impetus to work and endow them with a proper education.

This system, generally known as Copernican, is very ancient in India and, after learning from us, it was published and taught in Greece, after Pythagoras, in the development of science.

Of the five senses necessary to men, only that of sight seldom reaches the relevant object or matter under discussion. With regard to this system what should first be taken in considerationn is what Solomon says:

"Vidi afflictionem, quam dedit Deus filiis hominum, ut distendantur

in ea .... et mundum tradidit disputationi eorum, et non inveniat homo (is comprehensive and perfect) *opus, quod operatus est Deus ab initio usque ad finem*". (Book of Ecclesiasticus, ch. 3, v. 10).

It is really difficult because if a common man cannot reach beyond the temporary ideas formed by his senses, how can he say that those formed since birth, about the stability of earth, the movement of the sun etc. are false? They say it is absurd, that it cannot be believed. The wise people, on the contrary, who have the foresight to broaden their knowledge beyond their senses, are forced to accept them by the irrefutable correctness of their calculations and infallibility, without being able to contradict the notoriously manifest truth. However, these people also have to work hard and suffer hardships to attain the knowledge about the solar system from their birth onwards. Despite this, they are successful, but cannot understand the work of God.

This solar system has nothing against the Holy faith, nothing against Christian morals, on the contrary, it helps very much to increase the sphere of thoughts which God has bestowed on us that, guided by the wonderful knowledge of the marvellous creation of his omnipotence and kindness, we may learn better, what is, within itself, the supreme being, so that we may adore, praise and serve Him who is the only Lord.

The Sacred Scripture has many texts which, to those who pretend to understand, appear contrary to the system as "*Terra autem in aeternum stat. Oritur Sol et occidit et ad locum suum revertitur: ibique renascens gyrat per meridiem, et flectitur ad aquilonem*" (Book of Eccl. ch. 1, vs. 4-6), but anyone who wishes to understand such texts, in the strict sense of the word, will need to understand the corporal existence of the Holy Trinity because the holy written word gives, at every step, heart, eyes, ears, feet, hands, etc. to the supreme being.

The true understanding of such texts is based on theological principle: "*Scientia Dei, Deo locutio Dei, hominibus*" i.e. since science comes from God, as it really does, the infinite kindness of Our Lord which is transmitted to us becomes incomprehensible but it adapts itself to the smallness of our understanding, because, otherwise, when placed before us as they are, it would not be understood by us, given the limited sphere of our mental faculties. We do, likewise, when we speak to small children, using and modifying our words to suit their understanding and assimilation.

Jose Antonio Gonsalves.

Document No. 32

Letter from Fr. Caetano Victorino de Faria to António João Pinto.

Mr. João António Pinto.
Lisbon, 1 February 1772.

The fatherly affection that you have for me keeps your memory alive and drives me to confess an everlasting gratitude to you and your entire family. The filial duty makes me wish that these lines may find you and your family in good health. These are the prayers that I raise to Christ, everyday and on special occasions.

I reached this court of Lisbon on 23 November, after a pleasant voyage and good health, together with my companions with the exception of José de Oliveira who was sick all the time and to whom I rendered all possible help.

Upto now my son and I are in good health, always devoting to you the respect that you rightly deserve.

I spoke to Luis Manuel Tavares to whom you recommended me and who awaited my call with great pleasure. Due to the kind recommendation that you so insistently gave, though I have not yet had the occasion to trouble him, I still remain ever grateful to you and to him.

As I had an opportunity to talk to the Counts of St. Vincent, where I was well received with their sincere willingness to be of assistance to me in anything I needed, and for which I thanked them, I had occasion to convey to them, through their Majordomo João Evangelista Machado e Oliveira, the great affection and generosity that you and your family extended to Mr. Miguel Carlos da Cunha, confirming that your house was a sanctuary for the said gentleman and his family explaining in detail how and when you helped him, for which he was very grateful and awaited an opportune occasion to return your affection and maintain friendly relation with you. And to discharge my duty towards you I handed over a petition, on behalf of Ignacio Pinto, requesting that he be appointed General Treasurer of the Bull of Cruzada, which I got drafted by Luis Manuel Tavares, as I was not familiar with the system of the court, otherwise, I would have obtained it from Mr. Mendanha. I entrusted to the said Manuel Tavares the subsequent work, should the vacancy still exist with instruction to forward it to you, in case the Majordomo forgot it. I trust that he will write to you and your brothers and I hope you will reciprocate, maintaining the correspondence with this house through the same person who is like the door of the house and the best in this court.

I found in the said João Evangelista Machado e Oliveira a temperament identical to yours; he is serious, modest, solemn, affable, truthful and loyal and, therefore, controls everyone in this household and His Eminence the Cardinal adores him. It was through his influence that the annuity to Mr. Miguel Carlos of Sinquerim was approved, despite the objections from his own mother, and he is heard and listened to in the ministry. The affairs of the house are all in his hands, so you and your brothers may avail of that house through the same Luis Manoel Tavares for all that you may need, because though he is already old and deaf he loves that house very much.

The poverty in which I live does not permit me richer gifts than the rosary of blue beads with a cross in relief, with plenary indulgence at the hour of death, a poor gift from a poor priest, but sent with great love and filial devotion.

I had occasion to pursue, in this court all the requirements of my compatriots, as the ministry is inclined to consider favourably all my petitions, and, therefore, I applied to H. Majesty, on behalf of Mr. Ignacio Pinto, to issue an order allowing his and your daughters, grand-daughters and nieces to become nuns of the black hood, with the same dowry and honours as that of the white hoods and further requested that this facility be extended to cover all lay women. I also entrusted your work to Tavares and I am hopeful that he will do the needful, which is no more than submitting the application for approval and drawing up the Order. He asked me, though, if I was prepared to give some consideration to expedite it and I said that I had not been sounded in that respect but that if he could give the order right now I would be willing to contribute with some handkerchiefs, though I feel, it is not necessary.

José de Oliveira went from Angola to Rio de Janeiro to collect his money but left no instructions regarding what you were sending or ordering and, therefore, your parcels and dispatches will remain in India House without being released, as I have no documents or any receipt given by José de Oliveira. I was informed of this by Luis Manoel Tavares. I would have taken action if I had the time. You are, therefore, advised that you do not need to have business or correspondence with businessmen from here as they are not trustworthy.

Your faithful servant,
Fr. Caetano Victorino de Faria

Another letter from Fr. Caetano Victorino de Faria to António João Pinto.

Mr. António João Pinto
Lisbon, 14 February 1772.

I have already informed you, in my earlier letter, the great desire that Mr. João Evangelista Machado de Oliveira showed in being of assistance to you in obtaining favours from the house of the Counts of St. Vincent and especially from Cardinal da Cunha, which you will succeed in getting through the good offices of my friend, João Evangelista, because of the good treatment that you have given to Mr. Miguel Carlos da Cunha, helping him, unselfishly and without being asked to, indicating thereby, the consideration that you, your brothers and son place on his lineage and whose education he owes to my friend. For this reason he holds a special affection for you and to show how grateful he is, he has submitted a petition to His Eminence requesting that your brother Mr. Ignacio Pinto be appointed General Treasurer of the Bull, and not your son Salvador João Pinto, because he is otherwise very busy at home. I am sure he will get this appointment.

As I am not in a position to pursue your matter personally in this Court, and as my friend João Evangelista is also very busy, I have taken the liberty to delegate this to your representative Luis Manoel Tavares who, on obtaining the approval, will expeditiously hand it over to my friend who in his turn will dispatch it to you under cover of the letter he wants to write to you.

I do not have to stress on the capabilities and usefulness of João Evangelista, as experience will show to you. All I have done upto now is to discharge my duty towards you. This is what I mean. This is all for now.

God protect you.

Your obedient servant,
Fr. Caetano Victorino de Faria.

Letter from Fr. Caetano Victorino de Faria to Fr. Pascoal Pinto.

Rev. Fr. Pascoal Pinto.
Lisbon, 2 February 1772.

The many favours that, I must confess, I owe you, urge me to wish that on receipt of this you may be in robust health for which I raise my prayers to Our Lord that in His mercy He may keep you always so.

I have narrated the progress of my journey, as far as I could, to your brother Ignacio, as the very short journey to Genoa did not permit me to do as I wished and, therefore I shall avoid repeating it but I take this occasion to renew my gratitude which I owe to you and your family and I shall always keep on mentioning and showing it in all my actions how very much grateful I really am.

The personal conversation that I had with the Nuncio, the Archbishop of Tyro resulted in my being the proud owner of three rosaries of silver beads and plenary indulgence at the hour of death, one of which he gifted to my son, the other to my religious sister, and the third to me, without any obligation on us to gift it if we so wished to anyone. Out of veneration (for a gift from such a person), I feel that you deserve it and therefore offer it to you, requesting you to accept it as a token of my affection, as I am not in a position to gift you with something which may correspond with your merits.

You must have learnt from your brother, the good acceptance that I had from the Nuncio, who treated me with courtesy and great affability. All of this I owe to God in the person of Fr. João Baptista de S. Caetano, a Benedictine of whom I shall speak later.

I had the honour of dining, on various occasions, in his palace, followed by requests from him to come over at any time I wished, and for which purpose, he left instructions in the sacristy to give me the vestments any time I came. After mass, before going, the breakfast tray was always ready.

He asked me lot of information on the missions in Goa and on the bishoprics, on religions and on the entire ecclesiastical state and wanted all this in writing which, in fact, I managed through Bishop D. António, who, I think, will go to your house, this monsoon and will give my news. With the details that D. António gave and what the ex-Secretary of State remembered I managed to make a series on the missions, without mentioning their actual state, not to displease the one who did not want to listen to us, and submitted it to the Nuncio, who recognising the handwriting of my son, was very pleased. He forced us to stay in his house and to write on the existing situation, which I did, in accordance with my conscience, giving as proof the life of the venerable Fr. José Vaz, which I submitted with a recommendation that he liked very much. I proved to him that it was through the efforts of native ministers, born in the same land, and not of foreigners, that Christianity could remain and flourish, maxims practised by St. Paul and other apostles. I gave examples of Fr. Joaquim de Miranda, the progress he was making in the building of the hospital for which he brought material from his own house, in addition to other things that he did. In the same way, I wrote about Fr. João Francisco Gonçalves, founder of the church of Vaddy; the progress of the Theatines and the Filipinos and of the missions of Bengal, Timor and Costa. All this he had translated into Italian and sent to the secretariat at Rome, where he also recommended us, informing them of our arrival. He also sent us to the Archbishop of Genoa so that he could direct us to the Court and he gave us a city guide. We were directed to His Eminence the Cardinal Secretary, where, God willing, I hope to receive his orders and execute his precepts with the same willingness and submission that he deserves.

You will want to know how I came to know the Nuncio and I will relate it personally. As I reached this Court, the news of our arrival spread all over and I had to frequently visit the India House to talk to the Minister regarding the delivery of the effects of Mendanha. From this followed a procession of prominent members from the Court wanting to visit Mendanha, and I had through necessity to go to their houses. When I told this to professor Fr. Francisco, the poet, who lives at the crossroad, he advised me to avoid these meetings and to take a different course, to which Mendanha agreed. He sent me to Fr. João Baptista, whom I referred to earlier, with a request to him to hear me, and after four hours of discussions in the convent at Estrela, he decided to take me under his patronage and to help me in my aims, advising great caution, which was necessary in so delicate a matter in this Court. And, in fact, he personally spoke to the Nuncio showing my documents and those of my son touching on the subject of his passion which was excessive in regard to Goans, and after learning of the state of affairs of secular and regular ecclesiastics in Goa, went to the extent of saying that he would not rest until he bestowed the mitre and the staff on the said natives, imitating St. Paul and other Apostles. He was capable of doing this, since he enjoyed great consideration in the ministry and was listened to in the Board of Censors, was of high probity, a good religious man and of nobility by birth. I was honoured with his offer to be my representative, together with Mendanha, before the Court, to correspond with my religious sister and with those representatives whom you and your family already know. He will be pleased with your letters and those of your brother.

As a token of my affection, I offer to Our Lady of Agony, a marble slab out of the six that are being sent to be distributed. I handed them over to the reverend representative who assured me that they would be sent duly blessed with the relics of the saints. I am sure he will do so as I have kept money to defray the expenses but I am not sure if he will accept.

To satisfy my desire of showing my great affection for you, I had reserved two marble slabs, which looked like black damasks over white background, of 18 inches in length, 9 inches in breadth and 1 inch thick, both for two coins for which I kept a deposit of 16 *tostões* to carve a pair of buffets, but I had to give it up, losing my 16 *tostões* in the bargain, as I found myself short of money for expenses that suddenly cropped up. But I shall fulfill my wish when I reach Genoa.

A lay servant of the Nuncio requests me to arrange, through my representatives, the import into Goa of rosaries, crucifixes, bells from Loretto and other things, which are being sent in a carton, addressed to Ignacio Pinto. I request you to dispose of those things and with its proceeds to send handkerchiefs, bed spreads, and other things which he asks for in a list which he will give me today. He promises to pay any excess, about which I am writing to Fr. José Ribeiro to see if he can make up the difference.

The Neri priests have offered to help me in all I need, but so far I have not asked them anything. I am sure the three universities have been established in that city and provinces to teach Latin, Greek, French and Hebrew besides philosophy, theology and canon law, subjects in which one can obtain a doctorate.

I offer you a French book by Lima which I will send in the packet of the nun. It would help me, immensely, in the present circumstances, if you could send the work of Luis Caetano de Lima, and of Menezes, yet to be printed, and addressed to the said Reverend and as a gift to the Ministry, as I have already spoken to them about it.

I cannot go on more for lack of time and I hope you will excuse me. God protect you.

Embraces to Mrs. Agostinha and her niece.
Fr. Caetano Victorino de Faria.

Copy from the originals.

Note: These were written in a handwriting other than his, probably it was of his son and signed by him.

Document No. 33

Letter from the Secretary of State, Martinho de Mello e Castro to the Bishop of Cochin.

Your Lordship,

A representation was sent to H. Majesty that the Convent of St. Monica of Goa consists of religious who are daughters of both European and native people.

At the time of joining the convent the former are conferred black hoods while the latter are given white ones, though both of them bring the same dowry, the only difference between them being the colour of their skin.

Therefore, H. Majesty orders that immediately on your arrival in Goa you should find the best way to stop this abuse and that those who now wear white hoods be permitted to wear black ones, and that, in future, particular care should be taken to abolish such practice at the time of taking in new religious in the Convent.

God keep Your Lordship.

Salvaterra dos Magos,
6th March 1779.
Martinho de Mello e Castro, Bishop of Cochin.

Livro das Monções, no. 168, fl. 125.

Document No. 34

Text of the letter from Mr. Innocencio Francisco da Silva to Mr. Jacinto Caetano Barreto de Miranda.

I do not think that it is possible to tell in all truthfulness whether Fr. Caetano Victorino de Faria was at any time the confessor of the Queen D. Maria I, otherwise, you may see for yourself.

In 1757 when by decree of 19 September 1757 the Jesuits to whom the care of the conscience of the members of the royal family was entrusted, were expelled from the palace, among others, Dr. Fr. José Pereira de Santa Anna, ex-Provincial of Carmo, was chosen as confessor of the

Crown Princess D. Maria and of the princesses, her sisters. He was the confessor till his death on 31 January 1759, at the Palace of Salvaterra.

In February of the following year, Dr. Fr. Ignacio de St. Catharina, the prior of Carmelite Convent of Carnide, later Archbishop of Thessalonica, bishop of Penafiel, assistant Minister of the Inquisitor General etc., was appointed as his successor. He died in the Palace of Queluz at the age of 69 on 29 November 1788, and was the confessor of the Queen till his death.

He was succeeded by D. José Maria de Mello of the Oratory and Bishop of Algarve and it was during his time that the Queen became mentally unbalanced because of doubts and scruples, which it is said her father confessor created in the innermost mind of the august sinner. He was asked to leave the Palace in 1794, continuing in the displeasure of the Royal Court.

The Queen continued mentally unbalanced and did not take part, whatsoever, in the affairs of the State.

In the interval, therefore, between 1757 and 1794 it is not possible to place Fr. Caetano Victorino de Faria as father confessor much less thereafter. Therefore, I feel that any indications in this direction are ill-founded and completely incorrect.

Ultramar, 23 May 1867

Document No. 35

Comments of Fr. Caetano Victorino de Faria on the information of D. Fr. Manoel de St. Catharina, Bishop of Cochin and Governor of the archbishopric of Goa.

1. *Paragraph of Information*[2] : When that Bishop arrived in Goa, an Indian priest called Fr. Caetano Francisco do Couto was in charge of the affairs of the bishopric of Cochin. This priest had many controversies with the Franciscans, who were in charge of that mission, and with those of Propaganda. Presently, the priest is in Lisbon.

Comment: The priest who governed the bishopric of Cochin was Fr. Caetano Francisco do Couto, son of Pascoal Couto and Pascoela Pereira, Brahmin, born in Panjim, the island of Goa. This priest, well-known for his merits in Goa, did his minor studies upto sacred theology at the College of the Novitiate on the island of Chorao where there were as many as 500 students. He appeared for his final public examination under the guidance of D. António Taveira de Neiva Brum and of the secular court arguing with masters of religion of whom one is in this Court.

On concluding his Sacred Theology (to which the Archbishop was present) he was called as his personal assistant and Secretary of Inspections from where he was sent as Vicar Forane of Honavar in Kanara.

When D. Francisco da Assumpção e Brito succeeded him as Archbishop, recognising his talents and inclination to the ministry, he sent him as Governor of the bishopric of Cochin and he remained there for 12 years. He did a lot for the Crown and for the salvation of souls, keeping in check the arrogance of those of Propaganda, stopping the abuses which were being tolerated by the so-called missionaries and bringing more than 5,000 souls to the fold of the Catholic Church baptising them at a place called Vencort, besides the numerous apostates that were brought back to the church.

While in this task, he had to face stiff persecution from the Franciscans who lived in that bishopric, ostensibly as missionaries but in fact with scandalous behaviour, even to pagans, Muslims, Protestants, Calvinists and Lutherans.

The Catholics, finding in the new missionary priests a different behaviour, continuous sermons and courteous ways, realised how horrible were the ways of the Franciscans and therefore pleaded with their King to expel the friars from the parishes and, as proof of the friars' licentiousness, they produced the wives and children of these false missionaries, because they knew that the Governor had no powers to expel the Franciscans, since they lived under the protection of the pagan King. They went so far as to try to bribe their King, offering money (this has been testified by the two Malabar priests who are here for the last two years) but he though an ambitious pagan, yielded more to the persuasion and merits of the Governor, giving him powers even to expel the Franciscans from the country. The Governor, however, decided to proceed in accordance with the instructions received from his Archbishop sent on 5 December 1777 and on 18 April 1779. All this and other accomplishments, during his governance, should be transmitted for H. Majesty's knowledge.

While he was, thus, trying to pacify his flock, Fr. José da Soledade, a Discalced Carmelite, companion of the Bishop-Governor, came with instructions to take charge of the bishopric of Cochin as its Governor (before the said Bishop could take charge as Governor of the bishopric of Goa) and to whom Fr. Caetano, promptly, gave over the charge and returned to Goa. Fr. José da Soledade joined hands with the Franciscans and broke the peace and tranquility which his predecessor had built. He was arrested and, after four months in prison, he ran away and came to Goa, and it is doubtful if he would return to the governorship, for fear of the Catholics, but in the meantime, he succeeded in sending five more priests from Goa, to the Franciscans, together with six of the Congregation which were sent by their Superior to propagate the religion on the island of Ceylon.

The Bishop-Apostolic Vicar who expected such a blunder from Fr. José da Soledade, the new Governor, immediately sent his Vicar General to take over the charge of the bishopric of Cochin, claiming that it had been abandoned by the incumbent and advised Rome, from where he received a letter of confirmation, which he showed to H. Majesty. This Vicar General of Propaganda took charge of the church of Angenga which he turned into a metropolis of the bishopric.

One cannot understand what type of pacifying this is, as the Bishop Governor is wont to say.

2. *Paragraph of Information*: Similarly, another cleric from Goa, called Fr. Pedro de Figueiredo, was appointed Governor of the bishopric of Cannanore, but the people refused to accept him. He did not even cross Calicut and returned to Goa as Inquisitor. Because of the dissensions, the Bishop-Governor of Goa was forced to send Fr. José da Soledade back to settle the matters, as in fact, he did and returned to Goa to report on his mission. He was then appointed Governor of the bishopric of Cochin, where he proceeded to, taking with him seven clerics and six priests of the Congregation for the mission of Ceylon, in addition to those that were already there.

Comments: The Governor of the archbishopric of Cannanore is Fr. Pedro de Figueiredo of the Congregation of Oratory. He was teaching philosophy and theology, at the age of 22, until he was 45. A holy man in his habits and exemplary; in short a true picture of a Goan ecclesiastic, a solace to lay sinners, everything to everybody and himself to all. He was the Rector of the seminary of Rachol and of the school in the province of Salcete, where he left indelible marks on the church and for H. Majesty.

From here he was sent as Governor of the said archbishopric. He immediately set to take charge and fixed his residence in Calicut in the house of the farm manager, Mr. José de Amaral Carvalho, well known for his upbringing and merits. He remained in this post for the entire period of his two years' tenure.

This distinguished Governor was received by a huge crowd of his flock, but had to suffer immensely during his tenure of office, because the Jesuit, Mathias Excerpentel, a German, had arrogated for himself the governorship, and joining hands with those of Propaganda, tried in every way to harass him. With this intention, he joined the Franciscans who are to be found throughout the diocese, ostensibly as missionaries, and backed by Fr. António de Padua and his followers in Goa, tried to disturb the peace which he had built up. They tried their very best to remove him from the governorship. For this purpose, they accused him, before the court of Nawab Hyder Ali Khan of being a traitor, a Portuguese spy and of many other misdeeds, but he always came out victorious to the utter discomfort of his rivals. Despite the persecution by the friars, he continued to lead his flock untiringly until he was recalled to Goa to take charge as Inquisitor, a post which he presently holds.

While returning to Goa he had to save himself from many ambushes and had to escape from assassins ordered by Fr. António de Padua and his followers in Goa, which cost him a lot and delayed his arrival in Goa. The only thing that Fr. José da Soledade did was to hand over the governorship of that archbishopric, which cost so much sweat to his apostle, D. Fr. Aleixo de Menezes, and to Fr. Pedro de Figueiredo, to the Jesuit Excerpentel, factor of Propaganda, a suspect in faith and scandalous in behaviour.

It is not true, though, that seven clerics were sent from Goa to these missions, as stated in the paragraph above.

3. *Paragraph of Information*: Fr. Manoel de S. Francisco, a Franciscan, from Daman, of good reputation and sufficiently educated, was appointed Governor of the archbishopric of Cannanore, and five religious of Madre de Deus were sent with him for the mission of Mysore.

Comments: I knew Fr. Manoel de S. Francisco, a Franciscan very well. I found that his erudition did not go beyond the missal and the breviary. He was a naval chaplain and, as he was attached to the Tiracol fort, he resided with his mother. Every Saturday he would walk 18 miles to say the Sunday mass at the fort, and after the mass, would walk back the same distance. He was, therefore, nicknamed Fr. Manoel Tiracol.

This friar was a representative of his missionaries in the archbishopric of Cochin, or in other words, he was a protector and defender of friars who lived in that bishopric without any religion, and when Fr. Caetano

Francisco do Couto decided to discipline him, he ran away to Cannanore, where he was made a Governor of the same archbishopric, because they found him full of merits, particularly, scandalous ones, and, to enable him to live safely and at peace with his vices, he was given five friars of Madre de Deus. These friars of Madre de Deus are unfit for any such work, both because of their ignorance and their scandalous behaviour.

4. *Paragraph of Information*: Fr. António de Assumpção, a religious of Graça, 40 years of age, was sent to St. Thomas of Mylapore, as a man capable of filling up the vacancy created by the demise of the Bishop.

Comments: This priest was teaching philosophy and had no idea of curing souls. He was more interested in entertainment in Goa, as he had very little to do in the school where he taught. Therefore, in sending him out of Goa, they only reduced the number of nun-chasers, a pastime that kept the friars at Graça very much occupied, but certainly not desirable for the governance of bishoprics in India. Because the Bishop Governor found him competent to fill the place of his predecessor, that is precisely why he should be removed from this position as Governor. His predecessor, Bishop D. Bernardo, was consecrated Bishop in Goa, after he turned 50, far removed from the secular entertainments around which he lived, especially public games (this I witnessed) and he carried with him these entertainments to Madras and Mylapore.

In Goa, his first action was to request permission from D. António Taveira to ordain a boy, godchild of some of his friends and partners, whom the very Archbishop had earlier refused to ordain because he was unfit and unworthy. This ordination was so unfortunate that the very sacred oil used for his ordination served as poison to kill him before he could exercise his ministry.

At Mylapore he lived for 30 years or more and throughout his tenure, the licentiousness of the parish friars of his religious was such that it became loathsome even to heretics and finally many being disgusted, joined the Lutherans (I know of many) and one of them who was not accepted in the Lutheran society because of his detestable behaviour, later joined the Calvinists of Batavia. Those still living in that archbishopric have no law or regulation.

He had some businessmen as his partners. They were so haughty and scheming that Nawab Hyder Ali Khan was forced to lay a siege at Mylapore to catch them together with the Bishop, but the latter with some of his colleagues ran away to Bengal eight days earlier and the rest were caught.

A Catholic concubine who lived with a rich heretic, died a sinner leaving behind the children of her lover. She was denied a Catholic burial in a blessed grave, but that friend managed to get it done in exchange for more than 1,000 *pagodas*. The same bishop led the funeral service and made a speech which so compromised the Roman religion that the Protestants of India found it unbelievable.

To such a place goes Fr. António de Assumpção, who will faithfully fill the vacancy, as the Bishop-Governor of Goa assures us.

5. *Paragraph of Information*: Fr. Joaquim de St. Anna, a Dominican, who is in Macau and from whom no reply had been received, was appointed Bishop of Timor.

Comments: This mission was under the Dominicans of Goa. When Bishop D. Fr. Geraldo of the same Order, tried to discipline them they persecuted him to such an extent that he was forced one night to run away to Mysore, where he went out of his mind, threatening anyone who followed him. For 30 years there was no successor, so an order was issued recalling all Dominicans back to Goa, but they rebelled and took to arms against H. Majesty. In the conflict, one friar was killed with arms in his hands, and the case was reported to H. Majesty.

That mission was left in charge of the secular priests of Goa with Fr. José de Menezes, a Brahmin of Salcete, Goa, bachelor in sacred theology through a Jesuit school, a man of impeccable behaviour and good lineage, as Governor.

These are sufficient reasons to maintain that mission as it is.

6. *Paragraph of Information*: Fr. Amaro de St. Thomaz, a Dominican was appointed episcopal Governor of Mozambique, as a person capable of occupying that position. The Bishop Governor intended to send four or five clerics, if any capable could be found, to add to the two Dominicans sent there already.

Comments: H. Majesty is already aware, through some other source, how disorganised that diocese was under the Dominicans, both spiritually and temporarily. Those friars go there with the only intention of making money and to oppress the people of the Rios de Senna, without least caring about administering the sacraments and about spiritual guidance. Any Catholic needing them has to pay a good sum of money. Such is their lack of commitment to themselves and to the Catholic religion, that they feel that their tenure of service of three years and the title of chaplain of the Guard of the Emperor of Monomotapa, given by H. Majesty, give them the licence to acquire as much wealth as they possibly can in those three years, before they return to Goa.

Though the Emperor of Monomotapa was converted to the Catholic religion over a century ago, at the entreaties of H. Majesty, and his successors are also considered Catholics, and as such attend mass, bless themselves with holy water, and respect the chaplain. The present Emperor has not yet been baptised, his father and grandfather died without this sacrament, despite the continuous presence of the Dominicans. This same system will be carried on by the Governor appointed by the Bishop-Governor, because the friars of Goa do not easily bend to give spiritual food which they find below their dignity.

7. *Paragraph of Information*: The Prior of the college, along with a priest, and with two benefices needed to make up the shortage, was sent to Diu.

Comments: Since the Prior has not been appointed, I have no comments to make, but I feel that some priest should be sent, and if the Prior is the one, he will be considered a 'nobody' because he is a Canarim.

8. *Paragraph of Information*: To Daman, they sent a cleric, as parish priest of a church. But the four missionaries that were needed were not sent as the income was insufficient.

Comments: The priory of Daman is occupied by Fr. Sebastião de Albuquerque, appointed by Bishop D. António Taveira. He is from Goa, well-educated and well-bred. He has served Goa, H. Majesty and the city of Daman well and its people do not need missionaries but benefices. But the problem is that there is no one in Goa willing to go to Daman because the stipends are meagre, and therefore, I suggest that it should be brought on par with Diu.

9. *Paragraph of Information*: The same Bishop-Governor suggests the need to appoint a bishop of St. Thomas at Mylapore and an archbishop of Cannanore, as he has no authority to delegate the powers of the sacrament of confirmation to governors.

Comments: This suggestion from the Bishop-Governor is based solely on the need of confirmation. He, perhaps, is of the opinion that this is a sacrament of extreme need, when more urgent and important is that of a shepherd towards his flock, to watch over it, sustain it with sacraments, nourish it with the word of God, protect it against the wolves which surround Christianity and to save it from those who, in sheep's clothing create internecine fights. This matter should stir the person entrusted with it.

10. *Paragraph of Information*: The Archbishop (sic) suggests that the Governor he was sending to St. Thomas of Mylapore could become a bishop, and as a Bishop of Cannanore, he would wish someone from Portugal who would be amenable to live amidst the rudest and crudest people of Asia, because he had already made use of the best that were available in this State and there was none but the Fr. Provincial of Graça who was a sick man.

Comments: The comments under para. 4 cover in full what is suggested regarding the Bishop of St. Thomas of Mylapore. Regarding that of Cannanore, the learned Bishop errs when he suggests that a person from the kingdom should be sent as archbishop as those people are the rudest in Asia. But a foreigner who neither knows nor is able to assimilate their habits is of no use for such rude and crude people. On the contrary, one from the same region, educated in Europe, prone to assimilate the habits of such people and mix with them, is better equipped and more effective to tame those people and to teach and make them perfect. He says that the best that existed in that land were made use of. He thinks, I believe, that all those who do not wear the habit of some religious group are useless and only those (irrespective of the fact that they might be criminals wearing the habit of some group) are competent enough for any employment or ministry. Such maxims are carrots used to satisfy the regulars and encourage the seculars, an error that has shadowed the golden colour of the Church.

11. *Paragraph of Information*: That he found the secular priests were useless and even the natives of India did not accept them in those regions, as missionaries.

Comments: I should not have replied to this paragraph as it bares the passionate fanaticism with which you speak because no one but one out of his mind will believe or make himself believe that out of 3,000 clerics if it is not the tenth or the hundredth it would at least be the thousandth, and therefore one could easily select at least three, while you found none? This indicates that you are ill-advised because while you were able to appoint Fr. Joaquim Furtado of Salcete and Fr. José Felippe of Divar as teachers of the college of Chorao, if you wanted priests not only as teachers or bishops but also to teach others to become bishops, you would find at least a hundred of them.

Regarding what you say about native priests being unacceptable as missionaries in those regions, you are contradicting the actual practice in Goa, in Ceylon, in the kingdom of Cambay, Kanara and other parts of India. You contradict the Apostolic Archbishop, D. Fr. Aleixo de Menezes, the venerable D. António Taveira, you contradict the evangelical discipline of the holy fathers of the sacred canons and scriptures and of human intelligence, because any animal always wants someone to his likeness.

12. *Paragraph of Information*: That since white priests were being appointed, there were two very good priests. The first, Francisco Luis da Cunha, who being elevated to canon, renounced the canonship and is presently the Vicar of St. Lawrence.

Comments: This priest is the son of Fernando Teixeira da Cunha, a *mulatto*, adopted by Jeronimo Teixeira. His heir, Vicente Rebello wanted to sell him (Fernando Teixeira) but he was protected by the friars. He was made a soldier and thus saved himself from slavery. His birth certificate is recorded in the civil registry of Goa.

As he looked like a buffoon and had the face of a friar, he was married to a *mestico* woman and made an officer, and with this type of merits he managed to put his son in the seminary at Chorao, where he made no progress except in eating, drinking and dressing at the cost of the college. He created there so many scandals and disorders that the Governor of India was forced to send a squad of soldiers led by S.M. Miguel de Arroyos to discipline him. When he attained the proper age, he was ordained with no other qualifications but that of his having been in the seminary and of being white. On these merits he was elevated to Canon of the Sé.

This canonship curtailed his lustful freedom. The friars who were his benefactors and who also acted as synodal examiners passed on to him cases on moral law to study and answer for the test in the church of St. Lawrence, of which he is now the Vicar. This is why he renounced his canonship to have more freedom to pursue his vices at the cost of the friars. He is notorious all over Goa for his scandalous living and I refrain from commenting about his other simoniacal behaviour.

13. *Paragraph of Information*: The second priest was Fr. António da Silveira de Menezes, Vicar-General of this archbishopric and presently canon of that diocese. Any of these was suitable as Archbishop of

Cannanore, especially because they grew up here and therefore it would not be as difficult as it would to a person from the kingdom.

Comments: This priest was the son of Carlos da Silveira, a *mulatto* adopted by Martinho da Silveira. He also joined the Seminary of the Novitiate on the same merits as the one above and being an abetter in the crimes of the other, was accorded the same punishment. He was haughtier, though, than the other and went so far as to kill a native boy near the college with a shot from a firearm but managed to outwit the law and the misdemeanour because of his white colour. He was elevated to canonship of the Sé and because of this he managed to be appointed Vicar-General of D. Fr. Francisco de Assumpção.

This cleric always lived as the occasion demanded at home in public scandal; when he was Vicar General, he was the persecutor of justice, which he sold as in a shop, condemning and suspending clerics, and for whose lifting there was a commission for his concubine for the suspensions of the clerics, whom in his absence they would come to, as in a shop.

He was a partner in all crimes of D. Fr. Francisco de Assumpção and when he should have ended his life as a recluse or in a closed cell or as a religious to atone for his scandalous living, the Bishop Governor finds him suitable to be elevated to Archbishop of Cannanore.

These 13 points have been proved to the best of my ability. Regarding the facts though they are notorious, I shall testify to them as a witness.

The ingenuity of the Governor may be excused because he was educated in Bussaco, and therefore was ignorant of the ways of the world for which one needs the foresight of a serpent and without which one cannot handle properly the flock of the Lord especially in these parts of India.

What follows is a recapitulation of the thirteen paragraphs which Caetano Victorino de Faria made to be read by H. Majesty.

"Never was Catholic religion so chaotic and weakened in India as it presently is deprived of pastors, wallowing in vices, corrupted morally and persecuted by the very priests to the extent that one can say: *Filii Matris Meae Pugnaverunt Contra Me* (the children of my mother have fought against me).

The 13 paragraphs of information from the Bishop-Governor of Goa are by themselves sufficient proof of the lack of sincerity with which he pretends to advise Your Majesty. From the answers to these 13 paragraphs one can easily discern the lack of perception with which he conceives the episcopal character and the fanatic passion with which he behaves towards the natives both secular and ecclesiastical because of which he has become an anathema to the entire Christian community in India.

In paras 1 & 2, when he should have dealt at length, he deals very cursorily regarding what is essential for religion and conveniently hides the dissensions and controversies that he and his companion Fr. José da Soledade committed to the detriment of the religion and the Crown of Your Majesty.

In para 3 he praises and recommends as Governor of the bishopric of Cannanore a friar who is notoriously ignorant and scandalous.

In para 4 he hides the defects of the person he recommends as Bishop, a person who is otherwise unworthy of such a position and sanctifies his predecessor to the detriment of religion.

He hides or does not fully convey, in para 7 the information regarding the Prior of Diu Fr. Vicente Pereira of Chorao, a Brahmin and expert in ecclesiastical science, the same being true in respect to that of Daman at para 8.

In paras 12 & 13, he tells half-truths while disclosing the origin of the candidates as required by canon law for such high positions and at the same time conveniently ignores the scandalous and notorious vices of his preferred candidates, disregarding the needs of Catholic religion and the salvation of souls.

In para 9 he shows himself ignorant of the weight of the mitre, the worth of the ring, the power of the staff and the value of baptism, and only stresses on the need of the sacrament of confirmation as if this alone was the only and essential part of episcopal order. And he errs when he suggests remedies for the evils he complains of.

Finally, in para 11 he shows his contempt towards native ecclesiastics and seculars with a manifest error of judgement, in as much as if natives were not acceptable in their own country they should have been discarded a long time ago. Such passion is not only improper and unbecoming of a Governor but harmful and detrimental to public peace as it became evident in Goa.

Your Majesty was informed by the same Bishop in the last monsoon of the uselessness and unsuitability of regulars in Goa because of the general corruption of their customs and the same was apparently confirmed by the two priests of St. Vincent de Paul requesting their abolition. Your Majesty tried to certify it from other sources of Your Majesty's royal confidence from which Your Majesty learnt the truth. I do not know how this Bishop-Governor forgot his earlier information.

Christianity in India deserves the consideration of Your Majesty and it has the right to Your Majesty's mercy and compassion.

Ultramar, 30 May, 6 June and 13 June 1867.

Document No. 36

Letter from the Governor of State to the Governor of the bishopric of Cannanore, Fr. Pedro de Figueiredo of the Congregation of Oratory of Holy Cross of Miracles.

I received your letter of the 7th of last month and from what you write I am convinced of and very grateful for the great interest that you have taken on the state of my health which has been indifferent and afflicted by various other illnesses.

I am very happy to know that you have taken charge of the diocese of Cannanore and of the progress that you have made on behalf of the missions and Christianity and of what you propose to do, driven by the zeal that sustains you in your sacred ministry. As requested by you, and on my own initiative, I am making a special recommendation not only to the manager of the farm at Calicut but particularly to the Governor of Cochin requesting him to take you under his protection and to extend to you all transit facilities to your diocese at Serra where I wish you good luck.

Do not hesitate to contact me should you need anything more.

God protect you.

Goa, 1 December 1778.
D. José Pedro da Camara

Reis Vizinhos, fl. 98.

Document No. 37

Letter from the Governor of State to the manager of the farm at Calicut, José Francisco de Amaral de Menezes.

The ecclesiastical Governor of Cannanore who is there to look after the evangelical duties of the missions of Mysore and others belonging to that diocese, requests me to recommend you to render him all assistance in that holy ministry. As it is incumbent on me to do my utmost towards the propagation of faith it is (sic) equally my duty to ask you to extend to him such assistance that you can and in doing so you will be proving your zeal for which I thank you.

God protect you.

Panjim, 1 December 1778.
D. José Pedro da Camara

Reis Vizinhos, fl. 99.

Document No. 38

Letter from the Governor of the State to the Governor of Cochin, Adrinano Muns.

I am extremely pleased to write to you and to inquire about you. I hope you are enjoing very good health now that you are with your frigate in southern coast.

I avail of this opportunity to reiterate my consideration and to place my services at your disposal.

I request you to kindly take Rev. Fr. Pedro de Figueiredo, ecclesiastical Governor, Cannanore, under your protection and to extend to him all transit facilities to his diocese at Serra and any other assistance that you may deem necessary for which I shall remain very obliged.

Goa, 1 December 1778.
D. José Pedro da Camara

Reis Vizinhos, fl. 99.

Document No. 39

Letter from the Governor of the State to Budhu Khan, Governor of Calicut.

Fr. Pedro de Figueiredo and the manager of the farm, both residing in that port-town under your command, have informed me of the many favours that you have dispensed them with saving them from public disrespect which some troublesome Christians created, stirred by their unrestrained passions and lack of respect for law.

As I recognise that this action on your part had the sole aim of restoring peace and order among all, I cannot fail to be extremely thankful to you and to request you to take further action with a view to completely stop those troublesome from repeating such condemnable acts.

I reiterate the protestations of my high consideration and extend my special thanks, awaiting an opportune occasion of being of service to you.

May God enlighten you with His divine grace.

Goa, 16 March 1779.
D. José Pedro da Camara

Reis Vizinhos, fl. 116.

Document No. 40

Letter from the Governor of the State to the manager of the farm of Calicut, José Francisco do Amaral de Menezes.

I have received your letter dealing with the continuous troubles created by those of perverse mind who cannot realise the disastrous results and injustice they have perpetrated in order to satisfy their personal passions with such scandalous incidents which border on schism.

Since it is the Prelate who has to decide on the conflict of jurisdiction, which seems to be the main cause of the trouble, and I am sure that the actions he takes will be the most adequate and correct ones, all I have to tell you is not to interfere in it except where your express intentions are helpful in the measures taken, because those actions aim at safeguarding the royal right of benefice of H. Majesty.

I am sending the letter that you requested I should write to the Governor of that port town, and I hope that on learning of my desire he will act efficaciously to bring about a general peace to which you may also join with your natural caution, endeavouring in this regard ... that its end and its ... be an example to those who have no feelings ... as much as they lack in behaviour and upbringing.

I do not approve of Nicolau Delgado joining in this particular issue in which he presently is engaged on royal service. I would feel happy if he decides to leave the chaplain to occupy the position which those, without jurisdiction, intend to confer on him, both because his individual consent will not be to my liking and because the said priest is likely to be the cause of further dissentions. You use your efforts in calming down the Catholics and do not mix yourself in anything more nor even in giving advice, leaving your superiors to do what is just.

I await a report on the provisions for the farm, for which you may send me a list, so that I may arrange the provisions and keep it ready to be sent as soon as the rains cease.

God protect you.

Goa, 16 March 1779.
D. José Pedro da Camara.

Reis Vizinhos, fl. 116v.

Document No. 41

Letter from the Governor of the State to Fr. Pedro de Figueiredo, Governor of the bishopric of Cannanore.

I am aware of the continued disturbances that have taken place in that port-town and on my part I have written, today to the Governor to use his good offices in containing the disturbances which I hope he will do. I do hope that the disturbances will calm down and that you will succeed in the tasks you were entrusted with because I am much interested in its progress which will eventually go a long way to add to the power of our august sovereign.

I hope Nicolau Delgado has not permitted the chaplain who is the frigate Commander to remain in that port-town because he does not ignore the embarrassment that this may cause and I am not writing to him to warn him of this because by now I hope he is on his way to this capital.

I await an occasion to be of service to you and you may rest assured of my best.

God protect Your Reverend.

Goa, 16 March 1779.
D. José Pedro da Camara,

Reis Vizinhos, fl. 118.

Document No. 42

Letter from the Governor of the State to Manoel Bernardes.

Having an application made by some Christians residing in that port-town and addressed to H. Majesty reached my hands and having come to know that Manoel Bernardes is the man responsible for the success ... and the main cause, I cannot remain without warning him to cease taking part in that serious and delicate matter, i.e. heading a group of lay, uncouth, scandalous and licentious people to ostensibly defend the jurisdiction and the right of royal benefice of H. Majesty as they have no competence that they seem to arrogate to themselves. You must also realise that some of the protectors of those trouble-makers easily infiltrate from foreign dominions where they feel absolutely secure.

Manoel Bernardes should rather look after his own well-being with peace and calm in accordance with his own insignificant or unfortunate position bearing in mind that to put him in disgrace with others with whom he is now associated, it is enough to declare him a fugitive from the dominions of the Queen where he was born and in addition to be branded as mischief-maker and author of the most horrible schism among the faithful.

God protect Manoel Bernardes.[3]

Goa, 16 March 1779
D. José Pedro da Camara

Reis Vizinhos, fl. 118v.

Document No. 43

Edict

I, the Queen, in my capacity as Governess and perpetual Administrator of the Mastership Cavalry and Order of Our Lord Jesus Christ, make known to you, Bishop of Cochin and Governor and Administrator of the archbishopric of Goa, that I desiring to encourage to the extent possible, state that positions to various high posts of canonships and other ecclesiastical positions in the Sé Primate of that capital and in the parishes, benefices with or without curates, and other ecclesiastical posts in the archbishopric which are under your administration, be duly filled with persons worthy of such positions and who will better serve the church, will educate and edify the faithful with catechetical teachings and examples. Having asked to be produced before me the royal letter of 10 February 1774 and the rules framed thereunder and also the edict of 7 April of the same year of the King, my august father and lord, whom God has in His glory, I dispatched them to the Archbishop of Goa, D. Fr. Francisco de Assumpção e Brito and until further orders that I may deem fit to issue on the said royal letter and rules and edict, I now order and bind on you that everything that is stipulated there regarding the appointments to various positions, canonships and other benefices and ecclesiastical posts in the Sé and those in parishes, vicarages, chaplancies and other benefices with curates, in the provinces of Goa, Salcete and Bardez, as well as in everything connected with the missions established in various parts of the Orient, subject or suffragan to the archbishopric of Goa, be strictly subject to the following:

In conformity with what is stated in the edict, on the high positions in the Sé, I reserve the right of appointments to five posts, namely, of the dean, chanter, chief treasurer, archdeacon and choir master of the Sé and because of the great confidence that I repose on you, such persons as suggested by you for those positions shall be so appointed in that bishopric, provided they have distinguished themselves in letters and virtues, have served the church and accomplished all that could be reasonably expected of them. On being appointed, they will be good ministers in the altar and the choir and will discharge all their duties with dignity. I am, therefore, pleased to delegate on you the authority, in case any of the above posts fall vacant, to propose for those posts, names of priests born in India or in the kingdom who you may find worthy of occupying that position.

The proposals are to be sent by you for appointments to the above positions after simple consultation and without any formal interview with the names listed in order of their merit, depending on either their capabilities or education as well as services rendered to the Church and other accomplishments as are determined by canon law and the council of Trent, and with the education, behaviour, habits and merits of each candidate duly tabulated.

The report will be signed by you and sealed with your coat of arms, with all documents and certificates produced by the candidates duly attached, the certificate of baptism of each of them being mandatory. You will dispatch your proposals to my tribunal of the Board of

Conscience and Orders, in the first sailing, immediately after the vacancy for the post or posts takes place, and soon after the Board has examined your proposals and confirmed that they are in line with the provisions of the Edict. They will place before me for approval the names of the priests proposed by you. There will be no other interview or tests in this Court and the moment your reports are approved by the Board, they will dispatch the letters of my royal appointments to those I am pleased to appoint, be they from your list or from those I may decide upon. The appointees will be required to obtain or arrange to obtain the said letters of appointment and submit them to you within two years from the date of the sailing in which your reports were sent, failing which and unless satisfactorily justified, the said letters will become void and the appointees will lose their lieu on their appointments which would, otherwise, have entitled them to take up, if they had submitted them within the prescribed time. You will, thereafter, submit fresh proposals of other candidates to fill up the vacancies caused by the defaulters and the negligent.

However, if the said letters (signed by me and issued by the Secretariat) are submitted within the prescribed time, only then as ordinary and diocesan Prelate, you will cause the investiture of those whose names are mentioned in the letters signed by me. Regarding ten canons, four half-canons, two quarter-canons in the said Sé, I order that these appointments be made alternately, i.e. the first vacancy to be filled by one native priest and the next by one from the kingdom, and similarly other posts that may fall vacant, on the proviso that the appointees should always possess the same educational qualifications, behaviour, virtues and services rendered to the Church as mentioned above, preference being given, other things being equal, to those knowing plain chant or even to those possessing a good voice so that they may better serve the choir and the altar. The post of 12 chaplains, curates and decorators will be divided into three parts at least, two of which will be filled by the local people; the sub-chanter, choir master and everything connected with music and the running of the Sé will be within your jurisdiction, appointing to those places people who you may find able and capable to discharge their duties with decorum and respect due to the Church.

Regarding parishes, vicarages, chaplancies and other benefices in the provinces of Goa, Salcete and Bardez which are directly connected with the cure of souls, in accordance with the provisions of the said edict of 7 April 1774, I order and bind on you that all appointments be made from priests born in that State and who have the necessary educational qualifications to exercise their ministries. When there are local people suitable for the post, it is not just that, while they suffer the pangs of hunger, other secular or regular ecclesiastics should eat the bread which the Church earns with the sweat of their parents and relatives. On the other hand, knowing that they will be called to share in your pastoral work, they may apply themselves with fervour and diligence and learn to become capable to discharge all the functions and ministries wherever they are appointed.

The appointments should be made after a knowledge test, as indicated in old edicts of the kings, my predecessors, made mandatory by decree of 29 August 1776 and in accordance with the practice observed by the Board of Conscience and Orders of this kingdom. Accordingly, the moment there is a vacancy in any church or churches, you will fix notices calling for applications within 15 days, from all the priests who may wish to submit their applications, which should be accompanied by all necessary certificates and documents. Thereafter tests should be held which will be conducted by three examiners, chosen by you from among the best, in erudition and virtue, not because I am forced to order such appointments to be made on competitive basis but because of the better utility to the Church.

On completion of the tests you will send to me a list of the three best candidates, in order of their merits and whom you may find worthier both in their intelligence and other requirements, as determined by canon law and the Council of Trent, submitting your proposal in the same way as mentioned in respect of the posts for the Sé.

In order that parishes and churches which have been filled up do not remain without ministers, while the appointment letters are being signed by me and dispatched, you will send to such churches or parishes, those priests who figure in your list and whom you find best-suited to serve there, until receipt of the appointment letters. As soon as these are received, you will do the rest, exchanging if necessary those temporarily appointed by those chosen by me and you will see that they take charge of the benefices immediately.

Regarding missions established in different parts of the Orient, subject or suffragan to the archbishopric of Goa, it is a matter that above all needs your special pastoral care and vigilance. Since these missions are in the charge of the regular Orders established in that capital, and since in my view they should continue so, I issued orders to that effect to the Archbishop of Goa, the Governor and Captain-General of the State of India, by letters sent through my Secretariat of State of the Affairs of the Navy and Overseas Dominions dated 20 April 1777.

The progress and prosperity of the said missions consist essentially in sending missionaries who not only with catechetical teachings but also by their example will strengthen the Christian people in the preserverance of their faith, in the communion of Christianity and in the midst of and obedience to the Catholic Church. Their downfall arises mainly from missionaries who through laxity and the lack of regular and monastic discipline, instead of edification create confusion amidst the faithful and scandals before the pagans. Therefore, the moment you reach Goa you must advise me on the state of these missions, the number of missionaries that each of the said regular Orders ought to have and actually have. If you find it necessary, institute inspections and send inspectors to as many places as the distance permits using priests whom you may find fit for substituting you in your pastoral duties and who will report to you with impartiality and truthfulness about the behaviour, life and habits of all and each of the missionaries employed in those missions. They must also ascertain, minutely, whether they are particular and careful in the administration of sacraments, in the preaching of the gospel, in teaching catechetics to the people and in other precepts of the Church and, finally, if they discharge all their duties as true and exemplary shepherds or on the contrary, if they are missionaries only in name and solely interested in hoarding riches through the illicit means of business and commerce, oppressing and vexing people with extortions and other misdeeds, diametrically opposed to the sacred ministry which they have been entrusted with.

As soon as you have this information and have ascertained the facts, (beware of half-truths and perverse information which are very frequent in India), you must commend those who have behaved with apostolic spirit, imitating the virtues, sanctity, religious fervour of the holy patriarchs and founders of their religious orders and you must act with all severity, as permitted by the canons, against the perverse, unjust and incorrigible, not only dismissing them from the missions but also instituting disciplinary action against them and punishing them according to the gravity of their acts. You must order the prelates of the regular Orders to send immediately other religious to the missions which have been entrusted to them and you must exercise great care to see that there is no shortage in the number of missionaries that each mission is supposed to have. You must on no account permit the appointment of missionaries unless you are satisfied with the certainty of their exemplary behaviour, life and habits and you have duly interviewed them and approved their appointment to exercise the ministry of the parish and cure of the souls in the missions. And so that in the discharge of your episcopal jurisdiction you may not find hindrance, opposition and dissentions which have so far agitated my overseas provinces to the detriment of the Church and have been caused mainly by diocesan priests and the religious of regular Orders who keep on fighting about their privileges and exemptions, I have ordered the issuance of a decree which you will receive together with this. Among other provisions there, I have stipulated and determined the rules which will fix the power and authority of bishops over all the regulars who are in charge of the cure of the souls. Everything that has been stipulated should be carried out unfailingly in all my conquests and particularly in the State of India, by the missionaries of regular Orders.

I, therefore, order that you as well as others connected with it should discharge and obey my decree and cause all provisions contained therein to be obeyed. This replaces the letter, though it would have been valid for a period of one year, without any embargo on any law, edict, provision, rule, order or letter to the contrary. It will be recorded in the book of *Mercies of the Mastership* and issued by the Secretariat for orders.

Given at Salvaterra dos Magos

5 March 1779
The Queen.
Martinho de Mello e Castro.

Livro das Monções, no. 168, fl. 113.

Decree attached to the previous Edict

Whereas the King D. João V, my lord and grandfather, had in the resolution contained in the ordinance of 25 September 1732, issued a temporary provision to stop the continued fights regarding the jurisdiction between the regulars and the bishops from the overseas kingdom, while a final decision was awaited in this crucial matter, and whereas the delay and the absence of such an order have resulted in greater doubts, disobedience and disorders, prejudicial to the spiritual good and peace of my vassals, I was pleased to order that this matter be examined by theologians and jurists, and accepting the unanimous decision of all that were heard, and in conformity with the most sensible and truthful doctrine of the Church and provisions of the Council of Trent and the most recent bulls that have legislated in this matter, I am, therefore, pleased to declare that the regular priests to whichever Order they may belong cannot exercise their ministries or any other functions in their parishes without the prior permission and approval of the diocesan bishops. They are subject to the visits of their bishops, who are entitled to inquire into their lives and habits and also to punish them for any misdeeds committed by them in their churches, and any punishment imposed must be undergone by the regular priests without any right of dissent or protest or appeal. Similarly, the regular priests are prohibited from hearing confessions and preaching sermons without specific permission from their bishop except in their own churches, and after requesting permission and this being granted, they can hear the confessions of their room-mates who will include only those living in the same convent and lodging and boarding there permanently.

There is no exemption to those living in the farms, gardens and places of regulars. They will have to discharge their religious obligations in parishes, celebrate their weddings before the parish priest, receive communion and Extreme Unction. They are prohibited from arrogating to themselves any ecclesiastical jurisdiction. Finally the bishops are authorised to take cognisance of any acts of misconduct committed by the regulars outside their convents, provided that in cases when they are in their convents or within its precincts or are authorised to leave or are on duty of the community in the gardens or farms of the monastery. The bishops may forward the charges to their prelates for necessary action under advice to them for a stipulated time, failing which, the bishops may take independent action as delegates of the Holy See and punish them accordingly. They can also take cognisance of their misconduct and punish them when these are committed by the regulars who live outside the convents or are fugitives or are outside the precincts or even on extended leave and in far away places where they cannot be visited by their prelates.

I, further order that all these rules, which are determined by Pontifical Council and bulls, be faithfully obeyed and abided by, and for this purpose all bishops are accordingly informed that they may cause them to be strictly adhered to not only by virtue of their own jurisdiction but by the delegated one which I as Administrator of the Order of Christ do hereby delegate.

Similarly, all the regular prelates should also faithfully abide by all the above. Otherwise, you shall incur my displeasure and I shall proceed against you in accordance with the royal powers vested on me. And I order all the governors and ministers to render all help and assistance to the bishops who may request it in the discharge of my royal resolution and I likewise order the High Courts in my dominions not to take cognisance of any appeal that may be filed by the regulars on the jurisdiction of the bishops, which has been determined already.

The Board of Conscience and Orders is to record and cause execution of what pertains to them.

Salvaterra dos Magos,
5 March 1779.
Seal of H. Majesty.

At Our Lady of Help,
18 March 1779.
Martinho de Mello e Castro.

This decree was published by us in the book *A jurisdicção diocesana do bispado de S. Thomé de Meliapore nas Possessões Inglezas e Francezas,* p. 393, doc. no. 38, but here it is more elaborate because it is the copy which we found annexed to the previous edict.

Document No. 44

Letter from the Secretary of State, Martinho de Mello e Castro to the Bishop of Cochin.

Your Lordship,

The Queen, Our Lady, makes known to you by the edict on the Church that was dispatched to you the guidelines that will be in force in the appointments in that Sé Primate of that capital as well as in the parishes and other benefices which are concerned with the salvation of the souls, and also in the very important matter of the missions.

You will notice that the native priests of India are the ones who are the most contemplated in the distribution of the positions and ecclesiastical posts, and on the issue, I need to caution you that the debasement and contempt with which the natives have so far been treated in that State is the real cause for the sluggishness and uselessness which is often attributed to them resulting in H. Majesty having 200,000 and more of both sexes, useless for the service of the Church, the Crown and the State in the provinces of Goa, Salcete and Bardez.

Therefore, H. Majesty thought that the only way to turn those vassals useful was to motivate them and take them out of the sluggishness they are in, by sharing with them the work in the churches, for which they seem to have the right inclination (as they have for military and civil duties) in accordance with the merits and ability which each native may show for such employment, the difference in colour being no reason to disqualify them as is presently done.

This being the objective, H. Majesty determined that the natives of Goa should be contemplated for the offices in the Sé and parishes, but as you can see these are to be judiciously effected i.e. only those who are capable of discharging their duties should be appointed. In order that you may proceed with proper knowledge of the issue I feel it is indispensable that immediately on your arrival in Goa you try to find the number of native priests in that State and the education, virtues, etc. of each of them, making a list and a general roll of their names with remarks in the margin about their qualifications, education, qualities (good or bad) of each.

It is true that after many years there has been a great laxity in conferring the Sacred Orders in India without proper care being taken in the choice of persons for these orders. You will, therefore, notice that many or perhaps a great number of them are unfit for office of any type but at the same time it may be probable that among that great number of priests, you may find some with necessary qualities and merits to qualify for the service of the Church.

Your predecessor, in compliance with the orders he carried from this Court in the year 1774, appointed many native priests not only in parishes of Goa, Salcete and Bardez, many of whom are presently confirmed in their posts, but also sent administrators and missionaries from the same natives to missions of Cochin, Timor and Solor and to Mozambique and Rios de Senna. Till now there have not been any reports in this Court about those priests found wanting in any way, nor have any complaints been received against them from the people. One may, therefore, conclude that though there might be some who are difficult to live with and are useless there are many who are good for the service of the Sé and of the parishes.

These are the favours that H. Majesty desires should be presently conferred on them in conformity with the provisions of the edict which deals with such appointments. I must also warn you that there have been, and still are, fights between native priests of the State and the regular orders established there. However, since according to the terms of the notices and resolutions of 26 May 1759, 2 April 1761 and of 23 April 1763 and the edict of 7 April 1774, and recently in the orders issued by H. Majesty in the edict, which is enclosed herewith, you have been asked to institute, confer benefices and appoint secular priests born in India in all the parishes. You will have to carry out these orders very strictly, referring only such representations to H. Majesty that you may receive from regulars and natives so that H. Majesty may make known her desire.

Regarding the missions, I must say that though they are entrusted to the regular orders of St. Dominic, Graça, St. Francis, St. Felippe Neri, and though the august monarchs, predecessors of our Queen, might have neglected the zeal and care that those orders should have taken to hold, expand and promote our holy Catholic faith in those missions through missionaries expressly sent, gifted with learning and virtues and with a truly apostolic spirit, a sad and inexorable experience has shown just the opposite. The missions of Timor, Solor, Mozambique and Rios de Senna, under the Dominicans, those of Bengal under those of Graça, those of Cochin and the Malabar Coast under the Franciscans and those of Ceylon under the priests of St. Felippe Neri respectively, are all reduced to a pitiful condition barring the last one where the scandals are not public.

The remedy for these great evils is what our Majesty has prescribed in her edict and which is mentioned above. There is nothing more to add in this regard except to draw your special attention to the fact that the missions of Timor and Solor, being part of various kingdoms, each comprising of a small area and consequently having many parishes, need many priests. Similarly, the missions of Mozambique and Rios de Senna have a considerable number of parish churches and missionaries have accordingly to be proportionate depending on the greater or smaller number of them. In the case of Goa there is a lack of sufficient Dominicans. To make up for this shortage we have to bring missionaries from other orders, be they seculars or regulars, because it is unjust and it should never be allowed to happen that for lack of religious of a particular Order, the missions that are entrusted to them should suffer and remain without pastors to administer the sacraments.

This very same consideration should be given to the Franciscans. We are told that the number of parishes, along the Malabar Coast or in the kingdom of Travancore and along the Fishery Coast have as many as one hundred and forty churches of which seven since their foundation were administered by Franciscans. Ninety four belonged to the Society of

Jesus, which on orders from the Secretary of State dated 30 April 1772 were transferred to the Franciscans. Thirty nine still continue to be administered by the Jesuits in the guise of secular priests. In proportion to the parish priests of those churches who keep on dying or retiring, the Franciscans take over the parishes. After you make a study of the number of churches and compare those of the Franciscans established in the convents of Goa and the adjacent provinces, you will soon realise how many thousands of Christians who live along the Malabar Coast are forsaken and left in extreme need of pastors to administer the sacraments and teach them the mysteries of our faith. Despite this, the said Franciscans have requested that 24 parishes in the Bardez province be given to them.[4] It would be morally impossible for them to simultaneously look after these and satisfy the big number that exists along the Malabar Coast.

I am afraid you will find that what has been told about the Dominicans and Franciscans is also true of the missions under those of Graça and of the Congregation of St. Felippe Neri.

Care has to be taken to ensure that the missions entrusted to one order are not interferred with by other religious or secular priests and to send to those missions only persons who are able and exemplary, those who will edify and not scandalize, those who will shepherd the flock and not shear its wool, in short, those who will be good shepherds and not voracious wolves. All this till now has had little attention of the respective prelates and the reports and documents that exist in this Secretariat are constant reminders of the deplorable situation in which that said missions are and of how much vigilance and pastoral care they require.

God protect you.

Salvaterra dos Magos,
6 March 1779.
Martinho de Mello e Castro.
His Lordship, the Bishop of Cochin.

Livro das Monções, no. 168, fl. 113.

Document No. 45

Another

Your Lordship,

In the letter that I have just written to you and which begins with the words "The Queen, Our Lady, indicates ..." you will find some general guidelines on the very important subject of the missions. Continuing with the same subject in this letter I will recapitulate the points I discussed with you in the Secretariat which when placed before H. Majesty, she was pleased to approve. She instructs you to evince your best efforts to have them duly enforced and observed.

Fr. Victorino de St. Joseph, a religious of the Dominican order, very exemplary, learned, virtuous and with apostolic zeal, has been appointed by H. Majesty as episcopal Administrator of the jurisdiction of Mozambique and Rios de Senna to visit, discipline and correct anything that he may find amiss in the missions and deserving of correction or punishment. You must instruct him to submit to you a yearly report on the behaviour, life and habits of each of the missionaries employed in those missions and on the state of affairs of the missions in which each is.

There are at Mozambique and Rios de Senna 12 or 13 parishes entrusted to the Dominicans besides 2 hospitals of the same Order, one at Mozambique and the other at Rios de Senna. These churches require a minimum of 18 to 20 missionaries that you will have to send immediately to that land all at one time or in batches as circumstances may demand. The appointments must, however, precede personal scrutiny, tests and anything else that H. Majesty has determined in the edict which deals with this subject. They must refrain from sending any missionary of any Order that does not qualify for a ministry of that importance and does not come within the framework of the edict issued by H. Majesty.

The bishopric of Malacca is vacant and, therefore, it is necessary to have there an episcopal governor, and while a decision is not taken by H. Majesty on the appointment of a bishop, you may appoint Fr. Joaquim de Santa Anna, a Dominican residing at Macau, about whom the Provincial gave very good recommendations. The said religious should be asked to take special care of the missions of Timor and Solor and follow the same instructions as given to the episcopal Administrator of Mozambique.

As the missions of Timor and Solor comprise of 12 to 13 churches and as these are located in the kingdoms of various kings, they will require at least 20 missionaries, which have not been engaged for lack of priests, and since Goa may not have as many Dominicans suitable for that ministry, you may after ascertaining the extent of the shortage, fill them up with priests of other Orders or with secular priests, European or native as determined in the preceeding letter. You may do this not only with regard to Dominican Order in Mozambique and Rios de Senna but also with regard to other Orders.

Considering the fact that there are 140 churches in the missions of Cochin, Cannanore, the Fishery and the Malabar Coasts, all of them entrusted to Franciscans, you will realise the great number of missionaries that we will require in those places. As I have mentioned in my other letter, it is imperative to have, at least in Cochin, a vicar-general endowed with such virtues and zeal on whom we may confidently entrust such vast and extensive areas and who could also inform you of more important things that take place there with regard to the missions.

Even though from the letters from the Archbishop of Goa one learns that the Bishop of Mylapore is still alive, his advanced age will not permit him to take care as he should of his church and, under the circumstances, it would be worthwhile if you could write to the said Bishop and persuade him to appoint another person to look after it because without a bishop or because of his inability or the absence of a vicar-general to substitute him, nothing can be done which may be useful to the Church and to those forgotten and forsaken missions.

Regarding the number of missionaries to the missions of Cochin, Cannanore, the Fishery and Malabar Coasts and similarly to the bishopric of Mylapore, it is necessary that you discuss the issue and come to a final understanding with the Provincial of the Franciscans, about the total number of sufficiently qualified missionaries that he can spare for these missions enabling you thus to make alternate arrangements in case of need.

You must discuss with the Provincial of the Augustinians, who resides in Goa and who is in charge of the mission of Bengal, about which one has only good reports in this court, and ascertain from him how many parish churches there are in those missions, what the missions consist of, how many missionaries are presently there, the conduct, life and habits of each one of them, the number of parishioners belonging to each parish and, whether a vicar-general with the same authority and power for the purpose mentioned above will be of any practical use to the Church and to the Christians.

Regarding the mission on the island of Ceylon, it is equally imperative that you consult this matter with the Prepositor of the Congregation of St. Felippe Neri requesting from him a list of the number of churches, parishes, the composition of the missions, the number of missionaries employed to assist the many good Christians living on that important island and advising him to send as many missionaries that he may feel are necessary in those missions which being scattered have experienced a great shortage of ministers of the Gospel.

Since the immediate danger of laxity is the commerce that the missionaries indulge in under the guise of receiving from the country provisions such as ivory, sandalwood, powdered gold, silk, cotton and other fabrics, and since alms and donations that people contribute for the upkeep of the missionaries are exchanged for other goods necessary for life, like clothing and other urgent needs, and in order to remove such excuses from the missionaries, they must be compelled either by your direct order or by virtue of their obedience to their prelates, by means that you may deem more legal and efficacious, to hand over to their vicar-general and prelates the said provisions and donations received from the people. This must be done with the proviso that the vicar-general, after personally making the exchanges, will distribute among the missionaries all that they may need, limiting the distribution to what is indispensable and necessary for the maintenance and sustenance of the said missions and remitting the excess to their prelates, superiors or headquarters.

You must also prohibit the missionaries and vicars from keeping slaves and, if and when circumstances may so demand, you may allow them one slave each and with as much caution and moderation as is strictly required.

These being the measures taken in this court to give a beginning, in the State of India to the reforms of the regulars, who will be entrusted with the holy ministry of the missions. They will become deep-rooted and bear the fruits that H. Majesty so much desires, only if there is a direct involvement in it by the superior prelates. You must clearly draw their attention to the fact that the religious piety of our Queen, when she decided by letters dispatched by the Secretary of State on 20 April 1777 that the existing religious Orders that were in charge of the missions would be maintained, was not with the intention of allowing laxity that presently exists but that the prelates would join in your efforts to eradicate vices and establish virtue, propagate the doctrine of the gospel, not only with sermons but also with the purity of their actions and good examples.

God protect you.

Salvaterra dos Magos,
6 March 1779.
Martinho de Mello e Castro.
His Lordship, the bishop of Cochin.

Livro das Monções, no. 168, fl. 117.

Document No. 46

Another

Your Lordship,

Since you are expected, not only by virtue of the duties of your office of a pastoral minister but, more particularly, because you have been asked by the religious piety of our Queen to do your utmost and not fail in any way to help religion and virtue flourish in the missions of Asia and to root out all vices, it becomes necessary that we should not hide from you some of the vices which by their gravity deserve our special attention.

We have, in this Secretariat, many letters, complaints and representations together with some documents and proofs that all regular missionaries who are in charge of the missions routinely and openly carry a sort of business like the one normally carried in business houses. This business is as much of public knowledge as it is general and yet no action has been taken against them by their prelates. Therefore, it is evident that this business is carried out, if not with their full consent at least with their tacit knowledge and tolerance. This being so, what spiritual fruits can one expect from such missionaries who instead of occupying themselves with the work of the Church and the good of the souls, mix this sacred ministry with such profane interests? And, if it is a principle and a dogma of eternal truth that no one can serve God and Mammon at the same time, how can these missionaries be simultaneously ministers of God and businessmen?

It is therefore evident that as long as the prelates of the regular orders do not strictly (and not superficially) prohibit their subordinates from such sordid acts and if they do not sincerely join you in your efforts to eradicate this cancer, you may expect nothing in return but rocks and thorns for all your work and hardships.

Besides this scandalous abuse that has overtaken all missions and are diametrically opposed to the regular and monastic life and against all canons of the church, it is further learnt that the religious of the Dominican Order in the missions of Mozambique and Rios de Senna behave in a very disgusting and disorderly manner, as you yourself have heard in this Secretariat when letters from the Governor and Captain-General of India were read and as you will learn better when you reach Mozambique on your way to Goa.

The scandal that the said religious have created in the islands of Timor and Solor are also recorded in the investigations which were carried out there and submitted to the prelate of that order. It was found from the investigations that the spoils left by three of their religious were so immense that, after deducting a great portion as commissions to agents of this transactions and what was embezzled by others who did not miss the opportunity offered, the proceeds of the auction of what remained amounted to a staggering sum of 28,559 $ 800 *reis*, which is equal to 71,000 *cruzadas*. It is incredible that in such a small, poor and miserable mission, three missionaries had the ability to acquire so fabulous a fortune as mentioned above. And if this could happen in Timor and Solor, one wonders how much money other missionaries of the same order at Mozambique and Rios de Senna would have made with precious articles like gold and ivory which abound in those areas and which are the major items of their trade and commerce.

If despite these misdeeds they had at least endeavoured to teach people the mysteries of our faith showing them the duties of a good Christian and Catholic, drawing them away from sins and vices, as they were taught in their first years, one could at least say that though the missionaries had lost themselves, they did not fail to help and work for the salvation of their herd. But unfortunately what one finds is that they took greater care in shearing the wool and the skin without in the least worrying about their temporal and eternal damnation and ruin as one can gauge from the annexure nos. 1 and 2 which will give you a fair idea of the deplorable state to which the missions of Timor and Solor have been reduced.

With regard to the missions of Cochin, Malabar Coast, the kingdom of Travancore and the Fishery Coast, all under the Franciscans, it is further noticed that disorders and laxity are rampant, both in business as in other misconducts. From the translation, annexed herewith at no. 3, of a letter written by the Christians of the archbishopric of Cochin, you will find the extent of disregard of their duties as religious and ministers of the gospel, and the debauchery in which those missionaries live.[5]

Regarding the missions of Bengal, under the regulars of St. Augustine, it is said that it is very rare to find a missionary sent who is not involved in some open and free business, just like an ordinary shopkeeper, and they are accused of so many other misdeeds. Soon after your arrival in Goa, you should try to ascertain what is happening in those more or less remote and abandoned missions.

One of the proofs that show the little care that the prelates of St. Augustine have towards their church, is the appointment of Fr. João de S. Anna, who is presently in Lisbon, as inspector of the missions. This religious, after committing many misdemeanours in Lisbon was imprisoned, and after escaping from prison, remained a vagabond and apostate going from province to province in the kingdom. Pretending to be a brother of some important person in Portugal, he managed to dupe many persons, using this ploy to extort money and commit other misdeeds, until he was arrested a second time and put in the prison of his own Order. They eventually managed to get rid of him sending him to India where he continued to live the same way as in Portugal, committing, however, greater misdeeds and disorders and behaving scandalously.

You will find a resumé of all this in the summary attached as annexure no. 4, in which you will read of the horrible things he did which you should examine with circumspection because if they are proved they cannot remain without a severe and exemplary punishment.

We also learn there is a deep-felt need of missionaries on the island of Ceylon, under the Congregation of St. Felippe Neri, seen by the incessant outcry of the Christians living on that island and begging for priests. The missionaries here are, doubtlessly, more exemplary in their behaviour, conduct and modesty and in this they distinguish themselves from all other regular Orders in India, but it is equally true that in business transactions, profits and trade, they not only follow in the footsteps of the others, but surpass them all, though their business is not carried out in the open but through third parties, which is easy, because of the confidence they have in Indian settlers who are mostly their own relatives and compatriots. That is the reason why the body of this Congregation is the richest and wealthiest of all others in Goa.

But the means they use for acquisition of wealth is as much irregular as that used by the other Orders.

They live in constant fights and disunity among themselves and are well-known for breaking the seal of secrecy, as you will note from the attached annexure nos. 5-10, where among other accusations there are five made by as many priests of the same Congregation against their Superior and other religious. If these accusations are true, then they amount to a crime because it goes against the very foundations of our faith which is the Sacrament of penitence. If, on the other hand, they are false, there cannot be a bigger perversity than the one shown by the accusers, imputing such grave offences on their own prelates and colleagues, with the sole aim of denigrating them. The gravity of this matter requires that you examine the issue, with circumspection, in order that you may proceed with the guilty so that such behaviour against the tenets of the Church are stopped or the perverse accusers, who invented the offences, are duly punished.

This, in short, is the final idea that I can give you on the state of the missions and missionaries in India, and from it you will note how much the churches in Asia need your pastoral care, especially in the choice of good ministers of gospel, without which all your efforts will be in vain.

God protect you.

Salvaterra dos Magos,
6 March 1779.
Martinho de Mello e Castro.
His Lordship, the Bishop of Cochin.

Livro das Monções, no. 168, fl. 121.

Document No. 47

Letter from the Secretary of State Martinho ae Mello e Castro to the Archbishop of Goa and Primate of the East.

Your Lordship,

The Queen, Our Lady, has received representations from the Superior and from some religious of the Congregation of Oratory of Goa, that you have issued the order that you carried from this kingdom, empowering you to take away from them and from other Orders the missions entrusted to them, and that the missions entrusted to the Dominicans have already been withdrawn by you.

Since H. Majesty is not aware of the reasons under which these orders were based and considering the zeal that those religious have shown in propagating the gospel and protecting the Church against enemies of our faith and the religion that we profess, particularly, in the island of Ceylon, H. Majesty orders that all the missions so withdrawn from the religious of the Congregation of Oratory and from the Dominicans as well as from all other Orders, be given back, forthwith restoring the missions to the position prevailing at the time of your arrival in Goa, and further, that you shall not make any changes in the said missions without the express orders from H. Majesty.

God protect you.

Palace of Our Lady of Help,
20 April 1777.
Martinho de Mello e Castro.

Letter from the Secretary of the State to the Governor of India.

From the enclosed copy you will note the order that H. Majesty issued to the Archbishop of that city regarding the representations addressed to her by the Superior and by some religious of the Congregation of Oratory.

This is sent for your information and action to see that these orders of H. Majesty are carried out.

God protect you.

Palace of Our Lady of Help,
20 April 1777.
Martinho de Mello e Castro.
Dom José Pedro da Camara.

Livro das Monções, no. 158, fls. 944, 945.

Letter from the Governor of India to the Secretary of the State Martinho de Mello e Castro.

Your Excellency,

I acknowledge receipt of your letter informing me of the order issued by

H. Majesty to the Archbishop Primate of Goa to return the missions to the Congregation of Oratory to the Dominicans and to other Orders restoring the missions to the same position as prevailed when the Archbishop arrived in Goa.

The Lady having ordered me to see that her orders were duly executed, I wrote a letter to the Prelate, a copy of which is attached as annexure no. 1, in which I offered to extend all my assistance to him and requested him to confirm having executed the royal orders.

The Prelate sent me his reply which you will find as annexure no. 2 and which I am sending to you so that I may receive further orders from H. Majesty.

God keep you for many years.

Goa, 30 April 1778.
Seal of the Governor.

Livro das Monções, no. 158, fl. 278.

ANNEXURE 1

Letter from the Governor to the Archbishop.

Your Lordship,

You will see from the copy of the letter from Martinho de Mello e Castro, Secretary of the office of the Navy and Overseas Affairs, and also from the copy of the letter written to you, which goes herewith attached, that the Queen, our Lady, wishes that I extend to you all help in seeing that her royal orders are duly executed.

These orders enjoin you to restore all the missions to the position existing at the time of your arrival in Goa and to entrust them back to the religious of the Congregation of Oratory, to the Dominicans and to the other religious from whom they were withdrawn. I inform you that I am ready to be of any assistance in seeing that the royal orders are carried out and I am confident that Your Lordship will not fail to execute them, with your usual and exemplary obedience.

Please confirm, in writing, the execution of the orders that I may be satisfied of having discharged my duty.

God protect you for many years.

Panjim, 6 April 1778.
Yours faithfully,
D. José Pedro da Camara
His Lordship Archbishop and Primate o he East.

Livro das Monções, no. 158, fl. 279.

ANNEXURE 2

Reply from the Archbishop.

Your Excellency,

I refer to your letter dated the 6th instant, which I had the honour to receive last evening offering your entire assistance to me in the execution of the orders of H. Majesty regarding the restitution to the priests of the Congregation of Oratory, to the Dominicans and to the other communities of all the missions earlier withdrawn from them, and the restoration of the missions to the same position prevailing at the time of my arrival in Goa, and also prohibiting me from making any changes in the said missions without the express orders from H. Majesty. You also request me to confirm the execution of those orders in writing that you may satisfy yourself of having discharged your duties.

In reply, I enclose a copy of the letters sent by me to the Superior Prelates of the Orders of St. Dominic, St. Augustine, St. Francis, Mother of God, and to the Superior of the Congregation of Oratory, and also the copy of an identical letter sent by me in reply to some representation submitted by the Provincial of St. Augustine to be forwarded to Bengal and three others submitted by the Franciscan Provincial to be forwarded to Cochin, Cannanore and Mylapore in full compliance of the orders of H. Majesty

In case my action does not meet with your approval, I would appreciate if you could suggest another more adequate one so that I may execute it to your satisfaction and in full compliance of the royal orders.

I thought that my action in this respect was already known as by my letter of 27 February 1778 and addressed to the same minister and Secretary of State who advised me of the above order, I had not only confirmed that I was taking the necessary steps to restore the missions to the regulars and to the Congregations, as H. Majesty desired, but I also inquired from him if the said order restricted itself only to the missions or if I could extend it also to restore the churches to the regulars, from whom they had been withdrawn by virtue of the edict of 7 April 1774 and given to secular priests in accordance with the provisions of the same edict which in fact is the only source that empowers me to manage the churches of H. Majesty in Goa as Governor and life Administrator of the mastership and cavalry of the military order of Jesus Christ.

God protect you for many years.

Goa, 7 April 1778.
Yours faithfully,
Archbishop Primate of the East
His Excellency the Governor and Captain-General.

Livro das Monções, no. 158, fl. 280.

Copy of the letter addressed to the Superior Prelates of the sacred Orders of St Dominic, St. Augustine, St. Francis, to the Provincial of Mother of God, and Superiors of the Congregation of Goa regarding the restoration of the mission.

In accordance with the orders of H. Majesty whom God has in his mansion, when we began to govern this diocese, both in the instructions issued in royal name and confirmed by royal letter of 10 February 1774, as well as in the edict of 7 April of the same year, we were instructed that all churches and even those which previously were known as missions though they were actually parishes, should be filled up by us on her behalf. We sent you a letter dated 11 February 1775, advising you of the contents of that letter and requested you to submit a correct list of all the churches and of the parish priests whom we had appointed on temporary basis until a final decision to the contrary was taken in that respect. But since we have now received a letter from the Secretary of State dated 20 April of last year, in terms of which H. Majesty requires us to restore to all religious communities the missions that were taken from them bringing the missions to the position that prevailed at the time we arrived in Goa and that we should not bring about any changes in the missions without her express orders, we therefore advise you that the contents of our letter dated 11 February 1775 should be disregarded and instead in execution of fresh orders from H. Majesty, you are required to strictly abide by the royal orders at your early convenience.

God protect you.

Panjim, 3 March 1778.

Livro das Monções, no. 158, fl. 281.

Copy of the decision given on the representation submitted by the Vicar Provincial of the Order of St. Augustine and three others by the Provincial of St. Francis giving no objection to their subordinates to continue in the missions in the churches of Mylapore, Cannanore and Cochin.

By letter received by us from the Secretary of State dated 20 April of last year we were informed of the orders of H. Majesty that we should return all the missions taken from various religious communities and restore them to the position prevailing at the time of our arrival in Goa and that no change should be effected without her express orders; and as by our letter of 3 March 1778 of the same year, we had advised all the major prelates of the said communities of our prompt obedience to all the clauses mentioned therein, we accordingly enjoined all of you to strictly follow throughout the missions the royal orders as soon as conveniently possible. We feel that in the meantime this can be taken as our final decision on your present representation until their Lordships the Bishops, our co-Provincials and Governors of the suffragan bishoprics are not advised on this issue, after which, they may act as they deem necessary.

Livro das Monções, no. 158, fl. 282.

Letter from the Governor to the Secretary of State Martinho de Mello e Castro.

In execution of the order of H. Majesty, the Archbishop Primate has restored the mission of Timor to the Dominicans, those of the kingdom of Travancore to the Franciscans and those of Bengal to St. Augustine, some of the religious of their respective Orders are proceeding to their missions.

God protect you.

Goa, 28 April 1778.
Seal of the Governor

Livro das Monçoes, no. 158, fl. 81.

Document No. 48

Letter from Fr. Caetano Victorino de Faria to Rama Custam Naik, of Kumbarjua.

Mr. Rama Custam Naik & Co.
Lisbon, 4 April 1799.

I received, this monsoon, through our representative Mr. Rossi, three letters together with a statement of my accounts against some loans taken on my behalf by Mr. José Fructuoso.

In the same letter you confirm having received my letter of the corresponding monsoon and the copy of the earlier ones which caught the mail carried by the French vessel, bound for that port. In that letter I had informed you that I had received no money from José Fructuoso, your debtor, except the cloth sent, which is actually of no use to me because I do not deal in it. I received it solely to be of some help to my compatriot who would have otherwise lost his money if I had not decided to safeguard it in this way and also because another compatriot urged me to do this favour on your behalf because he knew you would lose the money if I had not extended my helping hand to protect you.

You state that you had not given me any authority to act on your behalf and I do not blame you for saying so because you do not profess that holy, true and unique law of Jesus Christ which is the only one that can open our eyes to see and follow the true path to our happiness and which has its foundations in charity which consists in loving God above all else and your neighbour as yourself for the love of God, our Creator and Redeemer. I have the good fortune of professing this holy law, through the infinite mercy of our Creator though I am unworthy. This law gives not only authority to help one's neighbour as I did for you but also enjoins that we do it the way we would wish ourselves.

If you had done the same for me as I have done for you I would not have condemned you for having done so but I would have remained ever grateful for the favour received for the love and interest taken without any special obligation or self-interest but only because of the affection for a compatriot.

Now I assure you with the purity of my heart that I shall not content myself only in safeguarding on your behalf this amount which I look down upon, and which would have otherwise been safe even if you had no accounts-book to confirm it, but also in assuring you of another bigger and incomparable happiness for which I have been fighting, for the past twenty two or more years and against all Europe which glories and turns your disgrace into their happiness, whilst gloating all the while in your lamentable ruin.

But I, as a true and good compatriot, will fight without being asked by you to find that happiness even at the risk of my life so that my compatriots may be truly happy because our Creator has made me realise the disgrace of our fatherland which has fallen into a lamentable blindness the kind of which does not exist in Europe.

I have endeavoured to wrest from the hands of Europeans our archbishoprics of Goa and India, which our Creator and Redeemer gave us eighteen thousand years ago, through his apostle St. Thomas and which Europe stole from us three hundred years ago, for their own worldly interests and to the detriment of our souls and salvation.

I shall take it away now against the wishes of entire Europe and this court not with my strength but with the omnipotent hand of our Creator and Redeemer, with the help of the Most Holy and Immaculate Mother of our Redeemer, who is our advocate, queen, protector and mother, and bring it to you to make you truly happy because this is my wish and also because, in his infinite kindness and mercy, our Redeemer wants to restore it to us, having pity on our plight and disgrace. I am going to baptize all Hindus, not only of Goa but of entire India, and I will give my life for them, so that they may be happy forever. Since I shall carry the books with me, I shall include the amount you say I owe you, and whatever I need to complete your work, I shall arrange here and will adjust with the amount that is due to you from the loans. I have written to Fr. Pedro Delgado, ex-Superior of the Congregation to whom I have sent one of the statements sent by you, to examine it against your books. He will be meeting you in this connection.

Even if I had wanted to indicate the price of the goods that you sent, it would not be possible, because the goods came mixed and damaged and they are not worth half the price.

You will lose much if you want me to sell. On the contrary, if I keep what is left, your money will be safe, though delayed. This is the best solution for you and entirely to your benefit and that of the fatherland and to my glory.

I wish you all happiness and hope to embrace you fondly and with all my heart, which is full of love for you. The Divine Redeemer will make you realise this sincere, pure and affectionate truth, which has no other interest than your happiness.

God protect you for many years.

Lisbon, 4 April 1779.
Your humble servant
Dr. Caetano Victorino de Faria

On the reverse: Received 21 December 1779, via *Conceição* docked on 19th.

Document No. 49

Certificate

I, the undersigned, acting Vicar of the church of Candolim, after checking the records of baptism of this church, find recorded on the reverse of fl. 123, the following:

"On 7 June 1756, I, Fr. Manoel de Jesus e Maria with permission from Rev. Fr. Manoel de Assumpção, Rector of this Church of Our Lady of Hope of Candolim, baptized and anointed with holy oils, Joseph Custodio, born eight days ago, son of Caetano Victorino de Faria and of Rosa de Souza. Fr. João Simões, resident of Serula and Celestina Maria Luisa de Souza, resident of this village, were his godparents.

Fr. Manoel de Jesus e Maria".

This is a true copy of the records in the book and it is issued at the request of Genezano António João de Souza.

Parochial House, Candolim.
22 April 1865.
The acting Vicar, Custodio Mathias do Rosario Dias.

Ultramar of 18 May 1865

Document No. 50

Theologicae Propositiones de Existentia Dei, Deo Uno et Divina Revelatione

Sub Augustissimis auspiciis Fidelissimorum Regum
Portugalliae et Algarbiorum
Mariae Franciscae et Petri III
A Josepho Custodio de Faria Goano
In collegio Urbano de Propaganda Fide Alumno
Defendendae
Praeside F. Thoma Maria Cerboni

Ordinis Praedicatorum Sacrae Theologiae Magistro & professore
in eodem Collegio
Romae CIC DCC LXXX
Tipis Sac. Congregationis de Propaganda Fide
Praesidium Adprobatione

Mariae Franciscae et Petro III
Portugalliae Algarbiorumque
Regibus Fidelissimis
PIIS Augustis Pacificis Potentissimis
Christianae Rei Amplificatoribus
Literarum Bonarumque Artium
Patronis Munificentissimis
Istas De Religione Theses
Suae in Ipsos Observantiae Memorisq Animi
Pro Immortalibus Beneficiis
In Se Petremque Suum Conlatis
Testimonium Sempiternum
Iosephus Custodius De Faria Goanus
In Colegio, Urbano De Propaganda Fide
ALUMNVS
OCQLM

Theological Themes on the Existence of God, One God and Divine Revelation

to be defended
under the High Patronage of the Most Faithful
Kings of Portugal and of the Algarves,
Mary Francis and Peter III
by Joseph Custodia de Faria from Goa,
student in the Urban College of Propaganda Fide
under the presidentship of
P. Thomas Maria Cerboni,
of the Order of Preachers,
Master of Sacred Theology and Professor
in the same College, Rome 1780.
From the Printing Press of
the Sacred Congregation of Propaganda Fide
with the approval of the Presidents.

To Mary Francis and Peter III
Kings of Portugal and of the Algarves
The Most Faithful Pious, August, Peaceful,
Most Powerful Propagators of the Christian Religion
Most Munificent Patrons of Letters and Arts

Joseph Custodia de Faria, from Goa,
Student in the Urban College of Propaganda Fide
Dedicates this thesis on religion
As a perennial testimony
Of his submission and gratitude
For the everlasting benefits
Conferred on him and on his father
OCQLM

Most Faithful Kings

I deem that no one who will come to know the reason and motives behind my decision to dedicate and address this my theological debate to Your Majesties, Most Faithful Kings, will attribute it to temerity or ambition, but will confess that it was done by dint of plain sense of duty. Which duty is in fact more necessary than to attribute to each one one's own due? On the other hand, what can ever flow from me, chiefly in this field, that does not belong to you in virtue of hereditary rights? For when as a young man I came to Rome from Goa, the capital city of the Portuguese empire, in the East Indies, in order to equip myself in this centre of religion and wisdom, so that, on my return to the motherland, I would be able to promote the Christian cause within my limited means, under God's protection, it was through the outstanding favour of your very august predecessor, Joseph I that I was admitted to the world-renowed Pontifical College of the Propaganda Fide, in order to be more fittingly trained, both in spiritual and literary matters. Thus since that time I decided to give, at the end of my studies, a public demonstration of my proficiency in theological subjects and to offer to the Most Benevolent King this small token, to express that I owe to him alone my literary proficiency, if any. This gesture would not seem to be worthy either of the majesty of such a great prince or the benefits that I had received, it was becoming to express my deep gratitude towards him, as I judged it to be my duty not to neglect any occasion to bear witness to it. It is true that the invincible king departed from this troubled world long before I spent the due time in the study of theology. That is why so to say the fruit of my studies, which I was unable to offer to Joseph I, I do now offer to you who are heirs to his dignity and virtue and I would like to request you that, on account of your highest benevolence towards me and my father, this my debate be adorned by your high patronage. This my debate regards the whole theology against the perversity which in this present age not only crawls secretly in many places, for the ruin of mankind, but also rages openly and, still worse, spreads more widely day by day. The thesis I selected to be defended are taken from the distorted sophisms of the most wicked men and I am confident that my decision in their selection will meet with your approval. As for me there is no reason whatsoever not to be confident. For, how few are there who fail to acknowledge that, the great variety of exalted deeds performed by you, in no other matter you work harder than to see that the Catholic faith which was welcomed, in the Portuguese empire, from its first beginnings with utmost diligence and kept unstained by any wickedness or superstitions, may continue to be strong and actively propagated? True, it is your deep conviction that it is not so much from the dissertations of the very sagacious men about the best way of ruling but rather from family upbringing and this you learned also from the examples about your illustrious predecessors — that this safety and security of human society are encompassed by one bond of the integral religion and that the empires which lacked this foundation are unable to stand for a long time. Thus as soon as you assume the reins of the kingdom amidst the unbelievable jubilation of the Portuguese people to whom your virtue was well-proved and since long known, you concentrated your whole attention and diligence in defending and propagating the religion. Witness to this is America where due to your munificence the gospel preachers of this humble and exalted king extend further day by day the confines of the Catholic Church. To this is the witness of Africa where no people or nation under your most prosperous empire is found without being illumined by the most radiant light of justice. Witness to this in Asia is the city of Goa itself, where a move by some people trying to restore the already uprooted superstitions was recently crushed by your authority, amidst public jubilation. Witness to this is this Congregation of the most eminent Cardinals to which in your extensive jurisdiction and its neighbouring territories you most willingly extend every help, means and patronage in the very many and important matters pertaining to the propagation or strengthening of the faith. And what should I say about Portugal? Is there any city, fort, beach or bay where do not exist rich monuments of your piety towards God? True, I proceeded imprudently much further than it was convenient risking to tarnish, on account of the poverty of my language the splendour and dignity of the very great and beautiful works. On this score I leave aside what I could mention here regarding the dedication and munificence with which you deal with the people under your care regarding the wonderful constancy in the defence of divine and human law as well as regarding the unique ability in dealing with internal and external matters and still regarding their extreme solicitude in promoting science and art which contribute to the needs and comforts of human life and finally regarding the remaining virtues by which the great expectations you had raised about your person, you not only upkeep but exceed a long way off. All the above I leave to be praised by others endowed with more abundant and forceful eloquence in order to be bequeathed to everlasting human memory. As so, returning to the beginning of this my discourse and being sure of your ardent desire to preserve and propagate the Catholic faith, a sure hope dawned in me that this my debate against wickedness by its very thing would be wholly acceptable to you and that you would encompass me with your most powerful patronage as I am about to start the fight against the most wicked enemies of religion. In case you will be so kind, as your benevolence towards me expressed in numerous and unequivocal signs ensures, then the benefits I already received and by which you bound me forever to yourself will attain their completion. From my part as I find myself in such unequal a condition and nothing to offer in return besides my will throughout my life, I shall be as extremely grateful as possible to you and I shall not neglect to raise to God wishes and prayers so that he may keep you for a long time safe and secure for the prosperity of the Portuguese empire.

Document No. 51

Letter from the Marquis of Pombal and the decision on the representation made by the Municipal Council of Salcete to H. Majesty on military service. An extract from the book Memorial, p. 179.

The petition submitted by the Municipal Council, dated 1 March of last year, was presented to the King.

For the first time, he saw a nation debasing itself before their own sovereign, firstly, confessing the secret weakness of their bodies and souls and belittling themselves in the general esteem of the public; secondly, showing their ignorance or pretending not to know the first principles of union and civil society, which requires every vassal to risk his life in the defence of his king, of his fatherland, and of the lives and properties of his countrymen; and thirdly, refusing to improve themselves in social positions or to increase their earnings like those in military professions who have earned and built up their social position and that of their families and have risen in the estimation of their monarch and were thus elevated to nobility. Fourthly, he saw the nation pretending not to know that military profession is not all-exhaustive, because in all monarchies where there are soldiers there is also a large court to assist the king, a big number of businessmen who fill the coffers of the kingdom, an infinite number of farmers, agriculturists and workmen who till the fields, a great number of artisans in all trades, and another big number of trainees who learn, all this being compatible with military service, because there are certain inflexible rules for recruitment and joining the services, and with such restraint that if one compares the small number of those who leave with those that remain, the former is but an insignificant parcel of the latter, and this being the rule of moderation, which the Governor and Captain-General of that State has been recommended to follow in India, H. Majesty hopes that as soon as the council realises the absurdity of their claim they will raise their spirits from the despondency in which they have fallen and will encourage the most distinguished sons of Brahmins and Kshatriyas to enlist, as it is done here by the sons of Marquises, Counts and persons of high society, and will also motivate the children to climb in their positions, rise in ranks and in personal esteem of H. Majesty and his entire court, bringing credit and honour to the country, because this is the path followed by all high families who are, today, the most distinguished in Portugal. H. Majesty cannot believe that the Portuguese have greater spirit and are more capable of bringing honours than the Indians.

God protect you.

Lisbon, 28 February 1776.
Marquis of Pombal.

To the people and the Municipal Council of the province of Salcete.

This letter was printed in *Bosquejo Historico das Comunidades* by Felippe Nery Xavier, Part II, p. 106, with many typographical errors which were corrected here.

Document No. 52

Representation of the Municipal Council of Salcete to H. Majesty, 1779.

Dear Lady,

With deep respect and humble submission, this Municipal Council, through its representatives appointed (vide the attached resolution) humbly prostrates before the most merciful and royal feet of Your Majesty, and assuring you with reverence and fervour to obey your royal and benefical commands, take the liberty to submit before Your Majesty, the following:

This Council has, since the monsoon of 1770 been praying with all humility before the royal throne of Your Majesty to wipe away the tears that the people of this province have been shedding for reasons detailed in this petition.

This Council complained, in the monsoon of 1770, before the royal throne of Your Majesty, about a very great problem and grief that the Governor, D. João José de Mello, caused to the people of this province, in creating a Corps of 600 auxiliary soldiers, which the edict of 1761 required of every province, except the province of Salcete, to be raised if they were really needed.

The Viceroy, Count of Ega dispensed with this Corps after satisfying himself the reasons why this Corps had been disbanded earlier, after an experience of over a century. The first such Corps was raised by Viceroy D. António Paes de Sande in 1680, and the second by Viceroy, D. Francisco da Tavora, Count of Alvor, who had a personal experience, when he had to beat a hasty retreat, while challenged by the enemy known as Shambhaji, a Maratha who had advanced into the island of Santo Estevao because of the cowardice of the auxiliaries. A similar incident took place, with the same auxiliaries, on another occasion when they could withstand the charge made by Shambhaji's cavalry. On this occasion, some ran helter-skelter into the forest while the others were crushed under the horses hoofs without their being able to defend the Count-Viceroy who would have been taken prisoner had not D. Rodrigo da Costa come to his rescue with a horse and saved him. No sooner did he reach the capital than he ordered the disbanding of the Corps of Auxiliaries as they were found useless.

Besides this, during the rule of Viceroy Caetano de Mello e Castro, 400 native children of important people of this land, were chosen for some regiments and all those who embarked, unable to bear the hardships and inconveniences on board died, while the others fearing that the same fate awaited them, abandoned the country, parents and family, and in order that important families should not become extinct. Many were discharged from the army on the ostensible pretext of their unsuitability for military service. Viceroy D. Francisco José de Sampaio tried to create for the third time, a Corps of Auxiliaries, following the suggestions from his advisors and he promoted some to the rank of captains but within a short time finding them useless, he withdrew the scheme and stopped further appointments.

The Viceroy, Count of Sandomil, raised two Corps of Auxiliaries in the province, each consisting of 600 men, one Corps drawn from the sons of Brahmins and the other from the Kshatriyas, all from important families. One was called the Frontier Corps, and the other, the Naval Corps. Similarly, two Corps were raised in Bardez and two in Ilhas of Goa. With these 3,600 men, which seemed a formidable force, the Viceroy wrote to the kingdom not to send more troops, which the King D. João V used to send each year. But a great misfortune befell them. Soon as news that Goa was being defended by the daring auxiliaries spread across the Ghats, suddenly and without being expected in the least,

Venkata Rao, a petty Maratha ruler, attacked this province on 24 January 1739. None but two Portuguese were left in the square of Margao, one of whom died of a bullet from the enemy and the other, sword in hand, broke through the enemy and went to hide in Rachol. Everything that the auxiliaries were supposed to defend was lost, including themselves. Some of them died and others were fatally wounded, because they were useless and cowards.

At the same time, our enemy Bhosale attacked Bardez and the Corps of Auxiliaries there was unable to halt them. The State suffered a lot in this invasion because the enemy in both provinces remained for over six months and would not free the prisoners unless a ransom of 800 *xerafins* was paid. The State, eventually, made peace with the intervention of respectable people, one of them being Dr. José Pedro Emauz, who helped in the squabble. Whatever silver was found in the churches, and all that was saved from the forts of Rachol and Mormugao was melted in the hospital and a peace treaty signed after giving this silver to them in payment of the amount promised, the shortage being met from the contributions of the rich.

Even after this, the enemy was not prepared to withdraw their men. On the contrary, they kept 200 soldiers at Cuncolim and at Assolna. They began to harass the population of that province. Accordingly, the remaining auxiliary soldiers, with the help of orderlies were sent to repel them but without any success. They were forced to retreat with many wounded and dead each time the enemy advanced.

This is the reason why the State was forced to part with the fort of Chaul in the north, together with a surety of 300 *xerafins* which was raised by this and other provinces in 1738, when the north was under the siege of the Marathas. The fort was being held by the State as a possible means of exchange for the recovery of the villages of Cuncolim, Assolna and other districts. The peace treaty under which terms these villages were returned, was signed on 24 November 1741, as one can find out from the records of the peace treaty filed in the Secretariat of the State.

If Portugal had not stopped sending troops for eight years, on the sole consideration that people from Portugal and those from here were equal, this State and her people would not have suffered such disastrous calamities that made them go crying to the feet of the image of the Redeemer in the convent of Santa Monica of Goa, when it was decided to abandon this city and take shelter at Mormugao. It was, then, decided to take the sacred body of St. Francis to that fort and preparations were being made to carry it by boat. However, when the time came to carry the coffin to the boat, there was no coffin at all. After this miracle, everybody decided to stay and save the city, at any cost.[6]

At Rachol, where there were orders to abandon the village, either the image of Our Lady of Snows, dressed as a plain lady, would appear, at the sight of which, the enemy would prostrate almost in a faint of amazement and fear or the image of Child Jesus, dressed as a young soldier, would appear and repel the enemy thrust. Thus Rachol was saved.

With this proven uselessness of the auxiliaries, as soon as D. Luis Caetano de Almeida took over as Governor, he disbanded both the Frontier and Naval Corps, and forced the people and the elected members of the Council on pain of eight days prison in the fort of Rachol, to pass two resolutions; one to maintain 60 soldiers of the garrison and 10 artillery soldiers, with their respective officers, and the other to pay, with effect from January 1743, the wages of 208 sepoys including horses and their officers, which would cost around 28 *xerafins* per year. This, after the people had suffered three invasions from the Marathas which had left them completely bankrupt, to the extent that they had no money to maintain themselves and to repay their debts.

To help us, the Viceroy, Count of Sandomil prohibited the sale of properties of the debtors till March 1741 after realising that everybody had become so poor that the properties or estates of the needy depreciated to about 1/8 of its real value, as one can see from the records in the edict of 3 September 1740 (Doc. fl. 6). However, as soon as the above Viceroy was replaced by Governor D. Luis Caetano de Almeida he ordered the payment of 28 *xerafins*, forcing them to pass a new resolution though it had been repealed by decree (Doc. fl. 7) for reasons mentioned therein.

A decision, confirmed through a decree can overide, in this Court, a simple order, yet the elected members of the Council were put in prison at Rachol for eight days and on pain of hard labour. The people were made to pay for a period of 11 years upto 1753, 308 *xerafins* for the maintenance of the soldiers of the garrison and sepoys at the frontiers, through a simple order.

Afterwards, by a decision (vide Doc. fl. 8v) and order of the Viceroy, Marquis de Tavora, the sepoys were replaced by a company of cavalry, for the maintenance of which and also for that of two assistants, a large sum of money is being spent each year. After the King, D. José I (may God have him in his glory) was informed of this, by a second ordinance, he appointed Henrique da Cunha de Attaide to command the unit until his death or promotion to a higher rank, as one can see in the transcript (Doc. fl. 10).

Though the Captain died in the year 1758, i.e. 20 years ago, the company has not yet been disbanded, because it is being maintained at the cost of the miserable public who, in the five years of the lifetime of the Captain, spent 97,500 *xerafins* which in these 20 years have exceeded 390 *xerafins*. Besides this, for the past four years, this troop is not in this province at all, but at Panjim, used as the Governor's guards and, inspite of that, we keep on paying for their maintenance as well as that of the soldiers of garrison, which was supposed to be abolished in 1775, an amount which we regularly deposit in the Exchequer.

In addition, 40 of them have been turned into couriers of the General of the province, which is not really needed, as there are the sepoys engaged to do this kind of work and is also availed of by the Auditor-General. Besides the large sum of money that the people are contributing annually, after the disbandment of the Corps of Auxiliaries, from 1580, the very vigilant Viceroy of this State stipulated that 200 Portuguese soldiers posted at the frontiers and sea front should be maintained by João Silva and his heirs to whom two villages of Cuncolim and Veroda were gifted and which today yield a net income of 30,000 *xerafins*. They were also required to defend the frontiers at their own cost with 100 soldiers and with guns and ammunition, and to contribute, proportionately, towards donations the same way as others did. (Cf. translated letters gifting the villages, Doc. fl. 11).

Similarly, three other villages namely, Assolna, Velim and Ambelim, with an income of 60 *xerafins* were also gifted to D. Pedro de Castro. These were administered by the religious of St. Ignatius of Loyola, on behalf of the college of Cochin, but after being confiscated, became property of H. Majesty. The villages have now been gifted, by royal letter from Viceroy D. Duarte de Menezes on condition that the owner should defend the creek and the dry area of Assolna with 100 white men, arms and ammunition at his cost because enemy ships frequently sail that side and can enter the province as it has no adequate defence. This is recorded in the gift letter (Doc. fl. 11v).

These landlords refused to contribute and did not arrange men to defend the coast as promised, therefore, the people and the Council submitted a representation to King D. João V who ordered them to adhere to all the terms and conditions. (Cf. copy of the letter, Doc. fl. 12) These orders and those sent in the next monsoon (in terms of which the Viceroy, Count of Ericeira was asked to put that province in proper state of defence, which could only be done if the landlords of the five villages were forced to keep the 200 soldiers, as agreed and to pay all their dues upto the present) were not carried out despite the fact that orders given by Your Majesty were issued immediately, and must override any decision of your ministers even if it was in favour of regulars. This is found recorded in the extracts of the letters (Doc. fl. 13), because the villages could not be defended, unless the promised defences were set up.

But, since there were not sufficient *lascarins* or sepoys or voluntary soldiers as was assured to Your Majesty by the Viceroy (Cf. his letter, Doc. fl. 12), on 24 January 1739 the enemy entered expectedly the five villages as they were contiguous to the frontier of the King of Sunda. They remained there for over two and half years with the result that the State lost this fort and its benefits, the people suffered untold miseries, but only the landlords found themselves richer by 90,000 *xerafins* which they saved because they did not have to pay for the defence of the land and they did not also pay their share of the donation and of their debts.

Prior to this, in 1753 when Custam Rao was at war during the governance of the Marquis of Tavora, the people of this Council paid 12 *xerafins* for 700 sepoys, sons of these five villages, whom they maintained so that the enemy should not invade the villages. This amount is still due to us.

Therefore, the regulars trained two Corps of Auxiliaries, one to defend the three villages of Assolna, Velim and Ambelim, and were known as Naval Corps, and the other to defend Cuncolim and Veroda and was known as Frontier Corps. This is found recorded in the terms of extinction (sub. sec. A & B, Doc. fl. 5). The latter replaced the 200 sepoys or *lascarins* at the frontier, and today they have been substituted by a Corps consisting of 60 horses, besides 60 garrison soldiers from the fort of Rachol, for which, since 1743, we paid 20 *xerafins* which added to 90 *xerafins* for the sevices towards the defence of this province, makes a total 118 *xerafins* which this province pays annually, only for the defence. Besides this we have other expenses like taxes, half taxes, interests and other payments which we refrain from mentioning, as it is outside the scope of this representation.

In addition to the money, the people of this Council also contributed with 240 men as volunteers in order to make a regiment in 1745, during the governance of Viceroy, Marquis of Alorna, as demanded by the Colonels and Captains. Some of these men were persuaded to join the services, others were rewarded, to pacify them. Similarly in 1760, during the governance of Viceroy, Count of Ega, we contributed with another 240 men, sons of Brahmins and Kshatriyas, born in this province. We also contributed with orderlies, whenever demanded, paying for their maintenance, arms and ammunition. On completion of their military duties, they would go back to their fields and maintain their families, in accordance with the royal letter of the most clement King, D. Pedro II (Doc. fl. 1 and Memorandum at fls. 2-3).

On these and other grounds, which may be taken as our pleadings, and which the people of this Council have submitted before the majestic throne of Your Majesty, we beseech, that our contribution of 28,000 *xerafins* be stopped because the Corps has automatically ceased to exist with the death of the Captain and even if it is being maintained at Panjim or elsewhere in Goa, the people should not be forced to pay for its maintenance. We also request the disbandment of the Corps of Auxiliaries, which was raised again, as this is composed of the same orderlies who are not paid their half wages, when not on duty or at home, nor their full wages, when on duty at the forts of Rachol or Mormugao, in 1771, as stipulated in the royal letter (fl. 1). These expenses by the State are superfluous because the people are ready to serve as orderlies, pay their maintenance, arms and ammunitions whenever called upon, and therefore they request that the general enrollment be stayed to avoid harassment from superior officers who create many problems for the auxiliary soldiers simply because they are their subordinates.

Instead of receiving a favourable reply, as eagerly awaited, the monsoon of September 1774 brought orders for recruitment for many regiments which was forcibly made, using violence and coercion, even dragging sons who had just received their minor orders, others who had just completed their philosophical and theological studies, others who were about to join the church and other religious convents, and still others who were about to follow their vocations, without making any distinction between sons of mechanics, tailors, masons, labourers, ordinary farmers, carpenters, blacksmiths and butchers, on the pretext that Your Majesty wanted to confer honours and even favour with kingdoms those who served the State, the only way for this being the army. In execution of this, they imprisoned parents and even fourth degree relatives of those unwilling to join, and drafted 396 men from the most important families, even middle-aged persons, and went about this in such a brutal and merciless way that, even today, neither has our grievance been redressed nor any action taken in the matter.

And when parents and wives approached the Governor, pleading with tears running down their eyes that Your Majesty never ordered that force and humiliations be used in the enlistment of our sons who were needed by us to look after our lands and continuation of their rights and royal undertakings, no decision was given nor any corrective measure taken, on the contrary, our representatives were jailed in the powder room for 22 days. When this grave insult and wrong was placed before the royal throne, in the same monsoon, Marquis of Pombal (fl. 13 of his letter)[17] reprimanded us on four counts that he found insulting in our representation, which, after all dealt only with the system of conferring honours, equating natives of Salcete with the Portuguese, rewarding them and their families for their military actions and of conferring titles and decorations on them and their families after serving Your Majesty satisfactorily.

If the said Marquis had examined the worth of a Portuguese vis-a-vis his Indian counterpart from the evaluations already made by knowledgeable persons, of his actions in campaigns in Asia, he would have easily accepted the decision of King D. Pedro II (fl. 1), but since he abolished everything and tried to establish a new system, he did precisely what had been given up earlier, as is clear from his reply of 28 February of 1776, where he brands our request as insults. We maintain it cannot be so for the following reasons:

(1) Because it is not a shame to confess before one's sovereign the reasons that compelled King D. Pedro II to establish the practice of exempting from military service, the sons of important persons who maintained themselves at their own cost and who always served the King when the occasion arose. This decision was taken 71 years ago, hence it is not something new nor something done for the first time, but something followed for over a century now. It would have been a manifest fraud, on the part of the people and this Council, to pretend before the most august lord, that we were a courageous lot and demand undeserved honours, and had the State relied on such deceitful assurances to defend the nation without the need of any help from the kingdom, we would have faced a similar calamity as the province did during the governance of Viceroy, Count of Sandomil, as it was mentioned earlier; and it was only because of regiment sent by H. Majesty, D. João V, that the State regained its lost prestige with the seizure of the fort of Sanguem in 1742 and the rout of the army of the Bhosale in 1745, and no native troop was deployed in this campaign. Therefore, in view of the above and the facts already known by all, can any one represent to Your Majesty that efforts put in by the natives are equal to that of the Portuguese?

(2) Because in a union and in a civil society vassals are bound to risk their lives in the defence of their monarch, their nation and the properties of their countrymen. All this has been fulfilled by the natives, both Brahmins and Kshatriyas, since time immemorial and they continue to do so, even now, as one can find from the chronicles and histories of military actions in Goa, because native soldiers and orderlies participated in all of them, with arms and ammunition at their own cost, including maintenance of the troops, risking their lives for the defence of the nation. Not to be lengthy, we will only recall the campaigns of Ponda, at the time of Viceroy, Count of Alvor, when everyone was in grave danger and many soldiers were taken prisoners and unable to bear the ill-treatment and whipping from the enemy were forced to sell their lands to buy their freedom. Similarly, at the time of three invasions, during the governance of Viceroy, Count of Sandomil, all the auxiliary soldiers were killed at the hands of the Marathas, and yet they did not discard their military uniforms. Others were taken as prisoners.

In the hostilities with Custam Rao, in 1753, during the governance of Marquis of Tavora, the orderlies accompanied the regiments and troops of Bardez, camped in that province, and marched against the enemy who had invaded the village of Cuncolim, belonging to the landlord, and other villages. They also guarded the frontiers with arms and ammunition at their own cost, without wages and provisions, thus serving the sovereign, the country and the countrymen, some helping with rations and arms in the forts of Rachol and Mormugao and others, who in peace time tilled their lands, enlisting in various regiments, in accordance with the Royal orders of the most pious King D. Pedro II (fl. 1).

But because they were of no help, on the contrary a hindrance to the regiments, allowing entry of the enemy through posts under their guard, they were withdrawn to the square and were replaced by a company of sepoys, for which the people spent 12,000 *xerafins*. Therefore, the Viceroy, Count of Ega, with this knowledge and experience he had during his governance, not to disobey the orders of the King, took only persons of officer's ranks refraining from taking any auxiliary soldiers.

(3) Because Portugal being a nation completely different from Asian nations, which have different castes like Brahmins, Kshatriyas, Sudras, Muslims, Malabaris and others, Asian nations can never have a union which one may consider homogeneous and this is the reason why the most pious king D. Pedro II ordered, by his royal letter (fl. 1) the extinction of mixed companies of native soldiers and Portuguese because of inherent differences. The two voluntary companies which offered to serve during

the governance of Viceroy, Marquis of Tavora, made no progress. On the contrary, they were disbanded as soon as the term of the government of the said Viceroy expired, as the Captains could no longer bear the rivalries among themselves and no lieutenant was promoted to Captain, but were transferred to other regiments with the Portuguese, and the subalterns were discharged.

What were the just reasons to deny promotion in ranks and wages to these military officers? Apparently, they were not as deserving as the Portuguese, therefore, they were kept behind in promotion. The value of a Portuguese soldier, who was put to fight the entire east, can never be surpassed by a native, nor will the natives ever attain high ranks and therefore, they will never be able to raise their names and that of their families. In this way, neither in justice or in merit can they ever shadow those soldiers of renown, ability and merit in all spheres, who have served the sovereign and India with equal distinction. To our mind, it is no shame to confess so naked a truth.

Seen in this light there is nothing wrong in the conclusion drawn by H. Majesty from one point made in our petition, which he made known in his reply sent by the Marquis of Pombal, in the last monsoon of 1777, to the effect that nowhere, in the political and civil tribunals and in the military hierarchy was there ever an example uptil now that natives occupied only inferior positions, and therefore, they bared their innermost weakness of mind and body. But this was only with regard to those people who were forcibly enlisted and not to those who volunteered. These were considered deserving, if sufficiently qualified. This was followed with regard to those seven hundred and odd volunteers offered by the people and the Council during the governance of Viceroys, Marquis of Alorna, Marquis of Tavora and Count of Ega. None of the volunteers, till today, ever complained because they were well aware that promotions were given to those deserving it and therefore the petitioners now wish to clarify that what they had actually placed for consideration in their petition was that promotions should be commensurate with merits, and we suggested that they be qualified for gradual promotion after a specified period of service so that the native civilian turned soldier should not feel disheartened and hope against hope to be equated to a Portuguese soldier known for his valour. This to us appeared more practicable than the system of the Marquis of Pombal who wanted promotions to be made irrespective of colour among the natives and the Portuguese.

Our line of reasoning was that if an Asian was made a captain, a Portuguese would not be prepared to work under him as he would feel belittled to be commanded by a weakling, one timid by nature, besides being frustrated with the feeling that Indians could live off their fields also, something they could not, as they were specifically sent by H. Majesty to defend this land since they were considered better equipped. Further, there have been many fights, even deaths, and some corporals, quarter-masters and even sergeants have resigned, in the last two years, and migrated to the territories of Kanara, because they were not preferred over their colleagues. In this way the State not only loses the best soldiers because justice has been denied, but it is forced to share this bread with the famished in India. For this and other reasons that Your Majesty is well aware of, we had been exempted by royal letter (fl. 1) and in fact with the money thus saved, the State could send more Portuguese soldiers to better defend the country.

(4) Because it is in accordance with normal practice, in all the courts in Europe, to exempt such persons who are of nobility, distinguished, of high lineage and merits, as are the Brahmins and Kshatriyas in India, who are normally engaged in business and other employments, like secretaries, advisers among the neighbouring kings, captains, priests and councillors of the municipalities and villages, farm managers, administrators of the coffers of the churches and chapels, which are employments, specially, carried out by Brahmins and Kshatriyas because of the unfailing honesty and loyalty with which they administer. Also to be considered is the decline of Brahmins and Kshatriyas, who are endowed with qualities and inclination towards teaching religion, missionary work, labour in the parish as confessors, curators, preachers etc. So that the progress and development of education should not suffer, these people should be exempted from military service, as is done with the nobility and illustrious people in Europe, who are normally inducted in the militia, lest the entire nobility becomes extinct. Such persons should not be called, with ignominy and humiliation, without first ascertaining if their presence is needed to look after their houses and families, on the only excuse that there are other brother or brothers who are priests and at home, or if he is married or about to get married, or the eldest of the two children of a respectable widow or the son of a decrepit father, as the Governor, mercilessly and without any consideration, did in 1775, not sparing seminary students who would have, today, filled the schools and religious houses and for which they had been trained with studies in philosophy and theology, not even those who were studying to become doctors, lawyers, professors of arts, and music. All these professions do no longer exist, and even ordinations have been suspended,

as the Bishop made this a very onerous proposition, increasing the patrimony to 3,000 *xerafins* which few, in this land, will be able to afford, and so, in a few years and with two more enlistments, the nobility of this land will be absorbed either for priesthood or for the army, as the recruiting officers do not look at artisans but only at those whom the country can use. This was the reason why the 720 volunteers, raised by the people and the Council on the last three occasions, were from this category, because if artisans from each village were chosen their number would be insignificant as compared with those tilling the land, as they are ten times more in number than the Brahmins that live in the twelve villages. Therefore, the fourth charge does not hold.

For these reasons, we feel, that what the Marquis of Pombal proposed is not practicable however, we beseech Your Majesty to consider our petition and the just reasons mentioned therein and to have pity on this poor and humble people, always faithful and loyal to Your Majesty who, for the past 40 years since 1766, have been living a poor and indigent life, and to order the landlords of Cuncolim and Assolna to maintain the 200 men to defend the frontier and the creek and to exempt the people from the payment of the contribution towards the company of 70 horses which does no longer exist, since it was abolished 20 years ago, as is recorded[8] in the Ordinance (fl. 10), nor is there any place or stable, in the fort of Rachol, for the horses. Additionally, there is no need for this because a full regiment exists in that fort. We also ask Your Majesty to exempt us from the maintenance of 60 soldiers and 10 of artillery because they are garrisoned by the Portuguese. Also of 40 couriers of the General and Colonel Commandant as we are not bound to maintain them and this work can be, easily, assigned to sepoys who have always done this work of messengers in this State and whose maintenance was the duty of the Exchequer. Finally, we request, for the love of God, that Your Majesty order the discharge of soldiers, forcibly enlisted in January 1775 and who presently live in regiments at very grave risk and loss to their families and that in future only those who have natural inclination and aptitude for military service should be enlisted, irrespective of their service, conduct, poverty, caste because military service does not preclude such qualities. Also the Corps of Auxiliaries raised by the Governor D. João José de Mello which has been proved of no practical utility be disbanded and the provisions of the royal letter from the most pious King D. Pedro II (fl. 1), regarding the orderlies be adhered to because, as stated, these are the difficulties which in these last years these people have suffered together with humiliations and extortions of large sums of money without any benefit or advantage to the Royal Exchequer and the public. Also that the patrimony for the ordinations should be reduced to 800 *xerafins* as existed for over 60 years.

Therefore, with great humility and respect due to the royal sovereign and majestic throne of Your Majesty, at whose feet we prostrate, one and one thousand times, the people and the Council, as representatives of the villages of their respective jurisdiction, beseech you to deign to hear the humble pleas made with full confidence in the royal greatness and magnanimity of Your Majesty and trusting that this petition will be favourably considered, we pray that God may increase the empire of Your Majesty and give you endless happiness.

Written in the Municipal Council,
6 January 1779.
Pascoal de Miranda — Salvador Barreto.

Livro das Monções, no. 162, fl. 1198.

Documents attached to the presentation. Assent given by the Municipal General, province of Salcete, in the current book at fl. 136.

On April 27, 1778, at the scheduled time, a general body meeting of all chief ganvkars was held. Present were Salvador Pinto and José Nicolau de Souza from Margao; António Caetano Alvares and João Antonio de Souza from Verna; José Vincent Pereira from Loutolim; Guilherme João Soares and Remedio Caetano do Rosario from Raia; Sebastião Furtado and Salvador Barreto from Benaulim; Manoel João de Silva and Felizardo Carvalho Leitão from Betalbatim; Manuel Leitão and Pascoal António Rebelo from Colva; Joaquim Felipe de Mesquita and José Francisco de Menezes from Cortalim; José Remedio de Cruz from Quelossim; Vincente Cabral and Jeronimo de Sena from Nagoa; Agostinho de Azaredo and João Vincente Xavier from Sancoale and treasurer Luis Gonzaga de Menezes. Of common accord, it was proposed that it was convenient and necessary to advise the Queen, Our Lady, of the sufferings that the people of this province were going through.

The assent by the Councillors was given and a committee with all the necessary powers and consisting of Pascoal de Miranda and Manuel João de Silva was set up to represent the feelings of the people to H. Majesty.

All the chief ganvkars having unanimously agreed on the above, sign the present assent in my presence, Jacinto Vaz, clerk of the Municipality under whose hand this is given.

The assent is duly and faithfully recorded as above without any alterations.

sd/ Jacinto Vaz
Another Assent

On 3 January at 1 p.m. a meeting of the councillors was held, as scheduled in the village of Margao, ward Mungul. The following chief ganvkars were present: José Nicolau de Souza from Margao; João António de Souza from Verna; António João Sequeira and José Pedro Coelho from Curtorim; Nicolau de Miranda from Loutolim; Guilherme João Soares and Remedio Caetano de Rosario from Raia; Sebastião Furtado and Inacio Pascoal de Cunha from Benaulim; Manuel Leitão and Pascoal António Rebelo from Colva; Joaquim Felipe de Mesquita and José Francisco de Menezes from Cortalim; Lourenço Rosario de Cruz from Quelossim; Vincente Cabral from Nagoa; Custodio Nicolau Mascarenhas from Sancoale; José Faleiro, substitute of the treasurer, acted as clerk.

The councillors gave their assent to set up a committee consisting of Salvador Barreto and Manoel Leitão, chief ganvkars who are present today, who together with Pascoal Miranda and Manuel João de Silva, appointed earlier (*vide* clerk's book, p. 136) would write to H. Majesty on behalf of the Municipality and the people. They were given all necessary powers and if needed to delegate such powers on others, under oath that they would abide by the provisions therein.

All the ganvkars, of common accord, agreed to the above on the first vote, and I do so record and sign.

This has been faithfully and recorded without any alterations and remains recorded in the *Memorial Book* of this Municipality General at fl. 26.

Given under my hand as above.
sd./ Salvador Pinto

Fl. 1. Copy of the Petition and order from the Viceroy and letter from H. Majesty, Our Lord, which is in the Memorial Book of this Municipality at pg 38v.

This Municipality states through its representatives that it requires for certain official purpose, a copy of the letter from H. Majesty, God guard

Him, which was received in 1707 regarding the relief to native soldiers who served during the term of Viceroy Caetano de Mello e Castro.

It is, therefore, requested that the Secretariat of the State may please issue a copy of the said letter.

With thanks.

Order: Copy may be issued if there is no inconvenience.
Panelim, 24 November 1707
Sd/ Viceroy

Among the letters that H. Majesty (may God guard him) deigned write to the Viceroy during the present monsoon and which are filed in this Secretariat of the State of India, there is one which is referred to in the above application, contents of which are as follows:

Viceroy of India, friend. I, the King, greet you. The Municipality General of that city of Goa in their letter of 18 December 1704 complained that you had violated the agreement reached during the term of Viceroy Count of Alvor to exempt locals from parades, exercises and enlistment in the garrison of the infantry and to discharge those that were still in the service at the time of writing to me and that instead the Municipality would contribute with 11,000 *xerafins* for the maintenance of troops guarding the province of Salcete, that in violation of the agreement you began recruiting local people to raise your companies and mixed Portuguese officers. This was against their interests and their lands which lay open. They also pointed that in case of any conflicts it was the orderlies of Salcete with their corporals and captains who were the first to assist with food, arms, gunpowder and ammunition, all at their own cost to defend the motherland. And, therefore, they requested me to stop the recuitment and disband the companies as it was against their interests and prejudicial to their lands, besides being a drain on the Royal Exchequer which is required to pay for the troops to defend the province when the people are ready to do so free. If the recruitment is stopped and the companies are disbanded the people will be free to cultivate their lands, earn their livelihood and when required will assist in the defence of their lands with whatever was needed and at the their own cost.

You are instructed to study and examine the privileges of the Municipality of Goa and if it is possible to enforce and to see that they are strictly carried out. However this will not preclude enlisting any available hand in case it is necessary for the defence of the State.

Given in Lisbon.
16 March 1707
King to the Viceroy, State of India, Count of Alvor.

a. *Reply from the Viceroy*

Sir,

After the present monsoon when the vessel sails for the kingdom, I shall examine the privileges of the Municipality General of Goa and if they are found to be enforceable I shall see that they are strictly followed as instructed by Your Majesty. However, I am afraid that I may not be able to do so because of the shortage of people in this State for the garrison and its defence. This is what I have to state to Your Majesty in this matter.

By the grace of God, may the royal person of Your Majesty prosper and have many and fortunate years. This is what I and all your vassals wish Your Majesty.

Goa, 7 January 1708.

sd/ Viceroy

Livro das Monções, no. 71, fl. 205.

Fl. 1v. Assent of the Municipality Council regarding the feed of horses. From the old book of Assents at fl. 167 onward, which follows in the same Memorial, fl. 26.

On the 30 May 1683, at the scheduled time, i.e. at one in the afternoon, in the same house, the following chief ganvkars of Margao were in session: António de Souza of Verna, Gaspar Pereira of of Curtorim, João Borges and António de Sequeira of Loutolim, Francisco Estevao and Salvador Pereira of Raia, Salvador Pereira and Custodio de Quadros of Benaulim, Theodosio de Mesquita and Francisco Pereira of Betalbatim, Gonçalo Cotta and Cosme Carvalho of Colva, Francisco Valle and António Francisco of Cortalim, João Pereira from Cortalim, Francisco Monis and António de Taura from Quelossim, João Castelo and António da Cunha from Nagoa, Nicolau Salvador de Moura and Braz Azaredo from Sancoale. Of common accord, all present gave their assent in the presence of Francisco da Taura (sic), the Viceroy, Count and Captain

General of the Navy (may God keep him), the Captain General of these lands, D. Felippe de Souza, the Field Marshal Manuel Furtado de Mendonça, the ex-inspector general of the Treasury Cristovão de Souza Coutinho, the captain of these lands Sebastião de Mello Sampaio, and Dr. Miguel Nunes de Mesquita, Attorney General of the Crown and Treasurer of His Highness (May God keep him). The councillors, in unison, complained to the Count Viceroy about the ill-treatment, insolence, indignities and violence which the people of these lands were subjected to at the hands of sergeant-majors, corporals and captains and other officers, and for no reason, who with the power of their office made everyone dance to their whims and fancies, and if these were not complied with, they let loose their vengeance and hatred presecuting them with false complaints, not allowing them to tend to their fields or carrying out their normal lives and thus preventing them from earning their livelihood, or repairing their houses and in this way making it difficult for them to pay their taxes to H. Highness. This led many to abandon, in despair, their lands. They now plead with the benign Prince to alleviate their sufferings so that they may be allowed to cultivate their lands in peace, carry out their other chores, treat themselves and their families as they are very weak both physically and monetarily, because of the heavy expenses they have incurred in the work of digging which they carried out for years on orders from ex-captain, General D. Manuel Lobo e Oilveira, and on which they spent over 60,000 *xerafins*, mortgaging their lands as H. Highness well knows. Over and above during these years, their fields and orchards had very poor yields because the common people were not able to tend their fields and lands as they were forced to work in the digging under the watchful eye of sergeant-majors and other officers, who enriched themselves tending the digging work, and with the power of their office brought communidade lands for a pittance as there was not a single ganvkar who dared oppose or challenge them. The local people who were thus vexatiously deprived of their votes lost the communidade fields over which they had perpetual lease. These underhand deals can be verified from the records available.

The Count Viceroy was fully aware of this sordid affair as the councillors had made a representation to him earlier. They now plead with Your Highness as merciful Prince, to lighten their burden, as you did when you visited these lands and immediately proposed to the welfare of the people and all other vassals, that, considering that these lands were open and presently a war against the neighbouring rebel Shivaji was likely, it was necessary, for the defence and fortification of the lands to have for a period of four years, two companies of 100 horses each with 50 horses, that Your Highness would provide the horses from Your Highness' stable as well as the horsemen, soldiers, sappes, arms and all that was needed and that the Municipality would only be required to supply the feed for the horses and the people would be exempted from the exercises and watch duty and the sergeant-majors and other officers disbanded, never to be taken back, their powers reduced so as to avoid further vexations, violence and other oppressions which could antagonise the local populace. And so that everyone should be duly aware of this order, a crier should announce throughout Salcete province that any infringement would make a person liable to a fine of 100 *xerafins* which would be used towards the works at the dockyard.

In this manner, all the vassals would live in peace, without harassments and they would be free to pursue their trade, enabling them to earn their living, pay the taxes to H. Highness, and look after their families and homes. So as not to lose practice with arms, the Count Viceroy, would appoint from among the ganvkars of each village, captains in the company, for a period of three years, disbanding the present captains. On the expiry of the first three years and so as one person should not remain in the same post for too long, others would be appointed. There would be two exercises per year, one, a week before Christmas, and another, before Easter, for which purpose a Portuguese officer would be deputed to Goa who would draw no salary and would not punish any native without prior notice to the persons and at no time would there be fresh recruitment of natives nor would they be prevented from tending their fields.

The Councillors after considering the proposal of the Viceroy explained the misery they were going through and because of the hard times the people would not be able to pay their taxes they are liable to, as this year their expenses on themselves, their cattle, seeds and oxen were very high, and therefore, they begged, for God's sake, to exempt them from supplying horse feed and instead to fix a certain amount which the Municipality could pay each year for a period of four years towards the maintenance of the two companies of horses. The Count Viceroy suggested that a sum of 10,000 *xerafins* for each year and an additional sum of 600 *xerafins* towards the purchase of grass for the horses be paid by the Municipality which for four years make a total of 42,400 *xerafins* which could be raised by one or the other Municipality with the proviso that in case the effective number of horses fell short of 100 they would only pay for the existing number of horses used for watch and ward duties on pro rata basis, and the Municipality would not be called upon to pay for all the 100 horses, as mentioned in the agreement and the clerk would make note of it, and begin to fix the contributions.

The Municipality General after duly considering the suggestion, gave its assent to contribute with 10,000 *xerafins* per year for a period of four years, in a total of 42,400 *xerafins* for the maintenance and feed of the said horses and in the event the actual number of horses falling short of 100 they would pay for only the actually existing number of horses, on pro rata basis as suggested by the Count Viceroy and gave their assent. Should a need arise to maintain these horses for a longer period the Municipality would be duly advised or alternatively the Municipality will not be bound to continue the payment. Accordingly, for the benefit of all and duty towards H. Highness, the first instalment would be paid, the moment the horses arrived and the company effectively raised. The contributions would be fixed by the clerk of the Municipality and be payable in quarterly instalments customarily on the third, sixth and twelfth months and the payment for the next year, again on pro rata basis. The share of the villages of Cuncolim, Assolna, Velim, Ambelim and Veroda will be credited to the account of H. Highness and will be collected by the cashier of those villages, since they fall within the areas and are subject to the contributions. These will be deposited in the Municipal coffers and will be used in accordance with the orders from the Viceroy. The contributions will be duly recorded in the books of accounts with all details of receipts and expenses made.

Accordingly the assent is hereby given and this document is being signed by the Count Viceroy and others present. Given under my hand, Francisco Xavier Pereira, clerk of the Municipality General and of the Treasury of His Highness. Signed by me and all chief ganvkars present Francisco Xavier Pereira, Count of Alvor, D. Rodrigo da Costa, D. Miguel de Almeida, D. Felippe de Souza, Manoel Furtado de Mendonça, Cristovam de Souza e Coutinho, Sebastião de Mello Sampaio, Miguel Nunes de Mesquita, António de Souza, Gaspar Pereira, João Borges, António de Sequeira, Franciso Estevão, Salvador Pereira, Custodio Quadros, Theodosio de Mesquita, Francisco Pereira, Gonçalo Cotta, Cosme Carvalho, Francisco de Valle, António Furtado, João Pereira, Francisco Moniz, António de Tavora, João Castello, António da Cunha, Nicolau Salvador de Oliveira, Braz da Azeredo.

This extract is a true and faithful copy of the original which is recorded in the old *Book of Assents*. Copy taken by me Pedro Mascarenhas, clerk of the Municipality General.

Fl. 4. Provision by Governor D. Luis Caetano de Almeida regarding the payments towards 60 soldiers of the garrison of the frontier, with extracts of the Assents of the Municipality, from the authenticated books at fl. 10v in the Memorial Book, fl. 117.

D. Luis Caetano de Almeida, of the Council of H. Majesty, Governor of India, etc.

I make it known to all who read this provision that the Municipality General of the province of Salcete has given two assents, one in which it agreed to pay towards the maintenance of 60 soldiers for duties in the fort of Rachol at the rate of 6 *xerafins* per month, to guard the frontier, after the withdrawal of auxiliaries, details of which are as follows:

Extract of the assent given by the Municipality on 16 November of the same year, and recorded in the authenticated book at fl. 10v details of which are as follows:

All the persons present, of common accord, went to the residence of the General where it was proposed, as decided earlier, to recruit 60 soldiers to guard the fort of Rachol because we faced many problems both of personal and monetary nature when it was guarded by the orderlies and auxiliaries and therefore agreed to give this assent to the proposal made by the said General to raise 60 soldiers on wages of 6 *xerafins* each per month, in relays of 3 months each, beginning from 1 January 1743. The choice of soldiers is to be left to the discretion of the General who will choose the ablest men from those who are prepared to live within the fort voluntarily so that the orderlies and auxiliaries may be withdrawn, and not be called upon for watch duty except in case of invasion by the enemy. It was under these conditions and the full knowledge of the General that his assent was given.

It was also stipulated that if at any time later, during the rule of any other Viceroy, these conditions were not adhered to, those elected at that point of time, would immediately cease payment of those 60 soldiers, and for the future general knowledge of these conditions, the Municipality will request His Excellency, the Governor to officially order that these conditions be always adhered to for the benefit and peace of the people.

This extract is a true copy of the original which I confirm: António Nicolau Mascarenhas, clerk of the Municipality.

Today, 29 November 1742,
ad/ António Nicolau Mascarenhas.

Extract of the assent given by the Municipality on 25 November of the current year, recorded in the authenticated book at fl. 13v, contents of which are as follows:

Having all assembled here, and of common accord, it was agreed to withdraw the orderies and auxiliaries thanks to the good offices of His Excellency, the Governor, of this State, who took pity and was moved by the representions made by the people. It was agreed, in exchange, that the Municipality would contribute towards the wages of 200 effective soldiers at the frontiers so that the orderlies and the auxiliaries together, as it was the custom here earlier could help the inhabitants without any distinction between rich and poor, big and small. The Council found that this proposal would be of great advantage of the people who would be able to utilise their time in a better way tending their fields and properties. Consequently all the ganvkars, of common accord, gave their assent to contribute with the wages of 200 soldiers or sepoys at the rate of eight *xerafins* each per month, since this was what was being paid by H. Majesty, and there were hard times, however, this amount would never be increased but would be reduced should H. Majesty desire to reduce the eight *xerafins* if and when better days come, and this will continue so that proper watch at the frontiers may be maintained and the people could live in peace and carry out their normal lives. The people will however, be required to assist with their arms whenever needed and during the parades.

The Captain General Agostinho de Mello Lobo has given enough proof of the great love with which he rules and protects us all and this Council and the entire populace expects complete peace under his rule, but since such provisions require confirmation from His Excellency the Governor, so that it may not be suddenly changed later, we have to approach His Excellency, the Governor to concede to the proviso, as was done at the time of the creation of the troops in this province, that the payment of the wages of the 200 soldiers in quarterly instalments will cease the moment regular troops arrive in this province. The withdrawal of the auxiliaries of the frontier and the navy requires official edict nullifying the present appointment and likewise the disposal of arms must also be regulated. These we feel, may be given to those who have the capacity to buy, and the remaining to the less fortunate, as was being done in the past.

Those who will be elected next year, that about to dawn, and during whose tenure this payment will be made, should ensure that all conditions are strictly adhered to before disbursing the payment of 200 soldiers and also of the third auxiliary sergeant-major so that there may be complete peace, and the people may live each in his village, within the jurisdiction of their corporals and other white officers, as usual. This extract is a true copy of the original, which I confirm, António Nicolau Mascarenhas, clerk of the Municipality.

Today, 29 November 1742.
sd/ António Nicolau Mascarenhas.

Whereas Nicolau Francisco Vaz, attorney of the said Municipality of Salcete, applied for my confirmation of the above assents, and that it should be issued free of cost, as it is on H. Majesty's service, after duly considering his request I am pleased to confirm the said assents according to which that Municipality will pay for the 60 soldiers for the garrison of Rachol fort at the rate of 6 *xerafins* each per month subject to the condition that the soldiers will reside inside the fort, that the orderlies and auxiliaries will never be called upon for the watch duty except in case of invasion from the enemy and if these conditions are violated the Municipality will not be bound to pay towards the upkeep of the 60 soldiers, the Municipality will pay for the upkeep of 200 soldiers or sepoys at the rate of 8 *xerafins* each per month for the garrison at the frontiers of the said province and this amount will never be increased, instead it may be reduced, the auxiliaries and their officers and the sergeant-major of the orderlies will be withdrawn, but they are however, bound to be ready to help in times of need with their arms and also during parades, that payment of 200 soldiers will cease if and when the troop of horses is restored.

I notify the general of the province of Salcete and the captain of Rachol fort and other parts, ministers and officers and other concerned people to strictly follow the provision of this assent. This will be duly registered as also the creation of the auxiliaries of the province. No order as to cost given under my hand.

Felippe de Albuquerque.
Goa, 11 December 1742.
Written by Luis Afonso Dantas.
sd/ D. Luis Caetano de Almeida.

Fl. 6. Official government grant by Viceroy D. Pedro Mascarenhas,

Count of Sandomil regarding the moratorium on the taxes due in the said Memorial at fl. 111.

Pedro Mascarenhas, Count of Sandomil, of the Council of State and War of H. Majesty, Viceroy and Captain General of the State of India, I make it known to all who read this grant, made into law, that having duly considered the great calamity that the people of the province of Salcete and Bardez have suffered with the invasions from the enemies and from which the province of Salcete is not yet fully free and having duly considered the representations made by the respective Municipalities and the people of each village detailing the miseries suffered by them and the heavy debts that they have incurred mostly for payment of royal taxes and personal needs, which debts have placed them in a very precarious position before their creditors, some of whom started recovery proceedings because they found themselves in such a position that they are unable to pay the interest accrued, much less the capital. Many landlords, in one or the other villages, have been issued recovery notices demanding repayment of the interest and capital within a time limit, especially when money is so scarce and lands have depreciated to about one eighth of its value and there is no one to buy them. All this has adversely affected all the people and will have an equally adverse and irreparable effect in future when the landlords will have to mortgage their lands to repay their debts. Since I feel it is imperative to avoid such a situation, I am pleased to order through this grant which is made into law no recovery proceedings will be initiated for a period of one year and a half from the date of this grant against the Municipalities General of Salcete and Bardez and the people in general, for the amount of capital taken on loan, recoveries though may be made for the interest accrued. I further order that during the same period of one and a half years no land in the provinces of Salcete and Bardez will be mortgaged for payment of the capital taken on loan but the produce of the said lands may be mortgaged or sold to repay the interest accrued, and those lands that are already mortgaged will not be sold during the above period of a year and a half. I notify the Treasurer, the Chancellor of the State, captains of those lands of Salcete and Bardez and the ministers, officers, and people concerned with this to strictly follow the provisions of this grant. No order as to costs as this is in H. Majesty's service.

This will be duly recorded in the Civil Courts in the Tribunals of the respective provinces, and in the books of the clerks of the Municipalities and in the Secretariat of the State.

This is being done in triplicate.

Given by João de Costa, at Goa on 8 September 1740.
Given under my hand, the Secretary, Luis Afonso Dantas.
sd/ Pedro Mascarenhas, Count of Sandomil.

Fl. 7: Decision

This is recorded in the Memorial at fl. 122.
Decision on appeal, etc.

The Division Bench hearing the appeal at fl. 25 has come to the conclusion that the petitioners have been proved, as according to the proceedings, and provisions of law, and the rules regulating the governance of the villages, the Municipality is but a mere administrator to ensure that all its actions are solely directed towards the welfare of the villages. It is not permitted to do anything that may be prejudicial to their interests of the villagers. They cannot make new bylaws or raise additional taxes beyond what is permitted by the rules and as directed by uses and customs which presently is every year. On the contrary, as a diligent and faithful representative of the people it should take utmost care to avoid illegal expenses and new taxes and instead endeavour to increase the revenues for the welfare of the people so that they are able to contribute better in times of need and in urgent contingencies of the State, as in effect they did many times, like on the occasion of Colaba, Mombassa, and in the current wars with the Marathas. There are the only occasions when the Municipality is entitled to raise extra taxes but not otherwise, much less demanding perpetual and successive contributions as the Municipality General of Salcete did while giving the latest assent at fl. 15, demanding a contribution of 28,000 *xerafins*, which besides being a perpetual and successive tax also affects the ecclesiastical churches and places of worship over which the Municipality has no jurisdiction. They can raise taxes and demand contributions from the Council of three states and only if circumstances so demand. In the present case there were no special circumstances or urgency and besides the Municipality did not take the councillors in confidence as it should have done. For reasons mentioned above the assent is declared null and void especially what is recorded at fls. 5 and 42 because it was carried out in the presence of the captain of Rachol while the ganvkars were forcibly confined within the fort for nearly eight days under threats and against their wills. The very fear and respect of the person who ordered their confinement besides the fact that the assent given in his favour were sufficient reasons to nullify the assent. In an identical case earlier the assent was also nullified (vide letter from the Viceroy dated 12 April 1736 and the certificate at fl. 44).

We, therefore, after duly considering the plea, declare the assent at fl. 5 null and void and without any effect.

To pay costs.
Goa, 8 January 1744.
Dr. Figueiredo, Dr. Pereira, Silva, Costa.

Fl. 7v. Petition of the Advocate General of the people of the province of Salcete in the Memorial at fl. 124.

Tadeu Mascarenhas, resident ganvkar and aggrieved cutumcar of Carmona, advocate general of the province of Salcete, state that an order has been passed by the High Court whereby the assent given by the Municipality in terms of which the people of the villages had to contribute each year nearly 38,000 *xerafins* towards the payment of wages of 200 sepoys and 60 native soldiers and also salaries of generals, has been declared null and void, the petitioner feels that despite this order the Municipality may continue to demand this or another contribution in some way or the other.

There are many royal orders and rules opposed by the public, yet there are persons who to curry favour from the influential persons, are prepared to change colours and help in flouting those orders. H. Majesty has prohibited new and extraordinary expenses, yet on the various pretexts, this is done and people are forced to come out with the truth and stop them from doing anything which is prejudicial to the interests of the people. Under such circumstances the petitioner finds no other solution, from experience he knows that these people fear neither God nor laws and do whatever they want.

The petitioner, therefore, appeals to the uprightness of H. Excellency to accept on his behalf and on behalf of the people, this protest and to require him to nullify everytime and as many times as necessary any assents or acts that the Municipality may make promising to spend or spending monies without the sanction of law or rules or edicts and consent of the people, on pain of the said elected persons being made directly responsible for total repayment of any monies given by the Municipality for any reason or on any condition whatsoever. And so that they should not any time claim ignorance the petitioner requests Your Excellency and the Honourable Judges of the Crown to accept this formal protest and complaint and to duly inform the Municipality and all others interested parties and to have this recorded in the current Memorial Book, an ordinance so that it may have the force of law, for which they gratefully thank Your Excellency.

Decision: Granted as requested. Dr. Figueiredo.

Fl. 8: Petition and Plea of the Municipality General recorded in the Memorial at fl. 123.

The Municipality states that by order of the General they are confined in the dungeon of Rachol because they have not yet paid the instalment for the upkeep of 200 sepoys and 60 native soldiers in accordance with Your Excellency's orders which they refrained from as there were counter orders, notifications and protests opposing the payment.

It was because of confinement that orders were issued for the payment and Your Excellency is aware of this from other petition made in which permission to take a loan on interest to meet this contingency was sought.

Despite this, we are still in prison for the last 18 days and, therefore, we requested the General to free us but he informs that he cannot do so without Your Excellency's permission. Since necessary action has been taken in this regard, we request that we be set free as we are suffering in the prison more so because now it is the time of the first harvest. We plead Your Excellencies to direct the General to free us accordingly for which we thank in anticipation.

Order: We have already ordered that on the payment of 12,000 *xerafins* in the coffers in repayment of the loan they may be set free.

sd/ Governors.

Fl. 8v. Order of His Excellency the Marquis of Tavora, Viceroy and Captain General of this State, on the restoration of the troops after discharge of 200 soldiers. In the said book at fl. 126

Francisco Assiz de Tavora, Marquis of Tavora, Count of St. John of the Council of State of H. Majesty, the King, my Lord, Viceroy and Captain General of India.

I make it known to all who may see this order that the Municipal Corporation of the province of Salcete made a representation attached here with their assent, in terms of which the Municipality was taking responsibility of contributing towards the feed and green and dry grass for the regiment of 60 horses, and also defraying expenses as detailed in the terms and conditions of the assent given, that for its implementation and execution they required my confirmation, which they request to issue free of cost as it is on H. Majesty's service.

I issued orders on the 18 August of the present year 1753 that the confirmation of the assent be duly issued in accordance with the request contained in their petition, details of which are as follows: Extract of the assent given by the Municipality General of the province of Salcete on 11 August 1753 recorded in the Book at fls. 146ff which among other things states. All the members who assembled at the request of Marquis of Tavora, Viceroy and Captain-General of this State, have duly considered the proposal made by the Viceroy to the Municipality General, namely, to restore the cavalry regiment which previously existed in lieu of the corps of sepoys which exists now because the province being open and extensive the cavalry is more suitable to assist promptly and more effectively than people of foot. The Councillors agreeing that the proposal was in fact sound and advantageous of common accord, gave their assent to contribute with the feed of a company of 60 horses at the rate of 22 *xerafins* and 3 annas and 45 pies per month for each live horse, also the wages of two helpers at the rate of 22 *xerafins* each per month, totalling 52 *xerafins*, in addition they would also contribute with 12 *xerafins* per month for the sergeant-major of the province and of the square, 16 *xerafins* per month for the crier of the State and of the fort of Rachol, 8 and a half *xerafins* for informers which in all adds up to 88 *xerafins* per month. By the same assent they also made provisions for 3 *xerafins* per month for green and dry grass for each live horse, as long as the company existed, to meet these liabilities, the Municipality will fix the contributions to be paid by each village, the same way as was done in the case of the 200 sepoys which liability now ceases and the Municipality will pay as above for the feed of 60 live horses to the extent of the number of actually existing horses. The cartage of grass will be the responsibility of the person under whose charge the horses are kept and not of the villagers, so that they may not be harassed by the corporals or officers as the amount fixed by the Municipality for the grass amply covers the cost of transportation. Should at any time the company of horses be withdrawn and those of sepoys or privates restored the payment for the horses and others will cease immediately on pain of those violating this, having to pay from their own pockets. For various reasons the

Municipality is unable to meet this year the above payments including the grass and instead the Municipality agrees to pay 3 *xerafins* for each live horse per month, as long as the company is in existence. Once the full complement of 60 live horses is reached, the amount pertaining to the number of horses withdrawn will be deposited in the coffers the same way as is done when any sepoy is withdrawn and this amount will be used towards the welfare of the company of the province and of the fort and if during this period any horse happens to die, the amount pertaining to it shall likewise be deposited in the coffers from the day of withdrawal or death. However, the amount so collected will never be used without prior sanction from the government and the Municipality General.

In view of the above, the Municipality begs His Excellency, the Marquis, Viceroy as representative and protector and Lord, the confirmation of the assent, which may please be issued and duly notified that payment of the 4 companies of sepoys should be debited to the Royal Treasury and that this Municipality will not be liable to pay for more than 60 horses. This extract of the assent, was taken by me, António Nicolau Mascarenhas, clerk of the Municipality General, from the original, which I confirm.

Today, 11 August 1753.
Given under my hand,
sd/ António Nicolau Mascarenhas.

Having considered the above, I am pleased to confirm the said. I also notify the General of the province of Salcete, the Captain of those lands, the ministers and people concerned, so that they may strictly follow all the provisions contained therein. This will be duly recorded in the Book with all the necessary declarations and in the Treasury of the Municipality of the province of Salcete. No order as to costs not even to the Chancellory as this is on H. Majesty's service. This will also be duly registered in the Secretariat of the State.

Nicolau Francisco de Sa
14 December 1753.
Secretary, Luis Afonso Dantas,
Marquis of Tavora.

Fl. 10. Letter patent which the Captain of this province received with copy to Henrique da Cunha de Ataide. From the Memorial fl. 196.

D. José, by the grace of God, King of Portugal and Algarve, of near and far seas of Africa, Lord of Guine and of Conquests, Navigation and Commerce of Ethiopia, Arabia. Persia and India. I make it known to all who see this letter patent and of confirmation thereat that having considered the representation made by Henrique da Cunha de Ataide who held the rank of Captain of Cavalry of the province of Salcete, a company which was raised by him and at this own cost, that he had been accused of having abandoned his post when commanding the garrison of Zambaulim, during the unfortunate campaign of Ponda, and was, for that reason, imprisoned by order, of the governors of the State, and was later absolved of that charge, on his apppeal to the High Court of Goa as is evident by the documents he produced and his present pleading to me to restore to him his earlier rank of Captain which was given by the Marquis of Tavora, then Viceroy of the State of India, I am pleased to restore to him (as I presently do) the rank of Captain of cavalry of the province of Salcete, which company he raised at his own cost, with direction that this rank and the company that the petitioner raised at his own cost, with due permission of the Viceroy, shall continue till his death or earlier if promoted to a higher rank, in the pay scale of his rank and in accordance with my orders he will enjoy all the honours and privileges, freedom, prerequisites and franchises which entitles him to his position.

I hereby instruct the Viceroy, and Captain General of the State of India to restore and to acknowledge him as Captain of Cavalry of the said company and give him the respect and honour that is due to his rank so that he may be able to perform his duties without incumberance and he will draw, as I have ordered the same pay that he drew when he took the oath of office at the time of joining and I order the officers and soldiers who are subordinate to him to obey him and abide by the orders issued by him on my behalf and for which they are duty bound.

As confirmation of the above I have this letter patent sealed with the royal seal of my coat of arms.

Given by me at Lisbon,
5 April in the year of birth of our Lord Jesus Christ 1760.
Seal.

Fl. 10v. Petition and order with transcripts of grants of the villages of Veroda, Velim, Ambelim and Assolna. In Memorial, fl. 30.

Sirs,

The Municipality General of Salcete, through their representatives state that they require for their official use extracts of the provisions contained in the grants that H. Majesty made of the villages of Assolna, Ambelim and Velim, Cuncolim and Veroda to the respective owners, so that the Corporation may make known the terms and conditions attached to the grants which are registered in the Secretariat of the State.

We request Your Excellency to please issue the above extracts.

Thanking you.

Order: The extracts may please be duly issued.

Panelim, 27 July 1700
sd/ Viceroy.

In the book of register of grants of the year 1585, during the term of Viceroy D. Duarte de Menezes and which is filed in the Secretariat of the State of India at fl. 25v, there is a grant of the villages of Cuncolim and Veroda made in favour of João da Silva contents of which are as follows:

"By letter dated 27 March 1585, H. Majesty having appreciated the meritorious services rendered by João da Silva, who spent a lot of his money on behalf of H. Majesty helping him with people, soldiers and vassals and arranging arms, ammunitions and other requirements, and personally accompanying with his own people as vassals, Count D. Francisco Mascarenhas in his journeys to the North and to Cochin, and returning from there with the Viceroy of India to this city of Goa, as a reward for his meritorious services H. Majesty pleased to endow him and his heirs, the villages of Cuncolim and Veroda with their gauncarias, situated in the province of Salcete and which belonged to the Treasury of H. Majesty because the ganvkars of these villages rebelled against the royal Crown and because during the term of António Moniz, they resisted the captain of the city of Goa and that of Rachol and on another occasion visited Agostinho Moniz, captain of that fort, fought on the side of the enemy during the war that Adil Shah waged against the State, enlisting as naiks or footmen and sometimes against the very fort where they lived violating the orders, laws of H. Majesty, evading payment of taxes, leaving the fort without permission to attend to their private work outside and above all for having resisted captain Gomes Eanes de Figueiredo and D. Julianes Mascarenhas creating trouble and killing some priests of St. Paul, and some Christians, of the fort of Rachol. For all the above H. Majesty is pleased to endow all rights that exist or may exist in the villages and gauncarias to João Silva, both he and his heirs will be bound to pay the taxes as the ganvkars did, namely 2278 white annas and 1 bargany per year for the village of Cuncolim and for that of Veroda 670 white annas per year. They will follow the same rules as the ganvkars did.

And in the same book at fl. 139 is another grant of the villages of Assolna, Velim, and Ambelim with their gauncarias made in favour of D. Pedro de Castro contents of which are as follows: By letter dated 6 August 1585 H. Majesty having appreciated the meritorious services rendered by D. Pedro de Castro, nobleman of the Court of H. Majesty, in various parts of India, where he was in the service of H. Majesty for many years continuously spending his own money, lodging at his cost and in his farm a large company of soldiers at Paço Seco during the siege put by Adil Shah during the term of Viceroy D. Luis de Ataide, accompanying him in his journeys to the forts of Honavar and Barcalore, in a galleon keeping a retenue of soldiers ever ready to serve H. Majesty and because of which he has fallen into heavy debts, the captaincy of Sofala given to him did not sufficiently compensate the many services rendered by him, as that did not yield much and he refrained from doing what other captains did in the past as evidenced from the huge debts he incurred to build at his cost the fort of Mozambique which had been entrusted to him by H. Majesty. The Royal Treasury has not yet repaid him the expenses he incurred. Not all these meritorious services rendered as detailed above, H. Majesty is pleased to endow for ever to him and his heirs the villages of Assolna, Velim and Ambelim with their gauncarias and other assets belonging to the villages, situated in Salcete and belonging to H. Majesty, because the ganvkars of those villages rebelled against the Royal Crown resisted at the time of António Moniz Barreto, ex-Governor, the captain of that city and that of Rachol and on another occasion reviled Agostinho Moniz, former captain of that fort and during the wars that Adil Shah waged against this State, enlisted as naiks or footmen and sometimes fought against the fort where they lived, violating the order and laws of H. Majesty and his officers evading payment of taxes, leaving the fort without permission to attend to their private work, created trouble, resisted Gomes Eanes and de Figueiredo and D. Julianes

Mascarenhas, killed many priests and Christians from those parts. For all the above services, H. Majesty is pleased to endow with all rights that exist and may exist in those villages and gauncarias and adjacent lands as detailed above the said villages, he and his successors will be bound to pay the taxes as the previous owners did and are fixed by the land revenue authority and will abide by all the existing rules.

In the margin of the grant is the following observations: This should not be registered as D. Pedro de Càstro has donated these villages to the College of the Society of Jesus of Cochin by public deed, and Viceroy D. Duarte de Menezes has issued the necessary certificate of transfer.

This is a true copy of the original.
Given under my hand, Francisco Gomes
6 September 1700
sd/ António Coelho Guerreiro.

These extracts were duly issued to Nicolau de Moura, representative of the Municipality General.

sd/ Nicolau Salvador de Moura.
Witnessed by Pedro Mascarenhas.

Fl. 12: Provision of Overseas Council

D. João, by grace of God, King of Portugal and Algarve, of near and far seas of Africa, Lord of Guine, etc..

I make it known to you, D. Luis de Menezes of Ericeira, Viceroy and Captain General of the State of India that I have duly noted what you have stated in your letter of 17 January of the current year regarding the order given to you about requiring the five villages of Assolna, Velim and Ambelim belonging to the priests of the Society of Jesus and the villagers of Cuncolim and Veroda belonging to the Count of Cuncolim to pay not only what they owe from their share of the contributions that other villages of the Municipality of Salcete have made, but that from now onwards they would have to pay whatever their share as was fixed as the Municipality of Salcete had already advised you of this but that you had not taken any action because the representative of Malabar to whom Assolna belongs and the Count of Cuncolim had contested this, alleging with documents that they were contributing towards the upkeep of the cavalry of Salcete and that they also paid towards the wages of certain helpers, that the Count of Cuncolim had built a fort with artillery at his cost, and was also defraying the expenses towards that of others villages, maintenance and a good number of helpers and was, therefore, contributing more than other villages. Additionally his villages were near the frontier and were therefore the first to be exposed to the thrust of the enemy and suffered more losses because the enemy seldom penetrated the interior of the province of Salcete and that presently only these villages and none of the others were contributing for the plantation of bamboo trees which in four years time will turn into a natural and impenetrable barricade. The benefits of this will benefit the succeeding Viceroys who will have peace of mind than the earlier ones, who had to live with a wide open province and with so little defence. This was the greatest service that was rendered unto the king and which cost over 10,000 to 12,000 *xerafins* without any onus on the Royal Exchequer and kept this part of the dominion free from invasions.

Despite all that you have stated I am of the opinion that you should strictly follow my orders as I issued requiring the five villages to pay the contributions that they owe and from now onwards to pay whatever the share of the contributions as fixed at, subject to the proviso that should these villages spend anything on any work that is of common benefit to all the villages of Salcete, and for which only these have contributed, the amount so spent may be deducted from the taxes due by them. You are further instructed that the moment a decision is given on the appeal preferred by the Society of Jesus on this matter before the High Court, you will see that the implementation of the decision is suspended and will send me a copy of the decision to enable me to take further action, as I may deem fit.

The King, Our Lord, had this issued in duplicate through João Teles da Silva and António Rodrigues da Costa, councillors of his Overseas Council.

Given under my hand, Miguel de Macedo Ribeiro,
Western Lisbon,
18 December 1729.
Secretary, André Lopes de Lavre.
sd/ João Teles da Silva, António Rodrigues da Costa.

a. Reply from Viceroy Francisco José de Sampayo e Castro

Sirs,

The bamboo plantation which the Viceroy my predecessor ordered be planted, is doubtlessly, of great advantage to the lands of Salcete which will become impenetrable to the enemies. However, from what I am presently told, this project needs more improvement because in some parts the seeds do not catch and on the others it was destroyed by casual or artificial fire. It is true that these villages contributed towards this project with over 20,000 *xerafins* but some villages have complained that not even half of this amount has been spent. As soon as the vessel sails from the kingdom, I have decided to visit the province of Salcete and to have the expenses examined and whatever amount the administrators have not spent in this work, will be utilised in the improvement of this project, appointing better administrators and regarding the contributors of the villages of Cuncolim and Assolna and other villages, I shall endeavour to strictly follow the instructions given by Your Majesty. I shall also suspend the implementation of the decision of the High Court which was given in favour of the Society of Jesus, copy of which I enclose as requested.

May God keep the highest and most powerful person of Your Majesty and give you many happy years.

Goa, 14 January 1721
sd/ Viceroy.

Livro das Monções, no. 86, fl. 339.

Certificate

I, Manuel Fructuoso Lima, clerk of Crown and Treasury of H. Majesty, may God keep him, in this court of the State of India and in my office certify that Fr. Hyeronimo de Moraes, representing the Society of Jesus of the South filed a writ petition in the High Court of Goa against that assent and report of the Municipality of Salcete and order of the former Viceroy, António Luis Gonçalves da Camara Coutinho, requiring the villages of Velim, Ambelim and Assolna which the Society of Jesus own by virtue of a grant, to pay their share of the contributions of donations and taxes fixed by the Municipality. They pleaded that the Municipality had exceeded their powers and to declare their orders null and void, adducing documentary evidence which forms part of the suit preferred by them.

The Bench heard their arguments and pursued the evidence tendered and came to the conclusion that the plea of the petitioners was fully established and passed the following order:

Order: of the High Court.

The prayer of the petitioners is allowed. They have proved with documentary evidence that the assent given by the Municipality requiring the petitioners to pay on pro rata basis their share of contributions and donations as assessed by the Municipality is in violation of the provisions contained in *Government Gazette*, fl. 6. The respondents have not adduced any evidence nor quoted any previous judgements in their defence and failed to prove that the petitioners were bound to pay the taxes raised and contradict their stand that they were exempted from the taxes as the villages were not within the jurisdiction of the Municipality. They asked for a stay of recoveries until their writ was heard as it was prejudicial to their interests. After hearing the parties and finding substance in their plea we absolve the appellants and declare the assent null and void. The respondents to pay the costs.

Goa, 22 December 1717.
Dr. Moreira, Abreu, Moraes.

Fl. 13: Order of the Overseas Council

D. João, by the grace of God, King of Portugal and of Algarve, of near and far seas of Africa, Lord of Guine, etc.

I make it known to you, Francisco José Sampaio, Viceroy and Captain General of the State of India that I have duly noted what you have stated in your letter of 14 January 1721 that you have followed my instructions regarding the five villages of Assolna, Velim and Ambelim of the priests of the Society of Jesus and the villages of Cuncolim and Veroda of the Count of Cuncolim that they should pay their share of the contributions as fixed and in case they spend any monies on any work which was of common benefit to all the villages of Salcete they could deduct the amount so spent from the taxes due, and also that you suspended the implementations of the order of the High Court which was in favour of the priests of the Society sending me a copy of the said decision so that I might take whatever action I deemed necessary and that the bamboo plantation ordered by your predecessor was of great advantage to the province of Salcete which now cannot be invaded by the enemy and that if you could obtain more funds than what was planned, you could improve the barricade as some parts of the bamboo plantation were destroyed either because the seeds failed to grow in some places or in the other the bamboo were destroyed by casual or artificial fire and that once the vessels sailed to the Kingdom you would undertake a visit to the province of Salcete and examine the expenses made, which the villages said has not exceeded half of the total amount collected, and would demand that the administrators pay the amount held by them and utilise it in the improvements of the bamboo barricade, appointing more honest administrators and finally about the villages of Assolna and Velim and other villages satisfying the payments of their dues orders which you have strictly followed as well as the suspension of the implementation of the decision of the High Court which went in favour of the priests of the Society copy of which you sent to me.

I am pleased with you and expect your continued zeal in turning the province of Salcete into a defensible one.

H. Majesty the King sends this letter in duplicate through João Teles da Silva and António Rodrigues da Costa, councillors of the Overseas Council.

Given under my hand, Manuel da Silva,
Eastern Lisbon, 27 February 1723.
Secretary, André Lopes de Lavre.
sd/ João Teles da Silva, António Rodrigues da Costa.

b. *Reply from the Governors*

Sirs,

In our endeavour to make the province of Salcete defensible in accordance with the recommendation of Your Majesty, we instructed the Secretary of this government to request the General of that province for a detailed information about the bamboo plantation in their borders by orders of Viceroy, Count of Ericeira, copy of which is enclosed. Not only the general but everyone is of the opinion that the bamboo grove is the most appropriate means to safeguard those lands and we have recommended utmost care in its implementation and ordered severe punitive action should they allow stray cattle in or fire to the bamboo grove. After the monsoon we shall verify the amount spent in this work.

May God keep the most high and powerful person of Your Majesty for many happy years.

Goa, 6 January 1721.
sd/ Governor.

Livro das Monções, no. 89, fl. 12.

Addendum

Further to the matter regarding military service we attach herewith another representation from the auxiliaries addressed to H. Majesty during the monsoon of 1772 which was intimated to the government of India by decision of the Overseas Council on 4 May 1773 (*Livro das Monções*, no. 151, fl. 53) which is as follows:

Sirs,

Prostrated at the royal feet of Your Majesty and with deepest respect and obedience we the auxiliaries of Salcete state that we were recruited in 1771 and were posted at the frontiers and squares of the province as evidenced from the certificate no. attached but we have not been paid the ammunition allowance nor any stipend for over two months now though in active service, as evidenced from certificate no. and another certificate no. As a result we are undergoing untold miseries and hunger and have been reduced to such a sorry state more because most of us come from poor families and by virtue of our being in active service we are unable to earn our daily bread elsewhere. Besides as against the usual custom followed in olden times, we are also not being supplied with a ration of rice, as evidence by certificate no. The stoppage of this custom right in the first year of our military service so alien to natives of this State, has increased the horror we always had towards military service.

As Your Majesty has ordered that the auxiliaries from this State would be brought at par with those of the Kingdom and the extra expense that the royal treasury of Your Majesty will incur with those posted at the frontiers would not amount to much, on the contrary would immensely mitigate our miseries and indigence therefore, we beg of Your Majesty who has always had a paternal love and is always ready to help his vassals and has with his magnanimity and benevolence helped the smallest of your vassals will certainly not permit that those who with so much love, zeal, and loyalty serve Your Majesty should die of hunger amidst calamities. Past experiences will justly compel the applicants to repeat what was done in the past against the general and universal customs and the royal commands of Your Majesty. They therefore humbly beg Your Majesty to hear their pleas and order that those engaged at the frontiers and squares of your province be duly given the ammunition allowance or a corresponding stipend so that they can sustain themselves and whenever on duty outside the province to be given the same pay as other paid soldiers.

The auxiliaries of Goa and Bardez also join us in this petition so that they may also be contemplated together with us.

Thanking you.

The Governor Felippe de Valladares Sotto Major in his letter of 9 February 1774 replies that all the auxiliaries should be supplied on the occasion of war and campaigns a ration and quarter rice and 12 pies, or 1 anna only per day.

Document No. 53

Notice from the Secretary of the State to the Governor.

On placing, before H. Majesty the attached representation, submitted by the Council General of the province of Salcete, in which it is requested that the natives of the same province be exempted from being enlisted in the army of the State, H. Majesty has been pleased to reject the representation.

This is for your information.

God keep you.
Palace of Our Lady of Help,
7 March 1781.
Martinho de Mello e Castro.

Livro das Monções, no. 162, fl. 1197.

Document No. 54

Royal Letter

To you, Francisco da Cunha e Menezes, Governor and Captain-General of the State of India, of my Council, I, the Queen, send my greetings.

Whereas by decree of 28 April 1773, in terms of which an Artillery Regiment was raised in that State, and whereas it was determined in paragraph six "that no posts of officers or ranks in the three companies of fire-fighters, miners and mechanics should be filled with persons who were not born in the kingdom of Portugal and Algarve, under pain of forfeiture of the post of officer and debarment from joining any other regiment, against those, either accepting or admitting to the said posts" and considering the representations made by you, on the disadvantages resulting from such provisions, and desirous of removing all and any such obstacles the natives might be facing in the progress of their studies and employment, I am pleased to repeal and cancel the said paragraph, maintaining, though, intact the rest of the provisions of the said decree.

This may, please, be duly executed.

Given at the Palace of Queluz,
5 October 1792.
The Prince.
To Francisco da Cunha e Menezes.

Livro das Monções, no. 175, fl. 207.

Document No. 55

Letter from the Governor to Mr. D. Montigni, Colonel, at the service of H. M. Christianissimo, in the court of Pune.

Goa, 24 October 1787.

Sir,

I was pleased to receive your letter dated 7 and 29 September, with your good news and of other military and political nature about the Marathas, Tipu Sultan and Nizam Ali, together with your judicious comments.

The illness I suffered and which kept me bed-ridden for some days and the medicine that I have to take for my blood pressure, are the reasons that caused this delay in replying to you and assuring you that your letters are always welcome and also of thanking you for the letter from Pondicherry that you were kind enough to send me.

The Nawab has really captured Kittur from where he has demolished the fortifications as well as the neighbouring territories and it appears that he will continue with his conquests.

The Marathas have, upto now, looked upon the capture with indifference. Who can know and guess the designs of these barbarous Sarkars? If politics, in Europe, hide the intentions of the cabinet, the good faith of people who are ignorant of the rights of a nation deceive us of their consequences. Your vivacity and experience can, alone, decipher this enigma.

I hope that you will keep me informed of the movements of the Sarkar, together with your views, which alone, can direct me in this maze.

I have the honour to remain your humble servant,

Francisco da Cunha e Menezes.

Mr. Montigni.

P.S. In the meantime, I have received your letter of 9 October, through which you inform me that the Nawab has, effectively, captured Kittur and congratulating me on having discovered, in time, the conspiracy which some natives had plotted against the State. I thank you, once again, for your letter and the assurances of your continued friendship.

Reis Vizinhos, fl. 70.

Another

Goa, 15 May 1788.

There is nothing more flattering to me than the kind eulogies which you honour me with, and I shall endeavour, I assure you, to maintain and reciprocate these sentiments, which are so dear to me.

I was glad to learn the good news that you give me regarding the return of the vessel *Adelaide* and I shall not deny any help that Mr. Dayot may need.

The latest news from Europe that we have had, dated 27 December, is good as it conveys the peace and good understanding existing between the two powerful rivals.

I remain your humble servant,
Francisco da Cunha e Menezes.

Reis Vizinhos, fl. 106v.

Document No. 56

Letter from Fr. Caetano Victorino de Faria to D. Fr. Manoel do Cenaculo, Bishop of Beja.

Reverend Prelate,

The Lord has not, so far, grudged me the good fortune that I always wished for, and among other wishes that I have been longing for, is to know you personally, which occasion has not, so far, materialised. But the same Providence that knows how to reward, bestowed on my compatriot, Dr. José António Gonçalves, who was returning from Rome, the good fortune of meeting you personally, which pleased me and my compatriots very much. We were glad to have good news about you and happy to learn of the fine hospitality given to him.

For this reason, I take the liberty to kiss your holy hand and to ask your blessings and prayers, before the Lord, and in turn, I offer myself entirely to your service. At the same time, I wish to inform you that the Marchioness of Angeja has entrusted me with the task of settling the problems faced by the nuns of St. Clare of this city. On investigating their complaints I came to the conclusion that if they were to live peacefully and work for the Lord and his spouse, the Catholic church, they should be placed under your ordinary, as the legitimate pastor, and also that you be their father and expert doctor. They are in full agreement with me on this matter, and they have asked me to intercede before you to give them this bounty, which they have been craving for, so long, and I keep on consoling these spouses of the Lord who are exposed to the wolves, that their pastor will not forsake them and will defend, shepherd and guide them.

One of the means used to frustrate their privy lives, was to take away two chapels, using one Joaquim as the accuser, and the worst part is, that this is being engineered by people who should have, otherwise, defended them. Your Reverend, will certainly, use his best efforts in taking these sheep from the paws of the wolves, forcing them to desist from the plaint, and I shall see to the rest.

Regarding their subjection to your Ordinary, I have already put it into canonical practice and hope to get your concurrence.

Please honour me with your precepts and allow me to remain your humble servant,

Caetano Victorino de Faria.

Reply from the Bishop

To
Rev. Fr. Caetano Victorino de Faria.

I thank you for the kind expressions, and please, congratulate, on my behalf, Fr. Dr. José António Gonçalves, for his safe arrival in Lisbon, after the fatigue of so long a journey he has just undertaken.

Regarding the matter of the abbess, you well know that my genial, impartial and prudent character does not allow me to give my opinion, unless it is officially asked for; if it were within the ambit of my person, I would not have minded it, but when my earthly superiors question, I have to act, as circumstances demand, because I am duty bound, in the discharge of my office, to see the truth, in such matters.

It is, however, undeniable, the zeal with which the Lord fathoms the origin of things and places them in their proper perspective. One has to put faith in divine providence and pray, fervently, because the cause is worthy.

Regarding the chapels, it was difficult to talk to the person concerned, but I did talk to the uncle of José Joaquim, unfortunately, there is nothing to hope for. According to me, it will be useless and even my ecclesiastical power (if it is worth anything) cannot prevail over the need of a person who has been forced to make the complaint to save himself from hunger.

You may rest assured of all my assistance, whenever possible.

Yours affectionately,

Seal of the Bishop.
Beja, 26 December (1782).

Another letter from Fr. Caetano Victorino de Faria to the Bishop.

Reverend Prelate,

Though I could not fail in my duty to inquire about your health, because your health is of public concern and the sole object of my interest, I, nevertheless, did not dare approach you, personally, not to inconvenience you. However, present circumstances force me to acquaint you with what I have done with regard to the matter of the abbess of St. Clara.

Confident of your support, I only tried to obtain the brief from Rome to redeem those nuns, despite the objections from this court, which I did not bother about, as I know your system and, in fact, I did manage the favour from His Holiness, in such an extraordinary way, that it looked as if it was a special favour from the Almighty. This revealed to me that our Lord had deigned show his mercy towards these spouses, keeping you, for their consolation, as their protector. Certain of this, I have decided to accompany her, even to Calvary, not afraid to die with her and for her because I know she is dear to our Lord.

His Holiness, after reading your information, was so convinced, that he ordered an official letter be dispatched to the Nuncio, granting therein, all the necessary and timely powers for the separation of the said nuns from the Regulars and their reunion to your flock and, at the same time, he asked the Nuncio to represent him before H. Majesty, the queen, in this matter, which the Nuncio discharged, immediately, but upto now there has been no final decision, — the usual style!

This news when conveyed to the friars caused a universal uprising and they made common cause. Forseeing the storm that would be raised against the innocent Abbess, I apprised the Nuncio and his auditor, as I have in them as much confidence as I have in Curia, nevertheless, I did not fail to advise them. The friars attacked the Marchioness. She informed me and seemed calm. Patience and endurance! In matters of the glory of our Lord we cannot win without swaying on the waves.

The prevention of reinstatement of the abbess was beyond normal. Repentance, which is like an arrow, will pierce the hearts of the provincial and his friars and the pain will cause such a frenzy in the current investigations that it will serve more as a noose with which they will hang themselves than cause any damage to the innocent Abbess.

In this situation, seeing how, in this court, the friars were blemishing honour, reputation and credibility of these poor nuns, I drafted a representation and sent it to the abbess, to return to me duly signed by her, which she did, and I submitted it to the Viscount and distributed various copies to the people I thought convenient and I am sending one, in one page, to you. I think this will defuse the uproar and restrain a hurried resolution.

I drafted another and showed it to Dr. Pegas of Beja. He added so much in it that it seemed to hide the flowers behind the leaves a habit of the curias who are accustomed to legalities. A copy, in four pages, is being sent to you, because a long oration does not go well with the judges.

I send another copy, in two pages, for you to read, and if you approve, please, have it signed by the abbess only, and return to me by return of post, without fail, because from the report I made to Queluz and recommendation to Mr. Mayne, who is of my confidence, I hope it will result in something favourable for us, as they have asked for information from here.

I request you to tell the abbess not to send any paper to the queen unless I have seen it, because two that came from there were not identical to the ones I wrote. I have told that they could obtain information from you, if needed, and the coming of the *Corregidor* was useful.

With deep respect, I kiss your hand and the same does my companion, Dr. José António Gonçalves, who had the honour to be your guest.

God keep you for many years.

3 August 1784.
Your humble and obedient servant,
Fr. Caetano Victorino de Faria.

Nota Bene

We are now able to clear the doubt at page 19 about the two Noronhas. Sebastião Paulo de Noronha, who died in prison was from Nagoa of Salcete. Sebastião de Noronha, sent in exile to Bengal was from Aldona, a corporal in the shore of Bardez. According to information given by a person from that village, it is said that this man, after being reduced to penury at Bengal, was forced to do menial work, but managed to accumulate a large sum of money which, after his death, was turned over to the State Public Fund in Lisbon. This amount was later withdrawn, with interest, and invested in government shares. After having overcome many difficulties and after deducting all the expenses and discounts and the premium of one third of its net value, paid to a powerful person from Goa, who arranged the collection, the balance paid to the family was in the region of Rs. 12,000 approximately. This was paid 30 years ago. He was married to Josepha Ferrão of whom he had, among other children, a son called Gabriel Joaquim de Noronha who, in turn had a son called Manoel Felicio de Noronha, presently dead and whose descendants live in the same village at Aldona.

FOOTNOTES

1. Thus one reads in the work like the *Manifesto* as well as in the *Refutação Analytica,* but it is seen to be an error of the copy, and should read "in the 14th article".
2. The extracts are done by Fr. Caetano Victorino.
3. This Manoel Bernardes de Almeida changed after a fortune. He was appointed factor at Alleppy by the King of Travancore, and well accepted by the Governor of Goa through whom he was nominated Portuguese director at Alleppy with the promotion of Captain of the sea and war. He built a chapel at Alleppy where he was buried with a tomb and epitaph which notes that he died on 31 December 1804. This chapel appeared abandoned and without a roof in 1863.
4. Truly the Franciscans pretented that they could preserve themselves in the churches of Bardez and not that they might manage like a new thing because they had the administration since they founded them.
5. It is a palm-leaf which is found in document no. 15.
6. Leaving this history and miracles from the account of the authors of this representation, it only remains to be seen that the plan of transferring the city to Mormugao was at the time of the Count of Alvor and was not made at the time of the Count of Sandomil, as the order of the narrative seems to show.
7. This is in document no. 51.
8. It is like this, but must read "extinct".

THE FAMILY OF THE PINTOS OF CANDOLIM

We owe Mr. Luis Manoel Julio Frederico Gonçalves, advocate of Panjim, a relative of the family of Pintos, the favour of the genealogical tree of that family collated from documents relating to that house.

We thank him for the kind offer and add it as a supplement to our Historical Records so that one may learn that while there was a breach of loyalty to the Portuguese Crown from some members of the Pintos family, many others served the nation with zeal and distinction and the precept of that loyalty had been inherited by various members of that family.

Notes on the Genealogical Tree

1. **Naru Sinay**: Born at Loutolim, Salcete, he came around the middle of the 16th century, and established himself with his father and two brothers at Candolim, Bardez, where he purchased the fifth vangod of the communidade, *Mazarfarós*, as mentioned in the records written in Konkani and dated 13 August 1604 (pp. 86-87 of the concerned book). The widow of Naru Sinay was converted to Christianity, together with her children, the eldest of whom was baptized with the name of Jeronimo de Souza. He died after 1624. He had a son called Manoel de Souza, as recorded in instrument of a transaction dated 23 February 1649. From then on there are no details about his progeny, with the exception of Quiteria de Souza, spinster and sole descendant that remains from that family and who lives at Candolim. The youngest was baptized with the name of Christovão d'Andrade. He was the head of the family which later took the surname of Mello. His family is, presently, extinct.

2. **Santu Sinay**: Son of Naru, he was born in 1577 and was baptized more or less when he was eight years old on the 3 November 1585 and given the name of Salvador Pinto. Fr. Manoel Pinto, Rector of the church and college of Reis Magos was his godfather. Fr. Pinto was the first to teach the boy, and Fr. Simão de Nazareth, father of Christians and rector of the church of Candolim, took it over from him. Both the priests were

Franciscans, and with their influence with the Viceroys, managed to obtain many life grants and concessions of properties of the Crown in favour of Salvador Pinto, (which are still owned by his descendants) in recognition of services rendered by him in the propagation of Christianity in Bardez.

He married Maria Pereira, the only daughter of António Pereira and Catharina Pereira of Candolim, in April 1595. António Pereira was the son of Gorea Sinay, ganvkar of 2nd vangod of the same communidade, as per the records dated 9 June 1604. (p. 7 of the concerned record) The husband and wife, through a deed, dated 15 June 1624, gifted half of the vangod to their daughter and son-in-law, Salvador Pinto and Maria Pereira, and made their three male children heirs of the remaining one third. The above mentioned Fr. Simão de Nazareth, as representative of Fr. Miguel de S. Boaventura, Custodian and General Commissioner of East Indies and Diogo Dias, syndic of St. Francis and procurator of His Holiness, granted to the father-in-law and the son-in-law and their respective wives, two perpetual graves in the church of Our Lady of Hope of Candolim — to the former in the transept, in front of the altar of Bom Jesus (the said Salvador Pinto had a special devotion to St. Francis, because, as a child, he was brought up in the College of Reis Magos and he rendered services in the propagation of Christianity and also because he was of the nobility in this land) as recorded in the respective title deeds of 20 May 1604 and to the latter, also in the transept, between the graves of Pedro Sequeira and Francisco de Souza, by another title deed dated 10 November 1609, both confirmed by an order from the Archbishop D. Fr. Francisco Martyres, dated 21 February 1639 and later by decisions dated 26 October 1753 and 12 July 1817. Salvador Pinto died around 1640, as can be seen from the details of the above decisions and property division deed among his children, executed in 1641. (There, still, are originals of these and of all the other above mentioned documents, in a perfect state of preservation.)

3. **Paschoal Pinto**: Was born around 1600. He was the first priest in the family and died interstate, between 1641-49, his two brothers becoming heirs, as recorded in the deed dated 23 February 1649 (In the cited documents, Paschoal was preordained by his grandparents to become priest).

4. **António Pinto**: Was born around 1604 and died in early January 1657, as is found recorded in the division of inheritance of the couple, dated 4 May 1669. He married Luiza de Sequeira, who died testate, her will having been executed on 2 June 1670.

5. **Francisco Pinto**: Was born on 22 August 1620 and baptized on the 29th of the same month. He married Luiza do Rego and, soon after built another house close to that of his parents in 1641. He was the head of another family whose known members figure in this genealogical tree. It was not possible to have a complete record of the branch of this family for lack of correct details.

6. **Maria Pereira**: She used this surname and the name of her grandmother. She married Feliciano de Bragança, advocate, son of João de Bragança from the parish of St. Bartholomeu, on the island of Chorao. A settlement was made from her father's inheritance, by deed dated 15 March 1659.

7. **Luiza de Sequeira**: She used this name and surname from her mother. She was married to Simão de Menezes, son of Diogo de Menezes, from the parish of Salvador do Mundo of Serula. A settlement was made from the legal paternal inheritance, by deed dated 19 July 1668.

8. **Clara Pinto**: Was married to António Pinto from the parish of Chorao. She received the share of her father's property, by deed dated 10 April 1669. She founded, at Arpora, a chapel dedicated to St. Sebastian, and instituted a trust of her estates, appointing her nephew, Fr. Salvador Pinto, its administrator and made her other male nephews, heirs of the remaining estates, as her only adult son, Sebastião Pinto had already, died. The above referred chapel still exists at Arpora in front of the house of the present administrator of the trust, and for purposes of worship it is managed by a fraternity.

9. **Pascoal Pinto**: Was born around 1645 and married Francisca Monteiro, daughter of Domingos Monteiro de Souza of Candolim. He died on 15 February 1717, leaving a will dated 10 September 1716. He founded a chapel dedicated to Our Lady of Sorrows, which still exists, next to his house, and was thrown open for public veneration, by virtue of a Papal Bull from Pope Clement XI, in 1714, with a plenary indulgence to those who, after due confession would visit it on the feast day (2 February).

10. **António Pinto**: Priest. He died at St. Inez, "in the wars" (so says a record) on 12 August 1739, and was buried at the main altar of the church of Candolim. By his will dated 13 February 1733, he made his brother, João Baptista Pinto, (sr. no. 18) his heir.

11. **Luiza Pinto**: Was married to António da Silva e Souza, from the parish of St. Matias, island of Divar. (This family is now extinct).

12. **Simão Pinto**: Was born around 1670. He was preordained for a ecclesiastical career, for which purpose he was studying in the royal

seminary of Chorao, when dazzled by Luiza Rangel, endowed with an extraordinary beauty, he married her. From this union he begot only one daughter, Izabel Pinto who married Caetano de Frias, customs agent in the city, by order dated 31 March 1735. He was born at Santana of Talaulim, Ilhas, son of José de Frias, procurator of the Queen (i.e. of some revenues with which the King favoured the privy purse of the Queen) by order of 20 March 1690, advocate of the High Court, solicitor of the Royal Treasury, by order of 18 March 1699 and customs agent, by letter of 14 March 1707, and of his wife D. Maria Cabral. He was grandson of Paschoal António de Frias, Lord-Squire, later Knight, by order of 1 March 1671, Professed Knight of St. Tiago of Espada, and presented with a coat of arms (a castle with two lions in relief) transferable, for life, to his descendants, by order of 7 January 1690. He had a licentiate in Law and was Collector of the royal revenue office, and besides the above positions he also held the position of public prosecutor of justice, settlements and three Military Orders. He was married to D. Izabel de Mello. The above mentioned Izabel Pinto died on 15 April 1733 and her only son, Simão Salvador de Frias was married, for the first time, to D. Roza Maria da Silva, and for the second, to Victoria da Silveira, daughter of Rodrigo da Silveira, advocate of the High Court. He came to live in the house of his grandfather, Simão Pinto, in a part of the original house of Pintos, later extended, on one side and, then, turned into an independent residence, by Victoria da Silveira and her son Luis Paschoal de Frias, Captain in the Regiment of the province of Bardez (whose units fought against the attacks of Bhosale) and Councillor of the Senate of the Municipality of the same province. He married Adriana Roza Gonçalves, daughter of Francisco José Gonçalves, from Navelim of Divar, senior officer and Registrar General of the revenue department, till 1774. Later he was an accountant in the administration of the Royal Navy and War Materials, till 1796 and served in the expeditions of Ponda and Meloudin in the North. He was the grandson of the above mentioned José de Frias on the side of his mother, Antonia Anna Izabel de Frias, wife of Bartholomeu Gonçalves, revenue official and Captain of the Auxiliaries (Navy) in 1735. Luis Paschoal, his wife and their eldest son, Caetano Maria de Frias, married to Maria Joaquina Pereira, daughter of José Felippe Pereira, Sergeant-Major of Infantry, Cashier and Assistant Registrar of Treasury, in the beginning of this century, born and resident of the parish of St. Matias of Divar, are today represented by their grandson, Luiz Hygino de Frias, professor emeritus, residing at Margao and D. Eliza de Frias, present administrator of the respective estate, residing at Candolim. Simão Pinto died on 4 December 1729, and his wife, Luiza Rangel, on 18 July 1746.

13. **Maria Pereira**: She took this name and surname from her great-grandmother, married André Caldeira from St. André of Goa Velha and had a son who was named José Caldeira who died issueless. His fortune was inherited by his nephew, Francisco José Caldeira, who willed it to his two daughters, Anna Rita Caldeira and Anna Avelina Caldeira, and on their demise, without heirs, to their present representative Luiz Manuel Julio Frederico Gonçalves, advocate in Panjim, by the deed of 18 November 1863 (Sr. nos. 13, 19, 23 and 48).

14. **Salvador Pinto**: Deacon, died on 18 November 1752, leaving a will dated 28 May 1738, instituting a trust, administration of which and that of the chapel founded by his aunt Clara Pinto, (Sr. no. 8) was given in the hands of his nephew, António João Pinto, on condition that all successors of the trust should be Catholics and loyal to the Royal Crown, and in the event any of them not being so or any one committing a crime, thus making the estate liable for sequestration, a reason for which this estate should never be lost, then "I shall not nominate, in fact, I refuse to nominate any one committing such crime and the estate should, instead, be given to the next successor, as if the person committing the crime was not born at all."[1]

15. **Anna Pinto**: She was married to António de Sa, from Neura-o-Grande, from whom she had a son, called Pedro Alcantara de Sa, and one daughter, Esperança de Sa, born on 19 March 1702 and baptized on 27th of the same month. She married João de Oliveira, of Arpora, (Sr. no. 21) on 17 February 1715. Pedro Alcantara had two sons, namely, António de Sa, who died issueless, and Dom Caetano de Sa, a Theatine religious, before 1770. By legal deed, the priest transferred, all the wealth to his cousin, Salvador João Pinto (Sr. no. 24).

16. **Manuel Pinto**: Priest, instituted a trust in the name of his nephew António João Pinto, with the condition transcribed, verbatim, in note 14, by his deed dated 1 September 1729. He died on 22 June 1738 (see note at Sr. no. 14).

17. **Esperança Pinto**: Single. She died at the age of 12, before 1716.

18. **João Baptista Pinto**: He was born around 1685 and died on 7 January 1734, leaving a will dated 10 September 1731. He was married to Joanna de Souza, daughter of Agostinho de Souza and Lucrecia Maciel from Calangute who died on 11 December 1754.

19. **Anastacia Pinto**: She died on 16 February 1717. She was married to Caetano Gonçalves, from Navelim of Divar, son of António

Gonçalves, senior official of the Royal Treasury, who also acted as Registrar in the same office from 1703 to 1737, being promoted to officer from 12 August 1682, in which capacity he accompanied the Viceroy, Count of Villa Verde, in the expedition against the Marathas in the North and to check the accounts of the farm managers, and accompanied Viceroy Caetano de Mello e Castro, in the capture of the fort of Bicholim being decorated, for these services rendered, with a knighthood of the Order of St. Tiago, and an annuity of 12,000 *reis*, a transferable property from the office of the Paymaster in the province of Salcete and appointment as Inspector of Finances and of Weights & Measures, all by letter dated 3 September 1729. He was the grandson of Manuel Gonçalves, senior officer of Treasury, by letter dated 27 August 1680, which position was also held by the first grandson of Manuel Gonçalves (brother of the said Caetano) by letter of 15 November 1735 and later by the great grandson, Francisco José Gonçalves, (Sr. no. 12) until the closure of the Tribunal of Revenue Department. The latter was the paternal grandfather of the present representative of this family Caetano Francisco Gonçalves (Sr. 48).

20. **Clara Pinto**: She was married to Aleixo Soares, ganvkar and resident of the village of Serula, Bardez. She died on 15 December 1763. Presently, there is only one male descendant, António Maria Soares lately, Administrator of a Trust.

21. **António João Pinto**: He was born on 3 March 1714 and baptized on 10th of the same month and year. He married Anna de Oliveira, daughter of João de Oliveira and Esperança de Sa, from Arpora, (Sr. no. 15) who died on 28 October 1737, leaving a will dated 24th of the same month and year. He was a bailiff of the Inquisition, a businessman with establishments in Lisbon and Bahia. He was entrusted, by the Government of the State to oversee the auctions and disbursement of wages to labourers engaged in digging trenches around the walls of the province of Bardez. He was decorated with the following coat of arms and nobility of Portugal, by letter of 2 April 1770 "for having served the State with arms, servants and slaves, for being the noblest and richest family in the State, given the privilege of a carriage by sea and land, a mansion with a private chapel where daily masses are held. The coat of arms consisted of a shield divided into four quarters. On the first and fourth quarter, the arms of Pintos, which comprise of five crescent blood stones in relief on a silver base, in the second, those of Sequeiras, with five golden shells in relief on blue base, on the third, the arms of Maciels, which are broken in palls, on the first two, a blue *flor-de-lily* on silver background and on

the second a half red eagle decorated in shade of black on the same base. An open silver crest bordered with gold, floral leaves of gun metal and colour of the arms. The crest of Pintos which is a silver leopard decorated with blood stones with a crescent shield on the shoulder and for contrast a blue blazon and a silver harpoon".

Deposing as witnesses on his nobility and on whose depositions the award of the decoration would be based, were: Chief Justice, João da Silva de Menezes Lobo, former Justices of the High Court of Goa, Jeronimo de Lemos Monteiro, José de Carvalho de Andrade, Bernardo Lopes Pereira Maldonado and Marçal José Machado, Infantry Captains, Sebastião Lopes Duarte and Teotonio Collaço, Lieutenant Alberto Pereira Gracias and 2nd Lieutenant Telesforo Alves Simões of Benfica. It is seen from the details of the correspondence exchanged between this house and the Court, that efforts to obtain this decoration were exerted by Ignacio Pinto the younger brother of António João, who showed himself least interested in this, but as the eldest in the family, administrator of the trusts and head of the family, he was the first to be decorated, on the same grounds as was, later, his younger brother.

The two coat of arms were sent from Lisbon, in the monsoon of 1771, and what took place before the decoration was awarded, will be narrated when we deal with Ignacio Pinto.

António João Pinto died on 18 December 1784 leaving a will dated 20 November 1783 and was buried in the perpetual grave near the altar of Jesus (Sr. no. 23).

22. **Pascoal Pinto**: He was born on 26 March 1718, became a priest and was bailiff of the Inquisition. He had a spirited fight with the Archbishop, D. Francisco de Assumpção e Brito, against whom he made a representation to Portugal, which resulted in an unannounced inspection visit of the Archbishop to the private chapel of Pintos at Candolim, who finding it, against all his expectations, clean and in order, caught hold of the purificator and declaring it old and unserviceable, took it as evidence against the chapel, whereupon Fr. Paschoal remonstrated, saying that it would be easier to throw the Archbishop out of this land than the purificator out of the sacristy. He used to correspond directly with the Count of Oeiras, after the Marquis of Pombal, as well as with the members of the General Council of the Inquisition at Lisbon. In 1762, he submitted to that minister a sealed petition (carried by the Chief Justice, João da Silva e Menezes Lobo) in which he asked: "In order to put into execution and practice the pragmatic decision of H. Majesty, given in favour of the natives, ordering that that they should be given employment in all

occupations and positions, presently held by the Portuguese in this land, because many Chinese, *mulattos* and others who think that they also belong to the same race as the Portuguese, are being employed there, there are many learned natives and of nobility who, if employed in those positions, would bring prestige to the monarchy of our king, and this State would have vassals qualified for those services" and further added, in the same petition, that in case the Court was inclined to approve this "some capable men should be preferred for the positions to be filled so that, beginning with more learned, others may get motivated to follow their suit, and this should start with the ecclesiastics because there are many clerics who are very learned, serious, noble and better than many Canons". This was the reason why he asked that many native priests should be elevated to canonships and that their appointments should come from Lisbon filling, first, the vacancies created by those canons that have died. These vacancies could be filled by Fr. Lucas Soares of Serula, Bardez, Frs. José Pedro Collaço and Nazario Caetano Collaço of Rachol, who could rise to the occasion with as much wisdom as those sent from the kingdom. It appears that his petition was granted, because the royal order in this respect was issued after this petition. The first native priest to be elevated to canonship was Fr. Nazario Collaço, who rose to become chanter of the Sé Primate. Fr. Paschoal Pinto lived in his father's house, together with his brothers, until Ignacio Pinto built his own house, with whom he went to live and in whose house he died on 4 November 1788. He created a trust which was given to his nephew, Joaquim Bernardo Pinto, while the rest of his inheritance was given to another nephew, Luis Miguel Pinto (Sr. nos 31 & 38).

23. **Ignacio Pinto**: He was born on 26 September 1723, and baptized on 3 October. He was a bailiff of the Inquisition from 1745, Treasurer General of the Bull of Santa Cruzada and was awarded the Coat of Arms described at Sr. no. 21, by decree of 6 April 1770, with a pension and privilege of the habit of Christ. In this respect there are the following passages in one of the letters he wrote to the Licentiate Luis Manuel Tavares, in the monsoon of 1771: "the same friend, José de Oliveira, handed to me the scroll with the coat of arms which I managed to get due to your efforts, and while I am happy with the contents of the parcel, I am very unhappy with the Governor of the State, because, when I sent it to him so that he might see it, he doubted the genuineness of my application to that Court. In his opinion, he felt that what was written there, was that my brother and I were descendants from the nobility of Portugal, which is not factually correct, and that, therefore, he had to investigate into this

misrepresentation. I sent the evidence that I had at home, identical to the one I sent to you. He replied that he did not doubt our word, but that it could, probably, be that our representative, to flatter us, might have conveyed that idea to the Court, and having I replied that the Governor could satisfy himself from the testimonies of those who deposed in Portugal, as they were all, presently, here, he said he did not also doubt the veracity of the application but that he had to consult the Registrar of the High Court before taking a decision. Since upto date my coat of arms has not reached me, I am, no longer, interested to have it, even if it comes cleared of doubts raised, therefore, I request you to take the trouble, once again, and use your best efforts to obtain a fresh order with clear provisions, because equivocal expressions make the genuineness of the application and the integrity of people appear suspect, as this land is full of jealous people. I also enclose some testimonies of people of unimpeachable character and of high probity, to adduce new proof, if need be, and you may also rely on my friend, José de Oliveira, who will produce all the witnesses that may be necessary. You will have to take great personal interest in this, as it is a serious matter affecting our honour and your credibility because, while the governor takes time to decide it here, he may, in the meantime, inform something different on this matter to H. Majesty. You will also have to be very careful because, in these times, the zeal of justice, sometimes, falls on innocent people. I think you will have made arrangements to send the habit so that I can take my vows and profess the cult as soon as I receive it, and in case you have not because of lack of legal paper, I enclose one, duly authenticated, so that you can use it and be able to send the habit, for which I shall remain ever grateful."

One finds, however, from another letter from Ignacio Pinto, written in 1772, to Domingos Ribeiro Neves, and from another addressed to Fr. João Baptista de S. Caetano in 1773, that till that year they had not confirmed the title deed of the Coat of Arms, despite the fact that the ex-Secretary, who went from here to that Court, and the new Secretary that came here, had, on various occasions, assured the Governor that there was not the least irregularity in it. In addition "while on the one hand he promises to give it, on the other, he protracts, ostensibly, awaiting receipt of fresh orders with clear provisions. I feel, he does not like to see his fellowmen happy nor the good of others."

However, later on, orders were issued to comply with them, as recorded at p. 152 of 2nd Book of Register of Applications from the Secretariat in India.[2] In the said letter to Luis Manuel Tavares, written by Ignacio Pinto in 1771, one also finds the following passage recommending Fr. Caetano Victorino de Faria: "In this monsoon, a priest called Caetano Victorino de Faria, who was a mess mate in this house for over seven years, goes to that Court, with his son, with intentions to proceed to Rome, and though he goes against our wishes because he was very helpful to our entire family and lived with dignity, however, considering his honest and meritorious intentions we are forced to agree with his desires. It is natural, since you have done so many favours to us, that you should also extend your assistance to him, advising and guiding him properly, so that he may be successful in his plans, for which we shall be very grateful".

Ignacio Pinto lived with his brothers in their father's house. He married, for the first time, Anna Collaço, who died on 13 March 1748, leaving two children, who are mentioned in the family tree, and, for the second time, Margarida Rodrigues, daughter of José Nicolau Rodrigues and Agueda Angela Liberata Collaço, of St. Mathias of Divar, (family that became extinct on the premature death of their son António Caetano Alcantara Rodrigues, chief physician in Mozambique and grandson of José Nicolau Rodrigues, alive till 1853, his mother and the widow of the former, Anna Clara Gonçalves, eldest daughter of Luis Manuel Gonçalves, cashier in the General Administration of the Navy War Materials, from 1795, and grandfather of Francisco José Gonsalves, outliving him) (Sr. 12 & 19). Of the second marriage, Ignacio Pinto had seven more children, while he lived in his father's house until 1767, when he separated from his brothers and built his own majestic and beautiful house, according to plans drawn by engineer Felippe Catalini, who had been entrusted by the Governor, D. João José de Mello, with the work of opening trenches outside the fort of Aguada, in which work he was assisted by the two Pinto brothers, as that formed part of their estate called "Ansalem Bhatt" which had been levelled at the time of his grandfather, Paschoal Pinto, by order of Gaspar Bayão, area Commander, though with the disapproval of the Viceroy, Count of Alvor, and without any indemnity. In this new house, which was the third of Pintos of Candolim, since their origin to date, Ignacio Pinto had his remaining children, who survived the misfortune which victimized two of them. He died on 16 February 1797.

24. **Salvador João Pinto**: He was born on 29 October 1733 and baptized on 12 February 1734. He married Celestina Maria Luiza de Lima, daughter of Jeronimo de Lima, parish of Graça, a ward of the island of Chorao, where the wedding was solemnised by Fr. Henrique de Santana, on 29 April 1754. She was born on 24 August 1740 and was

baptized by Rev. Domingos Correa da Graça, in the church of Mother of God of Pomburpa. The Chief Justice, José Pedro de Oliveira e Brito and Antonia Albuquerque, wife of Lucas de Lima, were her godparents.

Salvador João inherited the three estates administered by his father, and he took over the administration of his house and chapels. He died on 9 July 1795 his wife on 16 August 1819.

(Regarding Jeronimo de Lima see *Narrative of Inquisition of Goa* by Dellon, translated by Mr. M. V. de Abreu p. 87.).

25. **Francisca Rozaura Pinto**: She was born on 14 January 1737 and baptized three days later by Fr. José Vieira of Society of Jesus, Procurator of Malabar, while Fr. Gonçalo de S. José was the Vicar of Candolim. She was married, on 3 February 1750 in the private chapel of the house at Candolim, to António José Martins of St. Matias, grandson and heir of Manuel Martins, squire and knight, by decree of 29 March 1680. He was born at St. Matias of Divar. The wedding was solemnised, on behalf of the Archbishop, D. Fr. Lourenço de S. Maria, by Canon Victorino Cardozo Mainarte, in the presence of Canons Manuel Gomes and João Barboza Coelho, surveyor Francisco de Campos Coelho and Vicar of Candolim Fr. Manuel da Graça.

26. **Manuel Filippe Pinto**: He was born on 2 May 1743 and baptized on 10th of the same month. He died on 25 February 1758.

27. **Anastasia Pulcheria Pinto**: She was born on 27 October 1746 and baptized on 3 November by Fr. João de Madre de Deus, in the presence of canons, colleagues of the Archbishop Santa Maria. She was married on 14 May 1759 to Luiz Caetano da Lima, lawyer, son of Lucas da Lima of Chorao. She died on 2 November 1788.

(Regarding Lucas da Lima see *Narratives of Inquisition of Goa*, pp. 86-7).

28. **João Baptista Pinto**: Priest, he was born on 29 July 1756 and baptized by Rev. Fr. Francisco de St. Diogo. The Inquisitor, Manuel Marques de Azevedo was his godfather. He was involved in the conspiracy of 1787 and imprisoned in Lisbon in 1788 and was set free and returned to India in 1807.

29. **Manuel Caetano Pinto**: He was born on 19 October 1758 and baptized on 27th of the same month, by Rev. Fr. João d'Oliveira of Benfica, Chaplain of the man-of-war from the kingdom. He enlisted as

cadet in the regiment of Brig. Henrique Carlos Henriques on 1 March 1775; he was 3 feet tall, had black hair, brown eyes. He was promoted to standard bearer on 25th of the same month and year, to 2nd Lt. of the Legion of Volunteers on 1 April 1777, and to Lieutenant of the same Legion in 1780. He was suspected of being an accomplice in the conspiracy of 1787 and was tried on 21 December 1788.

30. **Emeliana Pinto**: She was born on 30 May 1760 and baptized on 6 June by Fr. Alvaro de S. Boaventura, while Fr. João de S. Quiteria was Vicar of Candolim. She became a nun of black hood in the Convent of Santa Monica of Goa, where she was professed in 1773, as is revealed by a letter from her father, Ignacio Pinto, written in the monsoon of that year, to his business correspondent in Lisbon, José Jelama.

31. **Joaquim Bernardo Pinto**: He was born on 13 August 1762 and baptized on 20th of the same month by Fr. Henrique de St. Anna, having as godparents, D. Gil Eanes de Noronha and his wife D. Anna Maria Pereira de Lacerda. He was married, for the first time, to Maria de Conceição de Menezes of Calangute and, for the second time, to Anna Clara Rodrigues of Candolim. He died on 12 January 1811.

32. **José António Pinto**: He was born on 2 March 1764 and baptized on 10th by Fr. Pedro Caetano Ribeiro, having as godparents, the Promoter of the Inquisition, José António Ribeiro de Motta and Victoria Luiza Rodrigues from Piedade, Divar. He was the first to be baptized in the new baptistery chapel of Candolim church. He went to Portugal in 1787 and in the same year proceeded to France. He, apparently, studied in Rome, devoting himself, especially, to mathematics. He returned to India before 1799 and joined military service at Pune, where he distinguished himself especially, in the last war, where the Peshwa was defeated by the British. He rose to the rank of Lt. Col. of Cavalry and was seriously wounded in the campaign of Sholapur on 10 May 1818. Left as dead in the battlefield, he managed to save himself and returned to Goa. It is said that he, not only refused the position of Professor in the Military Academy of Goa, offered to him by the Viceroy, Count of Rio Pardo, when the Academy was established here, but also refused the British, when they asked him to rejoin service. He lived a retired life, dedicating himself to agriculture, in which he had specialised and had books brought from France. He was also fluent in French and Italian. He introduced sugar mills to extract sugar from cane, like the ones still seen at Saligao. He married Anastacia Augusta de Souza of Siolim and died on 29 July 1834. The English authors, Grand Duff and Wallace, speak highly of him in their books *History of Marathas* and *Memories of India* respectively, describing him

as Major. (See *Naçao historica de alguns filhos distinctos de Goa* by M. V. de Abreu).

33. **Anna Joaquina Pinto**: She was born on 7 February 1766 and baptized on 14th by the Rector Fr. Luiz Madre de Deus. She married Manuel Pinto of Saligao, grandfather of Francisco Salvador Pinto, knight of the Order of Christ and President of the Municipal Council of Bardez. He was the son of Caetano António Pinto, who is the second son of the said Manuel, whose estate passing from his first born, Sebastião Pinto, to his grandson, Ignacio Pinto, is today administered by a grandson from his maternal side, Braz Bartholomeu da Victoria Pinto Lobo (Sr. no. 51).

34. **Vicente Felippe Pinto**: He was born on 17 March 1767 and baptized on 24th by Rector Fr. Bernando de St. Rita, having as godfather, Henrique José de Mendanha Benevides Cisne, Secretary of State. He was the last to be born in the original house. He died unmarried.

35. **Francisco Caetano Pinto**: He was the first to be born in the new house of his father in 1769 and lived there. He was an officer in the Maratha army, together with his brother, José António Pinto. He rose to the rank of major and distinguished himself in the last campaign of 1817-1818, both for his courage and humanitarian feelings, saving from the hands of Maratha officers and soldiers, two British officers of Cavalry of Madras, called Hunter and Morrison, when they were taken prisoners, by Gen. Gocleá chained and tortured cruelly. After the war, the British government, in consideration of services rendered by him, conferred on him a yearly pension of Rs. 2,500 (5,000 *xerafins*) and after his death, his widow received half of the pension. He was married, for the first time, to Mariana da Conceicão da Cunha, who died issueless. She was the daughter of Pedro António José da Cunha of Chorao, advocate of the Court and judge of communidades of Salcete. After returning from Pune, he married again Carlota de Souza from Calangute. (Regarding this Souza family see Sr. no. 18).

36. **Amalia Dorothea Pinto**: She was born around 1771 and was married to Lourenço Lino de Frias, captain of Auxiliaries of Arpora, son of António Felippe de Frias and Anna Margarida da Cunha, who established himself in that village, building a new house, near the chapel referred to earlier. He was a grandson, on his father's side, of Simão Salvador de Frias (Sr. no. 12) and of his first wife D. Roza Maria da Silva, and on his mother's side, of António Caetano da Cunha, field instructor of Auxiliaries of the province of Bardez from 1769 to 1796. Caetano Xavier de Frias was the eldest son and successor of Lourenço Lino and

Amalia Dorothea. He was the father of Gustavo Adolpho de Frias, doctor and surgeon and public notary of the same district and owner of the estate which was given from the original house of Frias to his great grandfather António Felippe.

37. **Leonarda Maria Pinto**: She was married to Deudato Mariano Ferreira of Arpora who was, probably, born around 1773. Presently, there is only one son of theirs, Luis Xavier Ferreira, who lives in British territories, after having sold his house and properties in Goa, a few years ago.

38. **Luiz Miguel Pinto**: He was born around 1775. He was a Lieutenant and died single.

39. **Bernarda Sebastiana Pinto**: She was born around 1777 and was married to António Felippe Gomes of St. Matias of Divar.

40. **Maria Antonia Pinto**: She was born around 1779 and was married to Caetano António Mathias Cabral, captain of Auxiliaries, of Goltim, Divar. His son, Vicente Xavier Cabral, doctor and surgeon, presently lives at Ribandar and is a retired doctor of the Misericordia Hospital. The said Caetano Cabral had two uncle priests, one of whom was Father of Christians and professed Knight of Christ and the other was Superior of the Congregation of Oratorians.

41. **Joanna Francisca Pinto**: She was born around 1781 and was married to Joaquim Luiz António Vaz of Navelim, Divar, a ward of Piedade, by proxy in the church of Candolim on 31 July 1799, as found from a letter from Pune dated 6 September of the same year and written by him to his colleague, José Joaquim Pinto, which reads as follows:

P.S. "On 31 July, your cousin Mrs. Joanna Francisca was married to me, by proxy of Joaquim Xavier Correa da Graça. A new bond with which Providence strengthens our friendship".

It is said that Joaquim Luiz António Vaz went to Portugal as a young boy, where he did his studies, and on returning to India, joined military service with the Marathas, and rose to the rank of General. He was favoured by the Peshwas who gave him the command of a Division and important lands. As he could not come to Goa to get married, he entrusted Fr. Gregorio Correa da Graça, of Chorao, Vicar-General of the North, cousin of his proxy Joaquim Xavier Correa da Graça, lawyer and captain of Auxiliaries, auditor and district magistrate, father of Luiz Xavier Correa da Graça, to do the needful. He stated that this wedding was solemnised over a sword, in military fashion. After the wedding and while preparations were being made for the bride to be taken to Pune, a skirmish broke, by the end of 1779 or beginning of 1800 with a potentate, because of the territories he held, where the General was killed. He was then not even 50 years. Mr. Luiz Xavier however, states that this is not true but that he was killed in a duel, as was reported in the paper *Ultramar* in the year 1873. After a year, more or less, the widow remarried Agostinho Manuel Pereira, of Navelim, Divar, physician and 2nd Lt. of the Navy in Goa.[3]

42. **Clementina Pinto**: She was the last daughter of Ignacio Pinto and was born around 1783 and died unmarried.

43. **Anna Joanna Pinto**: She was born on 24 October 1758 in the house of her maternal grandparents, at Chorao. She was baptized on 31st of the same month, in Graça church, by Rev. Fr. Manuel João de Oliveira, Chaplain in the man-of-war from the kingdom. The Vicar was Rev. Fr. Bernardo da Cunha and her godparents were 2nd Lt. Telesforo Alves Simoes of Benfica, and Anna Senhorinha Gomes, wife of Diogo Monteiro. (Sr. nos. 9 & 70). She was married to Gabriel Xavier da Gama, of Anjuna, Bardez. She is now represented by her great-granddaughter, D. Maria Augusta Luciana da Gama, married to her cousin, Alvaro José Xavier Pinto. (Sr. no. 65) who lives in the house of their in-laws, which was rebuilt two years ago. The said Gabriel and Anna Joanna are grandparents-in-law, by first marriage, of Luis Xavier Correa da Graça.

44. **João Xavier Pinto**: He was born on 11 July 1760, on which occasion a solemn Te-Deum was sung on the 12th in the church of Candolim at the cost of the co-villagers and the Rector, Fr. João de St. Quiteria and baptised on 20th by Fr. Henrique de Sant'Anna. His uncle, António José Martins, and aunt, Francisca Rozaura Pinto, were his godparents (Sr. no. 25). To celebrate the event a ball dance, followed by dinner, was arranged. He married on 18 May 1795, Deodata Maria Lucrecia Fernandes, daughter of Agostinho Luiz Fernandes and Joanna Maria Pinto of St. Bartholomeu of Chorao. The bride was born on 31 May 1779 and baptized on 7th June. She died on 20 July 1839. He was auditor, customs administrator and judge of communidade of Bardez, for three consecutive years till 1817, when Mr. Justice Manuel Duarte Leitão arrived and took over all the judicial functions, by decree of 25 January 1816. He died on 5 June 1822 and was buried in the permanent grave of the family.

45. **Pascoal Pinto**: He was a priest, born on 19 March 1764. He lived in his father's house and died on 3 March 1829. He appointed his unmarried brothers, José Joaquim Pinto and António João Pinto, his heirs (Sr. nos. 48-49).

46. **Clara Esperança Pinto**: She was born on 6 January 1765 and was baptized on 13th by Rev. Fr. Estacio de Christo. She died unmarried at the age of 89 years in 1854 leaving her nephews, Alvaro and Augusto, her sole heirs (Sr. nos. 65-66).

47. **Josepha Agostinha Pinto**: She was born on 28 August 1768 and died in 1850. She was married to José Maria da Cunha, captain of the militia and procurator of the Council of Bardez in 1835, son of field instructor, António Caetano da Cunha (Sr. no. 36) and his wife Pascoa Ribeiro, of Pilerne. They had, among others, the following children: Sebastião Xavier da Cunha, book-keeper in the Treasury Department in Mozambique, where he died; Camilo António da Cunha, Lieutenant in the Maratha army at Pune, who died on 27 July 1871; Joaquim Gabriel da Cunha and Francisco Caetano da Cunha, both Infantry lieutenants in this State who as cadets, took part in the campaigns of Uspa and Rarim. The former died at Diu and the latter in his house at Arpora, on 26 January 1872; one daughter, Maria Angelica da Cunha, married to António João de Noronha, of Pomburpa, captain of the militia. The above Francisco Caetano, who married D. Leopoldina Maria Gonçalves, daughter of Francisco António Gonçalves, book-keeper in the Treasury Department and granddaughter of Luiz Manuel Gonçalves (Sr. nos. 19 and 23) had twelve children, among whom were: José Gerson da Cunha, graduate in medicine, surgery and obstretics from the University of Edinburgh and Medical College of London and Bombay, where he resides with his wife D. Anna Rita da Gama, daughter of António José da Gama, knight of the Order of Conception of Villa-Vicoza, by decree of 5 September 1861, retired chief surgeon of this State, residing at Panjim; Fernando Claudio da Cunha (Sr. no. 48); Francisco de Sales da Cunha, assistant public prosecutor of the Crown and the State in the Court of Calangute; Joaquim Manuel da Cunha.who administers the house of his father and was therefore, made heir of the third part; D. Leocadia Maria Francìsca da Cunha, married to Luiz Manuel Julio Frederico Gonçalves (Sr. nos. 13, 19, 23 & 48); Victor Bernardo da Cunha, medical student at Porto; Pedro Zeferino da Cunha of the Commercial Institute of Liverpool and Margarida Henriqueta da Cunha, married to Alvaro Camillo Policarpo Vaz of Aldona.

48. **Jose Joaquim Pinto**: He was born on 14 October 1771 and baptized on 21st, having as godfather, Manuel Ignacio de Carvalho, cavalry captain. He was an Infantry Major in the army at Pune, in the division of General Joaquim Luiz António Vaz (Sr. no. 41) whom the latter in his letter to him addressed him as "Honourable Captain and true

Soldier". He died a bachelor on 7 June 1854, having appointed heir, together with his brother, António João Pinto (Sr. no. 49) (they were owners of 3/5 of the wealth not bonded in the original house too) his second nephew and godson Fernando Claudio da Cunha (Sr. no. 47) related to the same António João, with the condition "that he should live in that house, maintain, and keep the worship of the chapel and use his surname — Pinto — when he attained the age of 20". The remaining portion of 2/5 of the above estates, and the chapel and other properties were purchased by Fernando Claudio, lawyer of Panjim, from the heirs, João Xavier Pinto and Clara Esperança Pinto (Sr. nos. 44 & 46), two lands attached to the same house, a chapel and more property, thus becoming the sole owner of the original estate. Fernando Claudio married on 22 October 1867 D. Albina Ernestina Gonçalves, daughter of Caetano Francisco Gonçalves, knight of the Order of Christ, by decree of 26 October 1858, old lawyer, gentleman of the cavalry and with authority of Alvará of 23, 26 and 27 of April 1872, of Navelim of Divar and residing at Panjim and D. Mariana Henriqueta de Figueiredo, great granddaughter of Pedro António Alvares, field instructor of Auxiliaries of Salcete and squire and Lord by decree of 10 March 1803, with the coat of arms, given by decree of 29 March 1798.

49. **António João Pinto**: He was born on 22 July 1774. He was appointed deputy prefect of Diu in 1835 and died in 1852. (see preceding Serial)

50. **Ignacio Pinto**: He succeeded to the estates of his father of the same name. He married Catharina Joanna Pinto of Calangute. She went to live at the house of her mother. where she died a few years ago.

51. **Anastacia Pinto**: She married Braz Lobo, physician of Saligao. She is represented, today, by her priest son, André Avelino Lobo, Justice of the ecclesiastical tribunal and parish priest of Assagao and by her grandson, Braz Bartholomeu da Victoria Pinto Lobo, physician and surgeon and Vice-President of the Municipality of Bardez (Sr. no. 33).

52. **Luiz Caetano Pinto**: He was married to Maria Especiosa da Graça Costa, daughter of Sebastião Xavier da Costa and, Maria Izabel Pinto (Sr. no. 60). He lived in a part of his grandfather's house (Sr. no. 23) which was divided into two, between his father and uncle, Francisco Caetano, by deed signed by the children of the said Ignacio, on 11 August 1803. He died, incorporating the name of his widow and children in the family tree. Of them, his daughters Anna Clara and Penelope Honorina married, one after the other, Marcos Avelino Fernandes of Assagao.

53. **Joanna Josephina Pinto**: She lives at Candolim, with her brother

mentioned below. She is the widow of Nicolau Tolentino Correa of St. Matias, and left no issues.

54. **Pedro Paulo Pinto**: He was born around 1809, retired as infantry captain and knight of St. Bento d'Aviz, by decree of 19 March 1851. He is unmarried and lives in his father's house.

55. **Ignacio Maria Pinto**: He was married to Carlota Joanna Collaço of Rachol, both deceased, leaving no male issues. Of the four daughters that they left behind, the eldest married her cousin, Luiz Miguel Pinto (Sr. no. 58) the second, Manuel António do Rosario Affonso Dantas of this city, son of António Caetano do Rosario Affonso Dantas, director of Military Hospital and Professor in the Medical School of Goa. He had only one son. All of them died recently. The third daughter lives with her husband, Caetano Xavier da Rocha, at Divar. They have no children. The last daughter married Caetano Carlos da Sequeira of Socorro of Serula. She is dead. He built a new house (the 6th from the original at Candolim) which ended with him and his wife.

56. **Servulo Xavier Pinto**: He was married to Anna Luiza de Sa of Bombay. Both are since dead and left behind an only son, today 15 years old. His sister, Maria Sancha is a widow having married twice. She has no children from her husband Caetano das Dores e Santos of Candolim, and lives with the third and fourth sisters and the above nephew in his parental house (the 5th). Other sisters are dead.

57. **Constantino Pinto**: He was married to Emilia Barreto, daughter of Candido Barreto of Socorro (Sr. no. 61). He lives at Candolim, where he built a new house (the 7th). He has no descendants.

58. **Luiz Miguel Pinto**: He was married to his cousin, Maria Augusta Pinto (Sr. no. 55). They live at Candolim. Their eldest son married two years ago Cacilda Monteiro, daughter of Placido António Monteiro and Humiliana Pinto (Sr. no. 70).

59. **Sophia Narciza Pinto**: She was married to Vicente Xavier Cabral (Sr. no. 40). They live at Ribandar.

60. **Maria Izabel Pinto**: She married Sebastião Xavier da Costa of Arpora. They are represented today by their grandson, Dr. Caetano Xavier da Costa residing in the same village.

61. **Constantino Salvador João Pinto**: He was born on 7 June 1797 and baptized on 16th, in the private chapel of the house by Fr. João Salvador de Silveira, Commissioner of Inquisition and vicar of Calangute. He succeeded his father in the administration of the house and estates. He married on 24 January 1831 Anna Clara Christalina Barretto, daughter of Sebastião Xavier Barretto, the last field instructor of Bardez, who died

two years ago and D. Maria Aurora da Purificação Pacheco, and grand daughter of José Barreto, field instructor since 1796. He died on 13 February 1851. His widow lives with her son at Arpora.

62. **Celestina Maria Ernestina Pinto**: She was born on 23 November 1798 and married Lucas de Sa of Candolim, father of Francisco de Sa, former president of the Municipality of Bardez, residing in the same village of Candolim.

63. **Guilherme Paschoal Pinto**: He was a priest and was born on 6 February 1801 and died in 1860 or 1861, in the house of his brother, Alvaro with whom he lived and whom he appointed his heir. Until the death of his uncles, he lived in the paternal house with his sisters, Lucia Pulqueria, born on 21 July 1809, Eliza Ernestina, born on 21 August 1811 and baptized on 29th, having as godfather, Marshal Joaquim Manuel Correa da Silva e Gama, who died on 8 March 1830; and Maria Emerciana born on 14th and baptized on 23 December 1813, all of whom died unmarried.

64. **Angelica Emilia Maria Pinto**: She was born on 15 December 1806. The occasion was celebrated with a dinner offered by her father, Lt. Colonel Francisco Caetano Pinto to British officers, Commander William Boye, Dr. Hoyes, Adjutant Louis and Lts. Has and Wilson. She was married to António Izidoro de Souza of Aldona.

65. **Alvaro José Xavier Pinto**: He was born on 16 August 1815 and baptized on 23rd of the same month. He married on 17 February 1852 his cousin D. Maria Augusta Luciana da Gama (Sr. no. 43). He was an Artillery Major, retired in 1871, knight of St. Bento of Aviz, by decree of 7 February 1862. He was decorated with a military silver medal for good and exemplary conduct, by order of 10 April 1869, made a Lord by decree of 17 March 1866. He lives at Anjuna and has the names of his children incorporated in the family tree. His daughter, Islinda married in 1873 Victor Condorcet Ferreira, lawyer at Panjim, owner of the island of Ponulem, son of João Felippe Ferreira, former advocate, acting civil administrator of Ilhas and owner of the island of Corjuem, where he lives.

66. **Augusto Silverio Pinto**: He was born on 13th and baptized on 28 November 1816. He married Anna Graça Pinto of Saligao. He died in this village, without issues in 1873 preceded by his wife and after appointing his brother Alvaro his heir (Sr. no. 65).

67. **Michaela Pinto**: She was married for the first time to Miguel de Sa of Siolim, and for the second, to advocate Domingos João José da Sa who was civil administrator of Bardez. She was from Siolim where she lives as a widow.

68. **Joaquim Bernardo Pinto**: He is the present successor and administrator of the estates of his great grandfather (of the parts not bonded by law, abolishing bonds). He married Quiteria Pereira, daughter of João Caetano Pereira of Loutolim, Salcete, who died two years ago. He lives at Calangute with his children who have been incorporated in the family tree, and of whom the eldest daughter, Etelvina Amelia, is married to José António Lobo of Ucassaim.

69. **Anna Seraphina Pinto**: She was married to Manuel Silvestre Pereira, son of João Caetano Pereira. He died a few a few years after his marriage, leaving behind two sons of whom the eldest, João Vicente Pereira, married D. Irene Ferreira, daughter of João Felippe Ferreira (Sr. no. 65).

70. **Humiliana Pinto**: She was married to Placido António Monteiro of Candolim, son of José Maria Monteiro, field instructor, who was given a coat of arms by decree of 27 February 1802 (Sr. nos. 9 & 43).

71. **Miguel Caetano Pinto**: He was book-keeper, Grade I, of the Treasury Department, married two years ago Rita de Souza, daughter of Caetano Francisco de Souza of Aldona and Ernestina Monteiro and grand daughter of Placido António Monteiro (Sr. no. 70).

72. **Caetano António Pinto**: He was married to Idalina Costa, daughter of Vicente Caetano da Costa of Navelim, Divar and grand daughter of Lourenço Lino de Frias and Amelia Dorothea Pinto (Sr. no. 36). He died leaving behind his widow and children who live at Candolim. His sister Severina Pinto married and died issueless. Of his children who are incorporated in the family tree, the eldest, Anna Clara married Manuel Francisco da Conceição e Souza, lawyer, of Nachinola, where they live. The second, Maria Luciana married Frederico Alcantara de Lima of S. Pedro.

73. **João Xavier Pinto**: He was born on 12 May 1833, in the house of his maternal grandfather and was baptized on 19th. He married Rozalinda Hortencia Camilla de Almeida of Cunchelim and had his children's name incorporated in the family tree, of whom the eldest daughter, Irene was married to Manuel Francisco Salvador Collaço of Sancoale, grandson of José Francisco Hercules Collaço of Margao, squire and lord by decree of 13 March 1827, and the second, Lucilia to António Vicente Lobo, of Candolim, presently councillor of the Municipality of Bardez and grandson of José Paulo Lobo, knight of the Order of Christ by decree of 20 November 1840. He is presently Administrator of his estates and lives at Arpora where he built a big house in front of the chapel erected by Clara Pinto (Sr. no. 8). His eldest son

Salvador (the name of the first to be converted and head of the family) was born on 9 March 1868 and is a student in the Royal Seminary of Rachol, and is the immediate successor of the half reserved from the said bonds (Sr. nos. 8, 14 & 16).

74. **Eliza Deodata Pinto**: She was born on 29 March 1835 and married Remigio Caetano Dantas of Saligao, where she lives with her children.

75. **Theodoro Paschoal Pinto**: He was born on 3 June 1839 and died, unmarried, on 9 July 1869, at Arpora.

FOOTNOTES

1. It is to be noted that there was not a single person from this family involved in the conspiracy of 1787.
2. It appears to us that the Pintos did well in not accepting the coat of arms based on their relationship with the Portuguese. But the essential requirement of the Secretariat, at that time needed such proofs even if not true. Because of such requirements for the issuance of the coat of arms, the purity of blood of many native families who received such honours became tainted. Presently they are awarded without such requirements.
3. The biographies and actions of Goans who served with distinction in the Maratha army, have not been, properly, compiled. It is, perhaps, time that their compatriots endeavour to collect details and facts that may throw light on this aspect which is still unknown. Since among all others, Gen. Joaquim António Luiz Vaz was the most prominent and of whom the least is known here, we avail of the favour of Luiz Xavier Correa da Graça, to give, in full, the contents of a letter that the General wrote with hopes of further investigations in this matter, by others.

Mr. José Joaquim Pinto.
Pune, 6 September 1799.
My honourable captain and true Soldier,

I cannot explain to you the losses that we have suffered in our reputation and other things. I have no face to show, either before the darbar (Court) or before the Europeans, because of the disastrous failures of the unfortunate battalions, but amidst this maze of grief that surrounds me, I have the consolation to hear the praises that our sepoys (who come from here) bestow on your prudence and courage. One should not be disheartened with being in prison, as this is the fate of a soldier. Very soon you will be set free with your cousin Mendes, whom I hope you will console, young as he still is. Captain Gomes must have acquainted you with the happenings here as he has given me news from you. May God remedy everything, though my sins may require too much of it. With the loss of my land no one seems to trust me even a pie, neither does the government listen to me, on the contrary, I am blamed for the advance over Jalna. I hope to come out soon, in fact, in a few days to take revenge on the Pathan because unless we do so we will become an object of mockery on the part of men with hats (Christians), and what will the Portuguese in Goa think? I am not writing separately to my Salvador not to make this envelope bulky; tell him to consider this letter also for him and to rest assured that because I do not write frequently, it does not mean that I love him any less than I always did and with all my heart, even if he is in prison, which should serve as a lesson.

Your most sincere friend,

Joaquim Luiz António Vaz

P.S. On 31 July, I was married to your cousin. Joanna Francisca by proxy of Joaquim Xavier Correa da Graça. A new bond with which Providence strengthens our friendship.

On the Cover

To Captain José Joaquim Pinto. In his absence Lt. João Salvador Mendes.

No mention is made of the place where the letter was addressed to. From the letter one can note that military reverses had lowered the reputation of Goans before the Marathas and that some were imprisoned as responsible for the reverses. The very General lost his importance and influence before the government and also suffered monetary losses from the estates that were usurped by a Pathan ruler and against whom he was preparing to take his revenge but unfortunately he died before he could succeed.

INDEX